Forerunner of Freedom
Swami Vivekananda

Forerunner of Freedom Swami Vivekananda

Mohit Chakrabarti

KALPAZ

ISBN: 978-93-5128-234-1

Price: ₹ 990/-

First Published, 2017

Published by

Kalpaz Publications
C-30, Satyawati Nagar,
Delhi – 110052
E-mail: kalpaz@hotmail.com
Ph.: 9212142040
Printed at: G. Print Process, Delhi

Cataloging in Publication Data—DK
Courtesy: D.K. Agencies (P) Ltd. <docinfo@dkagencies.com>

Chakrabarti, Mohit, 1941- **author.**
Forerunner of freedom, Swami Vivekananda / Mohit Chakrabarti.
pages cm
Includes bibliographical references.
ISBN 9789351282341

1. Vivekananda, Swami, 1863-1902. 2. Liberty—Philosophy.
I. Title.

B5134.V584C43 2016 DDC 123.5 23

Contents

Dedicated to

Professor Dilip Kumar Dureha

Vice-Chancellor, Lakshmibai National Institute of Physical Education (LNIPE), Gwalior

&

Dr Ajay Tewari

Chancellor, Swami Vivekanand University, Sagar (MP)

"Give up the beggar's dress of the world; wear the flag of freedom..."

— Swami Vivekananda.

Preface

The philosophy of freedom is the inherent and all-round identity of man. It is, as it were, the real mirror through which the whole of every human being is visualised. To Swami Vivekananda, one of the most vibrant and radical exponents of ascent and excellence, fullness and poignance, it acts like a sentinel and guards against all odds and constraints of the advancement and refinement of man in every walk of life and action, involvement and contemplation. It takes a very important role in society and education. It serves as a hallmark to religion and spirituality. It embraces aesthetics as a pointer to genuine and everlasting progress and refinement of sensibilities. While humanism is at crossroads to undertaking newer challenges in terms of never-ending ukase, it unfolds newer agenda set against dire, dull and drab materialism by introducing mysticism that marks the passage of the beyond and the limitless, the embrace of the void in the voidless as Vivekananda characteristically upholds in an unparalleled and incomparable way. Added to all these, freedom paves an altogether new frontier in the philosophy of values that adorn man the wisest, worthiest and best. "Radical Thoughts on Freedom: Vivekananda's Viewpoints" is an in-depth and consolidated discussion.

That freedom and society are more often than not isolated and not at all in harmony as desired, can hardly be overestimated. In fact, freedom is yet to have its real meaning and expression, involvement and impression upon a society in quest of excellence and ascent. Like an ever uncompromising crusader, Vivekananda has shown in theory and practice that service to society calls forth the service of freedom well articulated in self-consciousness and self-service prioritised through devotion and dedication to society.

"Freedom and Society: Vivekananda's In-depth Vision" is an intensive study in this direction.

Education is a matter of askance and enquiry. To Swami Vivekananda, it is an unending quest for 'manifestation of perfection' inherent and absolute. In undertaking such a quest, one requires freedom in every aspect of manifestation. Otherwise, it turns out to be a matter of commonality and mechanical endeavour. How to exercise freedom in order to be truly justified to life and the beyond? How to be on the right track of freedom and education? How to have the education of freedom of the mind and that of the soul marvellously synchronised? All these and other allied points on education nursed in the natural warmth of freedom have been critically discussed in "Freedom and Education: Vivekananda's Introspection".

"Freedom and Religion: Vivekananda's Points of Vision" and "Freedom and Spirituality: Vivekananda's Quest" are two very intensive studies which might be very interesting, adventurous and brain-storming, and might attract the attention of any revered reader of Swami Vivekananda's philosophy of religion and spirituality.

Always serene and solemn, Swami Vivekananda is an incomparable and unparalleled aesthetic visionary. What prompts anyone to follow the hallowed footprints of his aesthetic thoughts and experiments in life and work is freedom associated with truth, beauty and goodness besides other aesthetic components of refinements and sensibilities in everything at any time anywhere. "Freedom and Aesthetics: Vivekananda's Uniqueness" is an introspective pointer in this direction.

The essence of humanism is freedom. Freedom dwarfed is humanity in peril. To be christened and cherished as man is to be blessed with freedom to be as everyone ought to be. The roads to humanism are always challenging and complex, hallucinating and ambiguous. This has been further aggravated by mockeries of maimed and macabre modernity. Under these perilous circumstances, Vivekananda's unique vision of humanism might show us the avenue of fullness and perfection in the light of freedom.

"Freedom and Humanism: Vivekananda's Radical Thoughts" is a critical and illuminating analysis for these ends-in-view.

"Freedom and Mysticism: Vivekananda's Poignance" is an humble quest for appreciating the role of freedom in the world of mysticism where the expansion of the concept of everything in the light of the lotus land of the beyond becomes serene and transparent, calm and poignant.

The philosophy of values in terms of freedom very often remains absent or ambiguous, complex and dubious. To Vivekananda, freedom sans values is no freedom at all. It invites indiscipline and absence of the vibrant mind seeking for self-expression and self-refinement through self-learning and self-advancement carefully crystallised in altruism. "Freedom and Values: Vivekananda's Suggestions" upholds some of the crucial and characteristic components of values cradled in freedom as Vivekananda emphasises.

I dedicate my book to Professor Dilip Kumar Dureha, Vice-Chancellor, Lakshmibai National Institute of Physical Education (LNIPE), Gwalior, and Dr Ajay Tewari, Chancellor, Swami Vivekanand University, Sagar (MP) as a token of my love and respect for them.

I recall in bliss, love and affection the prompt, patient and sincere service of Sobdo and Priyanka, my son and daughter-in-law, in processing the book through computer and allied activities. I also recall the strong vigil of Suktima, my five-year old grand-daughter *guardian* who has gladly allowed me to feel free in order to have an access to the study of freedom devotedly. A thousand kisses to Suktima!

If the book draws the attention of everyone interested in the philosophy of freedom as Swami Vivekananda highlights, I would be really rewarded with the spirit of his bold and boundless vision: "Give up the beggar's dress of the world; wear the flag of freedom..."

Santiniketan **Mohit Chakrabarti**

1

Radical Thoughts on Freedom: Vivekananda's Viewpoints

Unlike any other thinker and translator of freedom, Swami Vivekananda stands apart in conceptualising and practising freedom. He defines it principally and practically from two perspectives—one, from the psychological standpoint indicating the Sanskrit Desha-kala-nimitta, and the other, the European space, time and causation. This makes the point of definition of freedom clear and explicit. At the same time, it unfolds the true concept of freedom which more or less suffers from abstraction and ambiguity.

In terms of Karma-Yoga, Vivekananda highlights freedom as follows:

> Our universe is that portion of existence which is characterised by what the Sanskrit psychologists call Desha-kala-nimitta, or what is known to European psychology as space, time, and causation. This universe is only a part of infinite existence, thrown into a peculiar mould, composed of space, time, and causation. It necessarily follows that law is possible only within this conditioned universe; beyond it there cannot be any law. When we speak of the universe, we only mean that portion of existence which is limited by our mind— the universe of the senses, which we can see, feel, touch, hear, think of, imagine. This alone is under law; but beyond it existence cannot be

> subject to law, because causation does not extend beyond the world of our minds. Anything beyond the range of our mind and our senses is not bound by the law of causation, as there is no mental association of things in the region beyond the senses, and no causation without association of ideas. It is only when "being" or existence gets moulded into name and form that it obeys the law of causation, and is said to be under law; because all law has its essence in causation. Therefore, we see at once that there cannot be any such thing as free will; the very words are a contradiction, because will is what we know and everything that we know is within our universe, and everything within our universe is moulded by the conditions of space, time, and causation. Everything that we know, or can possibly know, must be subject to causation, and that which obeys the law of causation cannot be free. It is acted upon by other agents, and becomes a cause in its turn. But that which has become converted into the will, which was not the will before, but which, when it fell into the mould of space, time, and causation, became converted into the human will, is free; and when this will gets out of this mould of space, time, and causation, it will be free again. From freedom it comes, and becomes moulded into this bondage, and it gets out and goes back to freedom again.[1]

Freedom in the light of the above as Vivekananda has described also leads to another important idea associated with it. It demands a newer universe which is broader than this little one in which we live. It also wants elimination of our so-called life in joys and sorrows, happiness and sufferings and so on. What does that freedom mean? Here is Vivekananda's bold and radical answer:

> To acquire freedom we have to get beyond the limitations of this universe; it cannot be found here. Perfect equilibrium, or what the Christians call the peace that passeth all understanding, cannot be had in this universe, nor in heaven, nor in any place where our mind and thoughts can go, where the senses can feel, or which the imagination can conceive. No such place can give us that freedom, because all such places will be within our

> universe, and it is limited by space, time, and causation. There may be places that are more ethereal than this earth of ours, where enjoyments may be keener, but even those places must be in the universe and, therefore, in bondage to law; so we have to go beyond, and real religion begins where this little universe ends. These little joys, and sorrows, and knowledge of things end there, and the reality begins. Until we give up the thirst after life, the strong attachment to this our transient conditioned existence, we have no hope of catching even a glimpse of that infinite freedom beyond. It stands to reason then that there is only one way to attain to that freedom which is the goal of all the noblest aspirations of mankind, and that is by giving up this little life, giving up this little universe, giving up this earth, giving up heaven, giving up the body, giving up the mind, giving up everything that is limited and conditioned. If we give up our attachment to this little universe of the senses or of the mind, we shall be free immediately. The only way to come out of bondage is to go beyond the limitations of law, to go beyond causation.[2]

That our struggle for freedom is an unending one through knowledge remains blurred in the absence of our ignorance. This ignorance is bred in limited visions of knowledge and life. This life of ours is only a starting point of freedom which teaches us the great lesson of littleness of this world. It is the true design of the world which never gives us perfect freedom. Perfect freedom stands for infinity. "We are", Vivekananda adroitly observes in terms of knowledge and the soul:

> here for freedom, for knowledge. We want to know in order to make ourselves free. That is our life: one universal cry for freedom. What is the reason the...plant grows from the seed, overturning the ground and raising itself up to the skies? What is the offering for the earth from the sun? What is your life? The same struggle for freedom. Nature is trying all around to suppress us, and the soul wants to express itself. The struggle with nature is going on. Many things will be crushed and broken

in this struggle for freedom. That is your real misery. Large masses of dust and dirt must be raised in the battlefield. Nature says, "I will conquer." The soul says, "I must be the conqueror." Nature says, "Wait! I will give you a little enjoyment to keep you quiet." The soul enjoys a little, becomes deluded a moment, but the next moment it [cries for freedom again]. Have you marked the eternal cry going on through the ages in every breast? We are deceived by poverty. We become wealthy and are deceived with wealth. We are ignorant. We read and learn and are deceived with knowledge. No man is ever satisfied. That is the cause of misery, but it is also the cause of all blessing. That is the sure sign. How can you be satisfied with this world?...If tomorrow this world becomes heaven, we will cry, "Take this away. Give us something else."

The infinite human soul can never be satisfied but by the Infinite itself...Infinite desire can only be satisfied by infinite knowledge— nothing short of that. Worlds will come and go. What of that? The soul lives and for ever expands. Worlds must come into the soul. Worlds must disappear in the soul like drops in the ocean. And this world to become the goal of the soul! If we have common sense, we cannot be satisfied, though this has been the theme of the poets in all the ages, always telling us to be satisfied. And nobody has been satisfied yet! Millions of prophets have told us, "Be satisfied with your lot"; poets sing. We have told ourselves to be quiet and satisfied, yet we are not. It is the design of the Eternal that there is nothing in this world to satisfy my soul, nothing in the heavens above, and nothing beneath. Before the desire of my soul, the stars and the worlds, upper and lower, the whole universe, is but a hateful disease, nothing but that. That is the meaning. Every desire is evil unless that is the meaning, unless you understand its true importance, its goal. All nature is crying through all the atoms for one thing – its perfect freedom.[3]

True freedom is above any delusion. It is above senses and also above the body and the mind. That freedom stands for elimination of all delusions and its existence is beyond this universe and infinity must be its true identity. And that identity can only be explicit in going beyond Maya. As Maya is nothing but the network of unreality, freedom is to come out of this delusion. Vivekananda remarks:

> Our knowledge is within the network of Maya (unreality), and beyond that is freedom. Within the network there is slavery, it is all under law; beyond that there is no law. So far as the universe is concerned, existence is ruled by law, and beyond that is freedom. As long as you are in the network of time, space, and causation, to say you are free is nonsense, because in that network all is under rigorous law, sequence, and consequence. Every thought that you think is caused, every feeling has been caused; to say that the will is free is sheer nonsense. It is only when the infinite existence comes, as it were, into this network of Maya that it takes the form of will. Will is a portion of that being, caught in the network of Maya, and therefore "free will" is a misnomer. It means nothing— sheer nonsense. So is all this talk about freedom. There is no freedom in Maya.[4]

That freedom is never an outcome of Maya and is above delusion or hallucination all the time often remains ignored. Real freedom means freedom of the soul. It never remains arrested in space, time, and causation. It also remains far above the little self and always strives for the higher Self. There is no scope for freedom of the so-called atheist, because an atheist to be true to atheism must be assured of a denial to the world which is arrested by thought, speech, knowledge and intellect acting as constraints to freedom.

Freedom in the light of the above comes under the transparent scanner of Vivekananda who categorically observes:

> No work can go on until we begin to say we are free. It means that the freedom we talk about is the glimpse of the blue sky through the clouds and that the real freedom— the blue sky itself— is behind. True freedom cannot exist in the midst of this delusion, this nonsense of the world, this universe of the senses, body, and the mind. All these dreams, without beginning

> or end, uncontrolled and uncontrollable, ill-adjusted, broken, in harmonious form our idea of this universe. In a dream, when you see a giant with twenty heads chasing you, and you are flying from him, you do not think it is inharmonious; you think it is proper and right. So is this law. All that you call law is simply chance without meaning. In this dream state you call it law. Within Maya so far as this law of time, space, and causation exists, there is no freedom; and all these various forms of worship are within this Maya. The idea of God and the ideas of brute and of man are within this Maya, and as such are equally hallucinations; all of them are dreams. But you must take care not to argue like some extraordinary men of whom we hear at the present time. They say that the idea of God is a delusion, but the idea of this world is true. Both ideas stand or fall by the same logic. He alone has the right to be an atheist who denies this world as well as the other. The same argument is for both. The same mass of delusion extends from God to the lowest animal, from a blade of grass to the Creator. They stand or fall by the same logic. The same person who sees falsity in the name of God ought also to see it in the idea of his own body or his own mind. When God vanishes, then also vanish the body and mind; and when both vanish, that which is Real Existence remains for ever. 'There the eyes cannot go, nor the speech, nor the mind. We cannot see it, neither know it.' and we now understand that so far as speech and thought and knowledge and intellect go, it is all within this Maya, within bondage. Beyond that is Reality. There neither thought, nor mind, nor speech, can reach.[5]

The contradictory condition of man in terms of equality and inequality, between balance and imbalance is quite natural and this makes the urge for freedom more and more until perfect balance of the antithetical forces is achieved. But perfect balance is impossible in this world of ours. Therefore, human motivation will always remain adhered to the opposing forces in life. The difference between man and man is the outcome of opposing forces nurtured under different situations and varied experiences. This makes freedom more multidimensional in human life and work.

The genesis of freedom is based on creation. If creation is assured, freedom is safeguarded. If there is no creation, freedom becomes baseless and meaningless. So there is no possibility of absolute equality bereft of which perfect freedom is impossible. Vivekananda distinctly elucidates this point in the light of the relation between equality and freedom:

> Absolute equality, that which means a perfect balance of all the struggling forces in all the planes, can never be in this world. Before you attain that state, the world will have become quite unfit for any kind of life, and no one will be there. We find, therefore, that all these ideas of the millennium and of absolute equality are not only impossible but also that, if we try to carry them out, they will lead us surely enough to the day of destruction. What makes the difference between man and man? It is largely the difference in the brain. Nowadays no one but a lunatic will say that we are all born with the same brain power. We come into the world with unequal endowments; we come as greater men or as lesser men, and there is no getting away from that pre-natally determined condition. The American Indians were in this country for thousands of years, and a few handfuls of your ancestors came to their land. What difference they have caused in the appearance of the country! Why did not the Indians make improvements and build cities, if all were equal? With your ancestors a different sort of brain power came into the land, different bundles of past impressions came and they worked out and manifested themselves. Absolute non-differentiation is death. So long as this world lasts, differentiation there will and must be, and the millennium of perfect equality will come only when a cycle of creation comes to its end. Before that, equality cannot be. Yet this idea of realising the millennium is a great motive power. Just as inequality is necessary for creation itself, so the struggle to limit it is also necessary. If there were no struggle to become free and get back to God, there would

be no creation either. It is the difference between these two forces that determines the nature of the motives of men. There will always be these motives to work, some tending towards bondage and others towards freedom.[6]

In fact, the goal for freedom should always be strengthened and steered by the goal for unselfishness through performance of proper work.

The concept of freedom in terms of spirituality is very often misinterpreted. It falls short of its own incomparable identity. Vivekananda time and again calls it strength, absolute and most valuable strength. In fact, it is the only true religion of man. It idealises man as *Amritasya putrah.* It outright replaces man from ignorance to enlightenment, from sadness to happiness, and from temptations to elimination of personal longings and desires.

Referring to the Upanishads, Vivekananda clarifies the concept of freedom as a splendid force of the advancement of man. In his words:

> Strength, strength is what the Upanishads speak to me from every page. This is the one great thing to remember, it has been the one great lesson I have been taught in my life; strength, it says, strength, O man, be not weak. Are there no human weaknesses ? – says man. There are, say the Upanishads, but will more weakness heal them, would you try to wash dirt with dirt ? Will sin cure sin, weakness cure weakness ? Strength, O man, strength, says the Upanishads, stand up and be strong. Ay, it is the only literature in the world where you find the word "Abhih", "fearless", used again and again; in no other scripture in the world is this adjective applied either to God or to man. Abhih, fearless! And in my mind rises from the past the vision of the great Emperor of the West, Alexander the Great, and I see, as it were in a picture, the great monarch standing on the bank of the Indus, talking to one of our Sannyasins in the forest; the old man he was talking to, perhaps naked, sitting upon a block of stone, and the Emperor, astonished at his wisdom, tempting him with gold and honour

> to come over to Greece. And this man smiles at his gold, and smiles at his temptations, and refuses; and then the Emperor standing on his authority as an Emperor, says, "I will kill you if you do not come.", and the man bursts into a laugh and says, "You never told such a falsehood in your life, as you tell just now. Who can kill me? Me you kill, Emperor of the material world! Never! For I am Spirit unborn and undecaying; never was I born and never do I die; I am the Infinite, the Omnipresent, the Omniscient; and you kill me, child that you are!" That is strength, that is strength! And the more I read the Upanishads, my friends, my countrymen, the more I weep for you, for therein is the great practical application. Strength, strength for us. What we need is strength, who will give us strength? * * * Therefore, my friends, as one of your blood, as one that lives and dies with you, let me tell you that we want strength, strength, and every time strength. And the Upanishads are the great mine of strength. Therein lies strength enough to invigorate the whole world; the whole world can be vivified, made strong, energised through them. They will call with trumpet voice upon the weak, miserable, and the downtrodden of all races, all creeds, and all sects to stand on their feet and be free. Freedom, physical freedom, mental freedom, and spiritual freedom are the watchwords of the Upanishads.[7]

The ever forceful and optimistic concept of freedom as Vivekananda has highlighted as the watchword is the radical pointer to the advancement of man. To be free is to enjoy the warmth of broadened outlook and dissemination of culture in every direction. What is very important is to maintain and nourish a favourable and natural atmosphere of the exercise of freedom in thought, word and deed.

In a letter to "Kidi", the Maharaja of Khetri, on March 3, 1894, from Chicago, Vivekananda expands his liberal and radical viewpoints on freedom as follows:

> Whatever retards the onward progress or helps the downward fall is *vice;* whatever helps in coming up and becoming harmonised is *virtue.*

> We leave everybody free to know, select, and follow whatever suits and helps him. Thus, for example, eating meat may help one, eating fruit another. Each is welcome to his own peculiarity, but he has no right to criticise the conduct of others, because that would, if followed by him, injure him, much less to insist that others should follow his way. A wife may help some people in this progress, to others she may be a positive injury. But the unmarried man who has no right to say that the unmarried disciple is wrong, much less to force his own ideal of morality upon his brother.
>
> We believe that every being is divine, is God. Every soul is a sun covered over with clouds of ignorance, the difference between soul and soul is owing to the difference in density of these layers of clouds. We believe that this is the conscious or unconscious basis of all religions, and that this is the explanation of the whole history of human progress either in the material, intellectual, or spiritual plane— the same Spirit manifesting through different planes.[8]

The radical viewpoints on religion as Vivekananda explains above can also be well assessed in terms of the practice of patchwork in its practice as it is more or less done even now. There must be a strong protest against all odds in the name of religion; otherwise, freedom dies in its poverty of practice under an unhealthy climate of so-called satisfaction with dullness, passivity, ignorance, and falsehood. That man must not yield to patchwork is a vital force of freedom which must make life worthy of challenge in living and expanding the vision of enlightened humanity.

True religion is born in the womb of freedom. It finds its true platform of efflorescence in the abyss of hopelessness and desolation. As an incomparable optimist of the advancement of man, Vivekananda unfolds the radical vision of freedom. In this connection one might recall his vibrant observation:

> "Come unto Me all ye that labour and are heavy laden, and I will give you rest." This is the voice that lead us forward.

Man has heard it, and is hearing all through the ages. This voice comes to men when everything seems to be lost and hope has fled, when man's dependence on his own strength has been crushed down, and everything seems to melt away between his fingers, and life is a hopeless ruin. Then he hears it. This is religion.

On the one side, therefore, is the bold assertion that this is all nonsense, that this is Maya, but along with it, there is the most hopeful assertion that beyond Maya, there is a way out. On the other hand, practical men tell us, "Don't bother your heads about such nonsense as religion and metaphysics. Live here; this is very bad world indeed, but make the best of it" which put in plain language means, live a hypocritical, lying life, a life of continuous fraud, covering all sores in the best way you can. Go on putting patch after patch, until everything is lost, and you are a mass of patchwork. This is what is called practical life. Those that are satisfied with this patchwork will never come to religion. Religion begins with a tremendous dissatisfaction with the present state of things, with our lives, and a hatred, an intense hatred, for this patching up of life, an unbounded disgust for fraud and lies. He alone can be religious who dares say, as the mighty Buddha once said under the Bo-tree, when this idea of practicality appeared before him and he saw that it was nonsense, and yet could not find a way out. When the temptation came to him to give up his search after truth, to go back to the world and live the old life of fraud, calling things by wrong names, telling lies to oneself and to everybody, he, the giant, conquered it and said, "Death is better than a vegetating ignorant life; it is better to die on the battlefield than to live a life of defeat." This is the basis of religion. When a man takes this stand he is on the way to find the truth, he is on the way to God. That determination must be the first impulse towards becoming religious. I will hew out a way for myself. I will know the truth or give up my life in the attempt. For on this side it is nothing, it is gone, it is vanishing every day. The beautiful,

> hopeful, young person of today is the veteran of tomorrow. Hopes and joys and pleasures will die like blossoms with tomorrow's frost. That is one side; on the other, there are the great charms of conquest, victories over all the ills of life, victory over life itself, the conquest of the universe. On that side men can stand. Those who dare, therefore, to struggle for victory, for truth, for religion, are in the right way; and that is what the Vedas preach: Be not in despair; the way is difficult, like walking on the edge of a razor; yet despair not, arise, awake, and find the ideal, the goal.[9]

How to realise freedom as the most potent force of realisation of God? How to be justified to oneself in the exercise of freedom? Vivekananda explains the role of freedom in a figurative way and reiterates the spirit of optimism as above:

> Picture the Self to be the rider and this body the chariot, the intellect to be the charioteer, mind the reins, and the senses the horses. He whose horses are well broken, and whose reins are strong and kept well in the hands of the charioteer (intellect) reaches the goal which is the state of Him, the Omnipresent. But the man whose horses (the senses) are not controlled, nor the reins (the mind) well managed, goes to destruction. This Atman in all beings does not manifest Himself to the eyes or the senses, but those whose minds have become purified and refined realise Him. Beyond all sound, all sight, beyond form, absolute, beyond all taste and touch, infinite, without beginning and without end, even beyond nature, the Unchangeable; he who realises Him, frees himself from the jaws of death. But it is very difficult. It is as it were walking on the edge of a razor; the way is long and perilous, but struggle on, do not despair. Awake, arise, and stop not till the goal is reached.[10]

The challenging vision of the Self in the light of freedom makes one really conscious of being above any attraction and at the same time devoting to the cause of the happiness of others. Thus, denial of the little self thereby remaining above selfishness prompts him to do good to others. His sincerity of purpose to any act of benevolence becomes the hallmark of freedom of the self. In this connection, Vivekananda characteristically observes:

> The two phases of this distinction in life are—first, that the man who knows the real Self, will not be affected by anything; secondly, that that man alone can do good to the world. That man alone will have seen the real motive of doing good to others, because there is only one, it cannot be called egoistic, because that would be differentiation. It is the only selfishness. It is the perception of the universal, not of the individual. Every case of love and sympathy is an assertion of this universal. "Not I, but thou." Help another because you are in him and he is in you, is the philosophical way of putting it. The real Vedantist alone will give up his life for a fellow-man without any compunction, because he knows he will not die. As long as there is one insect left in the world, he is living; as long as one mouth eats, he eats. So he goes on doing good to others; and is never hindered by the modern ideas of caring for the body. When a man reaches this point of abnegation, he goes beyond the moral struggle, beyond everything. He sees in the most learned priest, in the cow, in the dog, in the most miserable places, neither the learned man, nor the cow, nor the dog, nor the miserable place, but the same divinity manifesting itself in them all. He alone is the happy man; and the man who has acquired that sameness has, even in this life, conquered all existence. God is pure; therefore such a man is said to be living in God. Jesus says, "Before Abraham was, I am." That means that Jesus and others like him are free spirits; and Jesus of Nazareth took human form, not by the compulsion of his past actions, but just to do good to mankind. It is not that when a man becomes free, he will stop and become a dead lump; but he will be more active than any other being, because every other being acts only under compulsion, he alone through freedom.[11]

Contrary to the normal belief that freedom is obedience to the laws of nature, Vivekananda makes us aware of the fact that there is no freedom arrested in eternal law. This will delimit freedom which will certainly turn into a bondage. In fact, bondage and eternal law are identical whereas freedom in the true sense of the term means emancipation from any bondage of law. Self-assertion is the only antidote to rules and regulations. Vivekananda advises:

> All fears will vanish when you assert your own nature. If you think that you are bound, bound you will remain. If you think you are free, free you will be.
>
> That sort of freedom which we can feel when we are yet in the phenomenal is a glimpse of the real but not yet the real.
>
> I disagree with the idea that freedom is obedience to the laws of nature. I do not understand what it means. According to the history of human progress, it is disobedience to nature that has constituted that progress. It may be said that the conquest of lower laws was through the higher. But even there, the conquering mind was only trying to be free; and as soon as it found that the struggle was also through law, it wanted to conquer that also. So the ideal was freedom in every case. The trees never disobey law. I never saw a cow steal. An oyster never told a lie. Yet they are not greater than man. This life is a tremendous assertion of freedom; and this obedience to law, carried far enough, would make us simply matter— either in society, or in politics, or in religion. Too many laws are a sure sign of death. Wherever in any society there are too many laws, it is a sure sign that that society will soon die.[12]

To return to the root of existence is to have the genesis of freedom. It stands for the motive and goal of the universe. Work, worship and knowledge act as the threefold means of attaining freedom. For that, three components— energy, love and beauty— act like a composite unit in the universe. Vivekananda unfolds the concept of freedom in the light of the Infinite Mother of this universe as follows:

> Every existence from the highest to the lowest, all manifest according to their degree as— energy (in the higher life), attraction (in the higher love), and struggle for equilibrium

> (in the higher happiness). This highest Energy-Love-Beauty is a person, an individual, the Infinite Mother of this universe— the God of gods— the Lord of lords, omnipresent yet separate from the universe— the Soul of souls, yet separate from every soul— the Mother of this universe, because She has produced it— the Ruler, because She guides it with the greatest love and in the long run brings everything back to Herself. Through Her command the sun and moon shine, the clouds rain, and death stalks upon the earth. * * * Freedom is the motive of the universe, freedom its goal. The laws of nature are the methods through which we are struggling to reach that freedom under the guidance of Mother. This universal struggle for freedom attains the highest expression in man in the conscious desire to be free.
>
> This freedom is attained by the threefold means of work, worship, and knowledge.[13]

The world of human thought rightly demands freedom for development of individuality. It should be given ample freedom to think and freedom to act without suppression and any other form of hindrance. If freedom is constrained by any authority forced or otherwise, the power to think freely and spontaneously suffers undesirably. The result is appalling. It destroys the normal mind-set in thinking freely and creatively. It also suffers from absence of originality and excellence in the warmth of freedom.

In clarifying the role of freedom to think, Vivekananda poignantly suggests:

> Whenever you suppress a thought, it is simply pressed down out of sight, in a coil like a spring, only to spring out again at a moment's notice, with all the pent-up force resulting from the suppression, and do in a few moments what it would have done in a much longer period.
>
> Every ounce of pleasure brings its pound of pain. It is the same energy that at one time manifests itself as pleasure, at another time as pain. As soon as one set of sensations stops, another

> begins. But in some cases, in more advanced persons, one may have two, yea, even a hundred different thoughts entering into active operation at the same time.
>
> Mind is action of its own nature. Mind-activity means creation. The thought is followed by the word, and the word by the form. All of this creating will have to stop, both mental and physical, before the mind can reflect the soul.[14]

Freedom for the reflection of the soul is the most essential component that is manifested in the exercise of spiritual excellence and ascent. If freedom succeeds in playing its proper role in the reflection of the soul, it is a blessing for man. If, on the other hand, it fails to do so, it loses its indomitable and unique force in the enrichment of spiritual development in man.

The spirit of freedom makes man restless. He cannot remain static and silent, passive and indolent. He must prove that he is a living force, and, to prove it, he must be dynamic and free. Unless he ignites himself, his existence will be at stake. The battle that starts in the mind of man is to master the mind in terms of time and freedom. "Everyone", Vivekananda shows the way to introspection:

> is trying to make himself and everybody else believe that this world is all very fine, that he is perfectly happy. But when man stops to question his motives in life, he will see that the reason he is struggling after this and that is because he cannot help himself. He must move on. He cannot stop, so he tries to make himself believe that he really wants this and that. The one who really succeeds in making himself believe that he is having a good time is the man of splendid physical health. This man responds to his desires instantly, without question. He acts in response to that power within him, urging him on without a thought, as though he acted because he wanted to. But when he has been knocked about a good deal by nature, when he has received a good many wounds and bruises, he begins to question the meaning of all this; and as he gets hurt more and thinks more, he sees that he is urged on by a power beyond his control

> and that he acts simply because he must. Then he begins to rebel, and the battle begins.
>
> Now if there is a way out of all this trouble, it is within ourselves. We are always trying to realise this Reality. Instinctively we are always trying to do that. It is creation in the human soul that covers up God; that is why there is so much difference in God-ideals. Only when creation stops can we find the Absolute. The Absolute is in the soul, not in creation. So by stopping creation, we come to know the Absolute. When we think of ourselves, we think of the body; and when we think of God, we think of Him as body. To stop the gyrations of the mind, so that the soul may become manifested, is the work. Training begins with the body. Breathing trains the body, gets it into a harmonious condition. The object of the breathing exercises is to attain meditation and concentration. If you can get absolutely still for just one moment, you have reached the goal. The mind may go on working after that; but it will never be the same mind again. You will know yourself as you are— your true Self. Still the mind but for one moment, and the truth of your real nature will flash upon you, and freedom is at hand: no more bondage after that. This follows from the theory that if you can know an instant of time, you know all time, as the whole is the rapid succession of one. Master the one, know thoroughly one instant— and freedom is reached.[15]

The study of the Atman is the study of the true Self, the ever free. Contrary to the idea that the body is free or the mind enjoys freedom, Vivekananda draws our attention to the true nature of freedom which stands for the Infinite. In case of man, it is his infinite divinity which is a pointer to his freedom.

The quest for the finer mind that enjoys true freedom is beyond any change. What is desirable for man is to be justified to the higher self, the Self free and everlasting. Vivekananda characteristically points out:

> The body is dying every minute. The mind is constantly changing. The body is a combination, and so is the mind, and

> as such can never reach to a state beyond all change. But beyond this momentary sheathing of gross matter, beyond even the finer covering of the mind is the Atman, the true Self of man, the permanent, the ever free. It is his freedom that is percolating through layers of thought and matter, and, in spite of colourings of name and form, is ever asserting its unshackled existence. It is his deathlessness, his bliss, his peace, his divinity that shines out and makes itself felt in spite of the thickest layers of ignorance. He is the real man, the fearless one, the deathless one, the free.
>
> Now freedom is only possible when no external power can exert any influence, produce any change. Freedom is only possible to the being who is beyond all conditions, all laws, all bondages of cause and effect. In other words, the unchangeable alone can be free and, therefore, immortal. This Being, this Atman, this real Self of man, the free, the unchangeable is beyond all conditions, and as such, it has neither birth nor death.[16]

Freedom as a continual and challenging force is always in man. He must find out the true spirit of freedom. He must trace out its effectiveness in terms of his involvements and activities. There is no obligation as such but what strengthens the spirit of freedom is to rise above any form of bondage, be it knowledge or power whatsoever. Vivekananda clearly asserts:

> Man has freedom already, but he will have to discover it. He has it, but every moment forgets it. That discovering, consciously or unconsciously, is the whole life of every one. But the difference between the sage and the ignorant man is that one does it consciously and the other unconsciously. Every one is struggling for freedom— from the atom to the star. The ignorant man is satisfied if he can get freedom within a certain limit— if he can get rid of the bondage of hunger or of being thirsty. But that sage feels that there is a stronger bondage which has to be thrown off. He would not consider the freedom of the Red Indian as freedom.

> According to our philosophers, freedom is the goal. Knowledge cannot be the goal, because knowledge is a compound. It is a compound of power and freedom, and it is freedom alone that is desirable. That is what men struggle after. Simply the possession of power would not be knowledge. For instance, a scientist can send an electric shock to a distance of some miles; but nature can send it to an unlimited distance. Why do we not build statues to nature then? It is not law that we want but ability to break law. We want to be outlaws. But if you are bound by laws, you will be a lump of clay. Whether you are beyond law or not is not the question; but the thought that we are beyond law—upon that is based the whole history of humanity. For instance, a man lives in a forest, and never has had any education or knowledge. He sees a stone falling down—a natural phenomenon happening— and he thinks it is freedom. He thinks it has a soul, and the central idea in that is freedom. But as soon as he knows that it must fall, he calls it nature—dead, mechanical action. I may or may not go into the street. In that is my glory as a man. If I am sure that I must go there, I give myself up and become a machine. Nature with its infinite power is only a machine; freedom alone constitutes a sentient life.[17]

The spirit of fearlessness is the essential component of freedom. It creates twofold sense in the mind of man— the sense of self-identity and the sense of self-respect. Together these contribute to the ascent of man. He realises that there is an infinite spirit in him which allows him how to stand against all narrowness and dishonour nursed and disseminated against the true nature of freedom. It also unfolds the truth that the All Fearless, the Atman beckons man to manifest in the warmth of freedom to be as one ought to be.

Highlighting his own personal experience of freedom, Vivekananda boldly idealises and stresses upon the true spirit of freedom in the light of fearlessness:

> In this embodied existence, you will be tossed again and again in the waves of happiness and misery, prosperity and adversity—

but know them all to be of momentary duration. Never care for them. "I am the birthless, the deathless Atman, whose nature is Intelligence"— implanting this idea firmly in your heart, you should pass the days of your life. "I have no birth, no death, I am the Atman untouched by anything"— lose yourself completely in this idea. If you can once become one with this idea, then in the hour of sorrow and tribulation, it will rise of itself in your mind, and you will not have to strive with difficulty to bring it up. The other day, I was a guest of Babu Priyanath Mukherjee at Baidyanath. There I had such a spell of asthma that I felt like dying. But from within, with every breath arose the deep-toned sound, "I am He, I am He." Resting on the pillow, I was waiting for the vital breath to depart, and observing all the time that from within was being heard the sound of "I am He, I am He!" I could hear all along "*Ekamevaadvayang Brahma neha nanasti kischana*-- The Brahman is One without a second, alone exists, nothing manifold exists in this world.[18]

What should one do in case one is under the spell of low spirits in the exercise of freedom? What should then be one's guiding spirit? In replying to a question made by one of his disciples on how to win over the low spirit, Vivekananda advises:

> Then think like this: "Whose child am I? I associate with him and shall I have such weak-mindedness and lowness of spirits?" Stamping down such weakness of mind and heart, stand up, saying, "I am possessed of heroism— I am possessed of a steady intellect— I am a knower of Brahman, a man of illumination." Be fully conscious of your dignity by remembering, "I am the disciple of such and such who is the companion-in-life of Shri Ramakrishna, the conqueror of lust and wealth." This will produce a good effect. He who has not this pride has no awakening of Brahman within him. Have you not heard Ramprasad's song? He used to say, "Whom do I fear in the world, whose sovereign is the Divine Mother!" Keep such a pride always awake in the mind. Then weakness of mind and

> heart will no longer be able to approach you. Never allow weakness to overtake the mind.[19]

The concept of the universe in terms of freedom becomes clear and explicit. In the absence of this clarity and explicitness, everything turns out to be Maya, and we are bound to realise and respond to our inner voice. That the whole world with its joys, sorrows, pleasures, pains, life and death is nothing but a mad struggle to reach the inner voice becomes inaccessible to us because we do not want to realise nature in terms of freedom. The manifestation of the power of freedom that governs the universe allows us to realise its nature not only independently but also from the right perspective of oneness of Being and beyond that. Vivekananda brilliantly expands the role of freedom as an incomparable exponent of man and religion:

> As soon as you know the voice and understand what it is, the whole scene changes. The same world which was the ghastly battlefield of Maya is now changed into something good and beautiful. We no longer curse nature, nor say that the world is horrible and that it is all vain; we need no longer weep and wail. As soon as we understand the voice, we see the reason why this struggle should be here, this fight, this competition, this difficulty, this cruelty, these little pleasures and joys; we see that they are in the nature of things, because without them there would be no going towards the voice, to attain which we are destined, whether we know it or not. All human life, all nature, therefore, is struggling to attain to freedom. The sun is moving towards the goal, so is the earth circling round the sun, so is the moon circling round the earth. To that goal the planet is moving, and the air is blowing. Everything is struggling towards that. The saint is going towards that voice— he cannot help it, it is no glory to him. So is the sinner. The charitable man is going straight to that voice, and cannot be hindered; the miser is also going towards the same destination; the greatest worker of good hears the same voice within, and he cannot resist it, he must go towards the voice; so with the most arrant

> idler. One stumbles more than another, and him who stumbles more we call bad, him who stumbles less we call good. Good and bad are never two different things, they are one and the same; the difference is not one of kind, but of degree.
>
> Now, if the manifestation of this power of freedom is really governing the whole universe— applying that to religion, our special study— we find this idea has been the one assertion throughout. Take the lowest form of religion where there is the worship of departed ancestors or certain powerful and cruel gods; what is the prominent idea about the gods or departed ancestors? That they are superior to nature, not bound by its restrictions. The worshipper has, no doubt, very limited ideas of nature. He himself cannot pass through a wall, nor fly up into the skies, but the gods whom he worships can do these things. What is meant by that, philosophically? That the assertion of freedom is there, that the gods whom he worships are superior to nature as he knows it. So with those who worship still higher things. As the idea of nature expands, the idea of the soul which is superior to nature also expands, until we come to what we call monotheism, which holds that there is Maya (nature), and that there is some Being who is the Ruler of this Maya.[20]

Freedom to visualise God in terms of work is also a contributor to freedom to expand in the light of work. This is also a revaluation of man in the spirit of work as worship. This concept of freedom enlightens the vision of religion as the altruistic force of man. This enables him to put God in everything, be it in work or in life as it ought to be as a radical visionary of freedom. This is the concept of freedom to work as the Vedanta teaches us.

Vivekananda exquisitely exposes the concept of God in freedom to work:

> I never read of any more beautiful conception of God than the following: "He is the great Poet, the Ancient Poet; the whole universe is His poem, coming in verses and rhymes and rhythms,

written in infinite bliss." When we have given up desires, then alone shall we be able to read and enjoy this universe of God. Then everything will become deified. Nooks and corners, by-ways and shady places, which we thought dark and unholy, will be all deified. They will all reveal their true nature, and we shall smile at ourselves and think that all this weeping and crying has been but child's play, and we were only standing by, watching.

So, do your work, says the Vedanta. It first advises us how to work— by giving up— giving up the apparent, illusive world. Thus, do your work. Desire to live a hundred years, have all earthly desires, if you wish, only deify them, convert them into heaven. Have the desire to live a long life of helpfulness, of blissfulness and activity on this earth. Thus, working, you will find the way out. There is no other way. If a man plunges headlong into foolish luxuries of the world without knowing the truth, he has missed his footing, he cannot reach the goal. And if a man curses the world, goes into a forest, mortifies his flesh, and kills himself little by little by starvation, makes his heart a barren waste, kills out all feelings, and becomes harsh, stern, and dried-up, that man also has missed the way. These are the two extremes, the two mistakes at either end. Both have lost the way, both have missed the goal.[21]

The relation between work and freedom leading to the beyond is an altogether radical concept that promotes man towards excellence and ascent. It leads us towards a new science of religion which was so long unknown to man. Reasoning as science prioritises in its quest for the unknown is not enough. There is a greater challenge for man. That challenge is the exercise of freedom that shows the way to our existence beyond reasoning. Freedom alone can show the avenues of going beyond thought, intellect and reasoning.

Vivekananda points out the fact that life begins with the beginning of our steps beyond thought, intellect and reasoning well-baked in the warmth of freedom. That is the true way to lead a religious life. But how can we exercise this religion of the beyond that stands for the real science of religion? Here is Vivekananda's clear and explicit answer:

> There are much higher states of existence beyond reasoning. It is really beyond the intellect that the first state of religious life is to be found. When you step beyond thought and intellect and all reasoning, then you have made the first step towards God; and that is the beginning of life. What is commonly called life is but an embryo state.
>
> The next question will be: What proof is there that the state beyond thought and reasoning is the highest state? In the first place, all the great men of the world, much greater than those that only talk, men who moved the world, men who never thought of any selfish ends whatever, have declared that this life is but a little stage on the way towards Infinity which is beyond. In the second place, they not only say so, but show the way to every one, explain their methods, that all can follow in their steps. In the third place, there is no other way left. There is no other explanation. Taking for granted that there is no higher state, why are we going through this circle all the time; what reason can explain the world? The sensible world will be the limit to our knowledge if we cannot go farther, if we must not ask for anything more. This is what is called agnosticism. But what reason is there to believe in the testimony of the senses? I would call that man a true agnostic who would stand still in the street and die. If reason is all in all, it leaves us no place to stand on this side of nihilism. If a man is agnostic of everything but money, fame, and name, he is only a fraud. Kant has proved beyond all doubt that we cannot penetrate beyond the dead wall called reason. But that is the very first idea upon which all Indian thought takes its stand, and dares to seek, and succeeds in finding something higher than reason, where alone the explanation of the present state is to be found. This is the value of the study of something that will take us beyond the world.

> "Thou art our father, and wilt take us to the other shore of this ocean of ignorance." That is the science of religion, nothing else.[22]

The new drama of the science of religion in the efflorescence of freedom must be aesthetically justified to the advancement of man. It must call forth a new platform where truth shines like a pole star in the refinement of man. It must assure him of elegance and simplicity well armed with straightforwardness and diligence. No great work can be accomplished by means of cleverness in life. Freedom as such must be oriented to the aesthetic spirit of refinement and transparency.

To be aesthetic and radical, man must understand and appreciate his Infinite nature. It is the blessing of freedom. Highlighting the Impersonal Man, Vivekananda characteristically observes:

> The whole universe is one person; let go the little things. Give up the small for the Infinite, give up small enjoyments for infinite bliss. It is all yours, for the Impersonal includes the Personal. So God is Personal and Impersonal at the same time. And Man, the Infinite, Impersonal Man, is manifesting Himself as person. We the infinite have limited ourselves, as it were, into small parts. The Vedanta says that Infinity is our true nature; it will never vanish, it will abide for ever. But we are limiting ourselves by our Karma, which like a chain round our necks has dragged us into this limitation. Break that chain and be free. Trample law under your feet. There is no law in human nature, there is no destiny, no fate. How can there be law in infinity? Freedom is its watchword. Freedom is its nature, its birthright. Be free, and then have any number of personalities you like. Then we will play like the actor who comes upon the stage and plays the part of a beggar. Contrast him with the actual beggar walking in the streets. The scene is, perhaps, the same in both cases, the words are, perhaps, the same, but yet what a difference! The one enjoys the beggary while the other is suffering misery from it. And what makes this difference? The one is free and the other is bound. The actor knows his

beggary is not true, but that he has assumed it for play, while the real beggar thinks that it is his too familiar state and that he has to bear it whether he wills it or not. This is the law. So long as we have no knowledge of our real nature, we are beggars, jostled about by every force in nature; and made slaves of by everything in nature; we cry all over the world for help, but help never comes to us; we cry to imaginary beings, and yet it never comes, but still we hope help will come, and thus in weeping, wailing, and hoping, one life is passed, and the same play goes on and on.

Be free; hope for nothing from anyone. I am sure if you look back upon your lives you will find that you were always vainly trying to get help from others which never came. All the help that has come was from within yourselves. You only had the fruits of what you yourselves worked for, and yet you are strangely hoping all the time for help. A rich man's parlour is always full; but if you notice, you do not find the same people there. The visitors are always hoping that they will get something from those wealthy men, but they never do. So are our lives spent in hoping, hoping, hoping, which never comes to an end. Give up hope says the Vedanta. Why should you hope? You *have* everything, nay, you are everything. What are you hoping for? If a king goes mad, and runs about trying to find the king of his country, he will never find him, because he is the king himself. He may go through every village and city in his own country, seeking in every house, weeping and wailing, but he will never find him, because he is the king himself. It is better that we know we are God and give up this fool's search after Him; and knowing that we are God we become happy and contented. Give up all these mad pursuits, and then play your part in the universe, as an actor on the stage.[23]

To play one's part in the universe like 'an actor on the stage' as Vivekananda observes is the sine qua non of freedom. This upholds freedom as the the victory of man. All religions of the world consider this victory as the ascent of nobler visions and higher prospects of man. That also simplifies Thou art That as the true identity of man the ever free.

The spirit of infinity in terms of freedom as above inspires man to worship his own self as the Infinite Self. It is the worship of the Universal Self as the blessed outcome of exercise of freedom. Vivekananda's radical and vibrant thoughts on freedom find soul-stirring exposition as follows:

> Be sensible. We make mistakes; what of that? That is all in fun. They go so crazy over their past sins, moaning and weeping and all that. Do not repent! After having done work, do not think of it. Go on! Stop not! Don't look back! What will you gain by looking back? You lose nothing, gain nothing. You are not going to be melted like butter. Heavens and hells and incarnations – all nonsense!
>
> Who is born and who dies? You are having fun, playing with worlds and all that. You keep this body as long as you like. If you do not like it, do not have it. The Infinite is the real; the finite is the play. You are the infinite body and the finite body in one. Know it! But knowledge will not make any difference; the play will go on…Two words – soul and body – have been joined. [Partial] knowledge is the cause. Know that you are always free. The fire of knowledge burns down all the [impurities and limitations]. I am that Infinite.
>
> You are as free as you were in the beginning, are now, and always will be. He who knows that he is free is free; he who knows that he is bound is bound.
>
> What becomes of God and worship and all that? They have their place. I have divided myself into God and me; I become the worshipped and I worship myself. Why not? God is I. Why not worship my Self? The universal God— He is also my Self. It is all fun. There is no other purpose.[24]

The real nature of man is revealed in his struggle towards freedom. This is also the nature of everything in and around us. This is because there is always a tendency to welcome freedom under any circumstances and eventualities. Vivekananda characteristically explains the real nature of freedom from this viewpoint:

> Everything that we perceive around us is struggling towards freedom, from the atom to the man, from the insentient, lifeless particle of matter to the highest existence on earth, the human soul. The whole universe is in fact the result of this struggle for freedom. In all combinations every particle is trying to go on its own way, to fly from the other particles.; but the others are holding it in check. Our earth is trying to fly away from the sun, and the moon from the earth. Everything has a tendency to infinite dispersion. All that we see in the universe has for its basis this one struggle towards freedom; it is under the impulse of this tendency that the saint prays and the robber robs. When the line of action taken is not a proper one, we call it evil; and when the manifestation of it is proper and high, we call it good. But the impulse is the same, the struggle towards freedom. The saint is oppressed with the knowledge of his condition of bondage, and he wants to get rid of it; so he worships God. The thief is oppressed with the idea that he does not possess certain things, and he tries to get rid of that want, to obtain freedom from it; so he steals. Freedom is the one goal of all nature, sentient or insentient; and consciously or unconsciously, everything is struggling towards that goal. The freedom which the saint seeks is very different from that which the robber seeks; the freedom loved by the saint leads him to the enjoyment of the infinite, unspeakable bliss, while that on which the robber has set his heart only forges other bonds for his soul.[25]

Buddha, with his radical thought of transforming the world, has based and exercised Karma-Yoga in the light of freedom par excellence. Vivekananda for the first time in the whole history of freedom for human ascent and excellence has drawn our attention to what Buddha shows the way to exercise and enrich freedom in life:

> All the prophets of the world, except Buddha, had external motives to move them to unselfish action. The prophets of the

> world, with this single exception, may be divided into two sets, one set holding that they are incarnations of God come down on earth, and the other holding that they are only messengers from God; and both draw their impetus for work from outside, expect reward from outside, however highly spiritual may be the language they use. But Buddha is the only prophet who said, "I do not care to know your various theories about God. What is the use of discussing all the subtle doctrines about the soul? Do good and be good. And this will take you to freedom and to whatever truth there is." He was, in the conduct of his life, absolutely without personal motives; and what man worked more than he? Show me in history one character who has soared so high above all. The whole human race has produced but one such character, such high philosophy, such wide sympathy. This great philosopher, preaching the highest philosophy, yet had the deepest sympathy for the lowest of animals, and never put forth any claims for himself. He is the ideal Karma-Yogi, acting entirely without motive, and the history of humanity shows him to have been greatest man ever born; beyond compare the greatest combination of heart and brain that ever existed, the greatest soul-power that has even been manifested. He is the first great reformer the world has seen. He was the first who dared to say, "Believe not because some old manuscripts are produced, believe not because it is your national belief, because you have been made to believe it from your childhood; but reason it all out, and after you have analysed it, then, if you find that it will do good to one and all, believe it, live up to it, and help others to live up to it." He works best who works without any motive, neither for money, nor for fame, nor for anything else; and when a man can do that, he will be a Buddha, and out of him will come the power to work in such a manner as will transform the world.[26]

The religious and ethical spirit of freedom well synchronised in aesthetics as Vivekananda advocates above, has its roots in freedom and spirituality. He does not isolate spirituality from freedom in the sense that the essence of spirituality is primarily the essence of freedom. That we are already free in our every aspect of life and work is the true outcome of spirituality. The spirit of infinity in every human being shows and ensures that something must be done to prove our spiritual power of positive approach to life and work endlessly. That we are never bound has been strongly emphasised by Vivekananda:

> How could the free ever be bound? It is a lie. [You were] never bound. How could the unlimited ever be limited by anything? Infinite divided by infinite, added to infinite, multiplied by infinite [remains] infinite. You are infinite; God is infinite. You are all infinite. There cannot be two existences, only one. The Infinite can never be made finite. You are never bound.[27]

Admittedly, this essence of freedom and spirituality makes man pro-active to make the aesthetic spirit of advancement boundless. He believes that his very worth is indicated by making a fusion between spirituality and goodness. He becomes aware of what he thinks and how he translates his thoughts into goodness. As Vivekananda elegantly observes:

> We have to do something; let us do good. [But] who cares for good and evil? Play! God Almighty plays. That is all... You are the mighty God playing. If you want to play on the side and take the part of a beggar, you are not [to blame someone else for making that choice]. You enjoy being the beggar. You know your real nature [to be divine]. You are the king and play you are a beggar...It is all fun. Know it and play. That is all there is to it. Then practise it. The whole universe is a vast play. All is good because all is fun. This star comes and crashes with our earth, and we are all dead. [That too is fun.] You only think fun the little things that delight your senses![28]

Added to the above is to be value-conscious. If one wants to be free, value-conscious one must be. That adds to the positive spirit of freedom. Like an unparalleled iconoclast, Vivekananda asserts in his address delivered in San Francisco on March 27, 1902:

> What is the end and aim of life? None, because I [know that I am the Infinite]. If you are beggars, you can have aims. I have no aims, no want, no purpose. I come to your country, and lecture— just for fun. No other meaning. What meaning can be there? Only slaves do actions for somebody else. You do actions for nobody else when it suits you, you worship. You can join the Christians, the Mohammedans, the Chinese, the Japanese. You can worship all the gods that ever were and are ever going to be...
>
> I am the sun, the moon, and the stars. I am with God and I am in all the gods. I worship my Self.
>
> There is another side to it. I have kept it in reserve. I am the man that is going to be hanged. I am all the wicked. I am getting punished in hells. That [also] is fun. This is the goal of philosophy [to know that I am the Infinite]. Aims, motives, purposes, and duties live in the background...
>
> This truth is first to be listened to, then to be thought about. Reason, argue it out by all manner of means. The enlightened know no more than that. Know it for certain that you are in everything. That is why you should not hurt anybody, because in hurting them you hurt yourself... [Lastly,] this is to be meditated upon. Think upon it. Can you realise there will come a time when everything will crumble in the dust and you will stand alone? That moment of ecstatic joy will never leave you.[29]

The multidimensional thoughts on freedom as Vivekananda spells out are always vibrant and interesting, poignant and stimulating. These open out newer avenues of askance and enquiry leading to ascent and excellence in all directions. Indeed, freedom in the light of acceleration of society promises enlightened and humane socialism— a must for any identity of man in terms of society and vice versa. The education of freedom starts with that promise of excellence and perfection and even beyond that. A variety of religions well nourished in spirituality is for what true freedom stands. The more involved we are with all sincerity of purpose tinged with dedication and humanism, the more fruitful is the role of freedom. Vivekananda takes up the challenges of freedom where all constraints turn into blessings of values translated into reality and relevance anywhere and everywhere. Freedom no longer remains a fiction but a real identity of man striving for fullness and ascent.

The paradise of freedom is in the heartland of efflorescence mystic and, therefore, for the beyond— a journey to nowhere except to the beyond. As Vivekananda serenely upholds:

Before the sun, the moon, the earth,
Before the stars or comets free,
Before e'en time has had its birth,
I was, I am, and I will be.

The beauteous earth, the glorious sun,
The calm sweet moon, the spangled sky,
Causation's laws do make them run;
They live in bonds, in bonds they die.

And mind its mantle dreamy net
Cast o'er them all and holds them fast.
In warp and woof of thought are set,
Earth, hells, and heavens, or worst or best.

Know these are but the outer crust—
And space and time, all effect, cause.
I am beyond all sense, all thoughts,
The witness of the universe.

Not two or many, 'tis but one,
And thus in me all me's I have;
I cannot hate, I cannot shun
Myself from me, I can but love.

From dreams awake, from bonds be free,
Be not afraid. This mystery,
My shadow, cannot frighten me,
Know once for all that I am He.[30]

Are we ready to become dedicated partners of freedom as Vivekananda beckons us: "I am He"?

References

1. Swami Vivekananda: *The Complete Works of Swami Vivekananda,* Advaita Ashrama, Kolkata, Mayavati Memorial Edition, 1989, Vol. I, pp. 95-96.
2. *Ibid.,* pp. 97-98.
3. *Ibid.,* Vol. IV, pp. 239-241.
4. *Ibid.,* Vol. III, p. 14.
5. *Ibid.,* pp. 14-15.
6. *Ibid.,* Vol. I, pp. 114-115.
7. *Ibid.,* Vol. III, pp. 237-238.
8. *Ibid.,* Vol. IV, p. 357.
9. *Ibid.,* Vol. II, pp. 123-124.
10. *Ibid.,* pp. 169-170.
11. *Ibid.,* Vol. V, pp. 285-286.
12. *Ibid.,* pp. 286-287.
13. *Ibid.,* pp. 433-444.
14. *Ibid.,* Vol. VI, p.100.
15. *Ibid.,* pp. 95-97.
16. *Ibid.,* Vol. IV, p. 256.
17. *Ibid.,* Vol. V, pp. 288-289.
18. *Ibid.,* Vol. VII, pp.136-137.
19. *Ibid.,* pp. 233-234.
20. *Ibid.,* Vol. II, pp. 126-128.
21. *Ibid.,* pp. 149-150.
22. *Ibid.,* Vol. I, pp. 198-199.
23. *Ibid.,* Vol. II, pp. 323-324.
24. *Ibid.,* p. 471.

25. *Ibid.*, Vol. I, pp. 108-109.
26. *Ibid.*, pp. 117-118.
27. *Ibid.*, Vol. II, pp. 469-470.
28. *Ibid.*, p. 470.
29. *Ibid.*, pp. 471-472.
30. *Ibid.*, Vol. VIII, pp. 163-164.

2

Freedom and Society: Vivekananda's In-depth Vision

Freedom is closely related to society. To Swami Vivekananda, a radical thinker par excellence of freedom and society, it is more than a mere close relationship. It is more than what one casually thinks. Freedom not only shapes a society but also shows newer avenues of excellence of every individual in the society. As such, it plays a very pivotal role in shaping the destiny of man and society. Any society, whatsoever developed and conscious of its very existence, cannot but provide ample scope for the role that freedom spontaneously plays. This also indicates the fact that an enlightened and humane society is best known by the freedom it cultivates and exercises in the spirit of togetherness side by side with the uniqueness of individuality.

Apart from the fact that Vivekananda has made a very significant and pioneering contribution to the advancement of man in many directions and from multi-pronged praxes, what is really most characteristic is that he has prioritised freedom not simply as an indomitable force for the excellence of the society but primarily as a radical pathway to progress and beyond that. He strongly believes in the great saying of the Upanishad *Charaiveti*, march ahead. This saying serves as an ever abiding force in shaping and reshaping the society in tune with freedom. Any society cannot but undergo a radical change to prove its dynamic role. And to prove it so, there is no alternative to freedom— freedom to think and act, freedom to ask and challenge, freedom to eliminate the unwanted and welcome the new, and freedom to be as one ought to be in a vibrant and living society.

To exercise freedom to be as one ought to be is to synchronise freedom and love in the society. Vivekananda has made this component of the concept of freedom in terms of the society absolutely clear and explicit:

> The man who works through freedom and love cares nothing for results. But the slave wants his whipping; the servant wants his pay. So with all life; take for instance the public life. The public speaker wants a little applause or a little hissing and hooting. If you keep him in a corner without it, you kill him, for he requires it. This is working through slavery. To expect something in return, under such conditions, becomes second nature. Next comes the work of the servant, who requires some pay; I give this, and you give me that. Nothing is easier to say, "I work for work's sake", but nothing is so difficult to attain. I would go twenty miles on my hands and knees to look on the face power of the man who can work for work's sake. There is a motive somewhere. If it is not money, it is power. If it is not power, it is gain. Somehow, somewhere, there is a motive power. You are my friend, and I want to work for you and with you. This is all very well, and every moment I may make protestation of my sincerity. But take care, you must be sure to agree with me! If you do not, I shall no longer take care of you or live for you! This kind of work for a motive brings misery. That work alone brings unattachment and bliss, wherein we work as masters of our own minds.[1]

The education of the masses in the society calls forth freedom to exercise dynamic and radical vision. It is really a very arduous task but it is thrilling and pays very worthy dividends in bringing about radical changes in the society. As Vivekananda transparently observes:

> Educate and raise the masses, and thus alone a nation is possible. Our reformers do not see where the wound is, they want to save the nation by marrying the widows; do you think that a nation is saved by the number of husbands its widows get? Nor is our religion to blame, for an idol more or less makes no difference. The whole defect is here: The real nation who live in cottage have forgotten their manhood, their individuality. Trodden under the foot of the Hindu, Mussalman, or Christian, they have come to think that they are born to be trodden under the foot of everybody who has money enough in his pocket. They are to be given back their lost individuality. They are to be educated. Whether idols will remain or not, whether widows will have husbands enough or not, whether caste is good or bad, I do not bother myself with such questions. Everyone must work out his own salvation. Our duty is to put the chemicals together, the crystallisation will come through God's laws. Let us put ideas into their heads, and they will do the rest."[2]

Self-dependence and radical thinking in the light of freedom go hand in hand in bringing about a sea-change in the mind-sets of the people of the society. To be bound by law is to go against freedom, and to go against freedom is to go against human nature. The essential component of both freedom and society is nature. Forsake nature, and you forsake freedom. Again, forsake society, and you forsake your own Self which epitomises the society enlightened and crystallised. "I am That I am" is the true outcome of nature in a serene society that enjoys love and individuality both outwardly and inwardly.

In a lecture delivered in San Francisco on March 20, 1900, Vivekananda poignantly remarks:

> What is the relation between me and nature? In so far as nature stands for name and form or for time, space, and causality, I am not part of nature, because I am free, I am immortal, I am

> unchanging and infinite. The question does not arise whether I have free will or not; I am beyond any will at all. Wherever there is will, it is never free. There is no freedom of will whatever. There is freedom of that which becomes will when name and form get hold of it, making it their slave. That substance— the soul— as it were moulds itself, as it were throws itself into the cast of name and form, and immediately becomes bound, whereas it was free before. And yet its original nature is still there. That is why it says, "I am free; in spite of all this bondage, I am free." and it never forgets this.
>
> But when the soul has become the will, it is no more really free. Nature pulls the strings, and it has to dance as nature wants it to. Thus, have you and I danced throughout the years. All the things that we see, do, feel, know, all our thoughts and actions, are nothing but dancing to the dictates of nature. There has been, and there is, no freedom in any of this. From the lowest to the highest, all thoughts and actions are bound by law, and none of these pertain to our real Self.[3]

The quest for the real Self in every one in the society by means of the exercise of freedom as Vivekananda upholds is the most challenging task. For a genuine foundation of the philosophy of radicalism in social vision, man must cultivate the spirit of freedom where religion finds a new language. The path of cultivating purity of mind and outlook for an enlightened society welcomes a new religion where there is no room for any form of superstition. It is only with Jnana-Yoga that one is hallowed with the blessing of the ever free Soul. Vivekananda advises us to follow that transparent path to fulfil the great mission for which every radical society continually strives:

> The sun [shines on the just and on the unjust]. Is he touched by the defective [character] of anyone? "I am He. Whatever [my] mind does, I am not touched. The sun is not touched by shining on filthy places, I am Existence."...
>
> Struggle on! Down with all superstitions! Neither teachers nor scriptures nor gods [exist]. Down with temples, with priests,

with gods, with incarnations, with God himself! I am all the God that ever existed! There, stand up philosophers! No fear! Speak no more of God and [the] superstition of the world. Truth alone triumphs, and this is true. I am the Infinite...

This society, that I see you before me, and [that] I am talking to you this is all superstition; all must be given up. Just see what it takes to become a philosopher! This is the [path] of [Jnana-]Yoga, the way through knowledge. The other [paths] are easy, slow, . . . but this is pure strength of mind. No weakling [can follow this path of knowledge. You must be able to say:] "I am the Soul, the ever free; [I] was never bound. Time is in me, not I in time. God was born in my mind. God the Father, Father of the universe— he is created by me in my own mind.[4]

With such a radical vision as above, society gets a new platform of selfless and unbiased service for humanity. Indeed, in his in-depth vision of individual and social regeneration, Vivekananda prioritises non-attachment as the touchstone of excellence in service. In his invaluable words:

In whatever you do for a particular person, a city, or a state, assume the same attitude towards it as you have towards your children— expect nothing in return. If you can invariably take the position of a giver, in which everything given by you is a free offering to the world, without any thought of return, then will your work bring you no attachment. Attachment comes only where we expect a return.

If working like slaves results in selfishness and attachment, working as master of our own mind gives rise to the bliss of non-attachment. We often talk of right and justice, but we find that in the world right and justice are mere baby's talk. There are two things which guide the conduct of men: might and mercy. The exercise of might is invariably the exercise of selfishness. All men and women try to make the most of whatever power or advantage they have. Mercy is heaven itself; to be good, we have all to be merciful. Even justice and right should stand on mercy. All thought of obtaining return for the work we do hinders our spiritual progress; nay, in the end it brings misery. There is another way in which this idea of mercy and selfless charity can be put into practice; that is, by looking upon work as "worship" in case we believe in a Personal God. Here we give up all the fruits of our work unto the Lord, and worshipping Him thus, we have no right to expect anything from mankind for the work we do. The Lord Himself works incessantly and is ever without attachment. Just as water cannot wet the lotus leaf, so work cannot bind the unselfish man by giving rise to attachment to results.[5]

The spirit of unattached service to man and society that Vivekananda serenely expects from every human being is the only hope of regaining the paradise lost in the hapless society. When he speaks about liberty, he unfolds the truth of altruism which stands for liberty that challenges against any odds in social understanding or advancement among the members of the society. There is no room for liberty exercised by a few in the society at the cost of others. As Vivekananda significantly explains the role of freedom in realising and practising social customs:

> Rishi, Muni, or God— none has power to force an institution on society. When the needs of the times press hard on it, society adopts certain customs for self-preservation. Rishis have only recorded those customs. As a man often resorts even to such means as are good for immediate self-protection but which are very injurious in the future, similarly society also not unfrequently saves itself for the time being, but these immediate means which contributed to its preservation turn out terrible in the long run...
>
> Is it for the good of the public at large that social rules are framed or society is formed? Many reply to this in the affirmative; some, again, may hold that it is not so. Some men, being comparatively powerful, slowly bring all others under their control and by stratagem, force, or adroitness gain their own objects. If this be true, what can be the meaning of the

> statement that there is danger in giving liberty to the ignorant? What, again, is the meaning of liberty?
>
> Liberty does not certainly mean the absence of obstacles in the path of misappropriation of wealth etc. by you or me, but it is our natural right to be allowed to use our own body, intelligence, or wealth according to our will, without doing any harm to others; and all the members of the society ought to have the same opportunity for obtaining wealth, education, or knowledge. The second question is: Those who say that if the ignorant and the poor be given liberty, i.e. full right to their body, wealth, etc., and if their children have the same opportunity to better their condition and acquire knowledge as those of the rich and the highly situated, they would become perverse— do they say this for the good of society or blinded by their selfishness?[6]

For a radical improvement of the conditions of the masses denied in exercising freedom, education— living and loving— is the only alternative, and freedom such exercised always shows the avenues of efflorescence in social culture. Only the role of freedom well backed in and through education of the free mind and free approach can guarantee a cultured society. As Vivekananda reminds us:

> You can put a mass of knowledge into the world, but that will not do it much good. There must come culture into the blood. We all know in modern times of nations which have masses of knowledge, but what of them? They are like tigers, they are like savages, because culture is not there. Knowledge is only skin-deep, as civilisation is, and a little scratch brings out the old savage. Such things happen; this is the danger. Teach the masses in the vernaculars, give them ideas; they will get information, but something more is necessary; give them culture. Until you give them that, there can be no permanence in the raised condition of the masses.[7]

To be an optimist in social involvement and social responsibilities is to exrrcise freedom in the expected right way for the right direction towards excellence and ascent of the society. Vivekananda has never given importance to orthodoxy nor has he at any time sacrificed freedom for the society without caring for the right basis of social advancement. This is why he dreams of a society sans superstition sans crystallisation of social sensibilities. In his address delivered at the Triplicane Literary Society in Chennai, Vivekananda explains the dream of his life in terms of cooperation and freedom to eliminate all social superstitions:

> A broader and more generous conception of life is before us; and although at first we have been deluded a little and wanted to narrow things down, we are finding out today that these generous impulses which are at work, these broader conceptions of life, are the logical interpretation of what is in our ancient books. They are the carrying out, to the rigorously logical effect, of the primary conceptions of our own ancestors. To become broad, to go out, to amalgamate, to universalise, is the end of our aims. And all the time we have been making ourselves smaller and smaller, and dissociating ourselves, contrary to the plans laid down in the scriptures.
>
> Several dangers are in the way, and one is that of the extreme conception that we are *the* people in the world. With all my love for India, and with all my patriotism and veneration for the ancients, I cannot but think that we have to learn many things from other nations. We must be always ready to sit at the feet of all, for, mark you, every one can teach us great lessons. Says our great law-giver, Manu: "Receive some good knowledge even from the low-born, and even from the man of lowest birth learn by service the road to heaven." We, therefore, as true children of Manu, must obey his commands and be ready to learn the lessons of this life or the life hereafter from any one who can teach us. At the same time we must not forget that we have also to teach a great lesson to the world. We cannot do without the world outside India; it was our foolishness that we thought we could, and we have paid the penalty by about a thousand years of slavery. That we did not go out to compare

things with other nations, did not mark the workings that have been all around us, has been the one great cause of this degradation of the Indian mind. We have paid the penalty; let us do it no more. All such foolish ideas that Indians must not go out of India are childish. They must be knocked on the head; the more you go out and travel among the nations of the world, the better for you and for your country. If you had done that for hundreds of years past, you would not be here today at the feet of every nation that wants to rule India. The first manifest effect of life is expansion. You must expand if you want to live. The moment you have ceased to expand, death is upon you, danger is ahead. I went to America and Europe, to which you so kindly allude; I have to, because that is the first sign of the revival of national life, expansion. This reviving national life, expanding inside, threw me off, and thousands will be thrown off in that way. Mark my words, it has got to come if this nation lives at all. This question, therefore, is the greatest of the signs of the revival of national life, and through this expansion our quota of offering to the general mass of human knowledge, our contribution to the general upheaval of the world, is going out to the external world.[8]

What Vivekananda said more than a hundred years ago has come true to our any endeavour at social advancement in tune with the radical spirit of freedom at the national or the global level. Indeed, the mind-set for social enrichment is now very keen for a social bond of humane relationship where the national and the global vision is based on the great truth: unite and expand. The spirit of fostering the emancipation of the individual in tune with national and global social relationship has extended the horizon of human relationship where 'the contribution of the general upheavel of the world' as Vivekananda reminds us has extended a warm welcome to whatever we call external or otherwise. As a matter of fact, with broadened social vision and widened social outlook, today's social panorama has greeted freedom in a newer context of man and the world.

The concept of freedom necessitates a practical approach in terms of the society. Unless the society is adorned with the spirit of freedom, whatever emancipation of man and society is expected turns out to be a myth. Progressive reforms indicate an earnest exercise of freedom by every individual in the society. As Vivekananda points out:

> We do stand in need of social reform. At times great men would evolve new ideas of progress, and kings would give them sanction of law. Thus, social improvements had been in the past made in India, and in modern times to effect such progressive reforms, we will have first to build up such an authoritative power. Kings having gone, the power is the people's. We have, therefore, to wait till the people are educated, till they understand their needs and are ready and able to solve their problems. The tyranny of the minority is the worst tyranny in the world. Therefore, instead of frittering away our energies on ideal reforms, which will never become practical, we had better to go to the root of the evil and make a legislative body, that is to say, educate our people, so that they may be able to solve their own problems. Until that is done all these ideal reforms will remain ideals only. The new order of things is the salvation of the people by the people, and it takes time to make it workable, especially in India, which has always in the past been governed by kings.[9]

The quest for a new meaning of freedom starts with the individual. If every one in the society is aware of the value of freedom in life, the end-in-view of life for superconsciousness becomes a reality. Then we can be blessed with an enlightened human society of enlightened and serene individuals. "We are", as Vivekananda poignantly observes:

> too busy trying to mend the ways of our neighbours, that is the difficulty. We must begin with our own bodies. The heart, the liver, etc., are all atavistic; bring them back into consciousness, control them, so that they will obey your commands and act up to your wishes. There was a time when we had control of the liver; we could shake the whole skin, as can the cow. I have

> seen many people bring the control back by sheer hard practice. Once an impress is made, it is there. Bring back all the submerged activities – the vast ocean of action. This is the first part of the great study, and it is absolutely necessary for our social well-being. On the other hand, only the consciousness need not be studied all the time.[10]

This is not all. The spirit of freedom working for strengthening social consciousness and elevating man to superconsciousness leads to a certain sense of socio-spirituality whereby man gets a new vision of passing from natural phenomena like life and death to a new freedom of knowing the Real and becoming the Real as Vivekananda explicitly spells out:

> Then there is the other part of the study, not so necessary in our social life, which tends to liberation. Its direct action is to free the soul, to take the torch into the gloom, to clean out what is behind, to shake it up or even defy it, and to make us march onward piercing the gloom. That is the goal—the superconscious. Then when that state is reached, this very man becomes divine, becomes free. And to the mind thus trained to transcend all, gradually this universe will begin to give up its secrets; the book of nature will be read chapter after chapter, till the goal is attained, and we pass from this valley of life and death to that One, where death and life do not exist, and we know the Real and become the Real.[11]

Freedom to serve the society in order to serve God is the road to the ascent of man. This is the road to exercise freedom of the heart that should always be prepared for dedication to love and service of others in the society as the real service to the All Good. This is the freedom exercised to eliminate all innate inhibitions appearing in the form of selfishness.

In his elucidation on real worship, Vivekananda significantly remarks:

> 'He who wants to serve the father must serve the children first. He who wants to serve Shiva must serve His children—must

> serve all creatures in this world first. It is said in the Shastra that those who serve the servants of God are His greatest servants. So you will bear this in your mind.'
>
> Let me tell you again that you must be pure and help any one who comes to you, as much as lies in your power. And this is good Karma. By the power of this, the heart becomes pure (Chitta-suddhi), and then Shiva who is residing in every one will become manifest. He is always in the heart of every one. If there is dirt and dust on a mirror, we cannot see our image. So ignorance and wickedness are the dirt and dust that are on the mirror of our hearts. Selfishness is the chief sin, thinking of ourselves first. He who thinks, "I will eat first, I will have more money than others, and I will possess everything", he who thinks, "I will get to heaven before others, I will get Mukti before others" is the selfish man. The unselfish man says, "I will be last, I do not care to go to heaven, I will even go to hell if by doing so I can help my brothers."[12]

The new religion of man is the religion of service to the society in an ambience of freedom. How to think and act freely as an individual is the essence of a sound and evolving society. Every society demands such a radical approach to advancement where every individual enjoys the absolute right to develop himself/herself for the cause of the greater role it demands from him/her. Explaining the role of the individual in the society in terms of freedom of the soul as one comes across in the Upanishads, Vivekananda characteristically observes in his lecture delivered in London, 5th November 1896:

> Although all the systems agree so far that we had the empire, and that we have lost it, they give us varied advice as to how to regain it. One says that you must perform certain ceremonies, pay certain sums of money to certain idols, eat certain sorts of food, live in a particular fashion to regain that empire. Another says that if you weep and prostrate yourselves and ask pardon of some Being beyond nature, you will regain that empire. Again, another says if you love such a being with all your heart, you

> will regain that empire. All this varied advice is in the Upanishads. As I go on, you will find it so. But the last and the greatest counsel is that you need not weep at all. You need not go through all these ceremonies, and need not take any notice of how to regain your empire, because you never lost it. Why should you go to seek for what you never lost? You are pure already, you are free already. If you think you are free, free you are this moment, and if you think you are bound, bound you will be. This is a very bold statement, and as I told you at the beginning of this course, I shall have to speak to you very boldly. It may frighten you now, but when you think over it, then you will come to know that what I say is true. For, supporting that freedom is not your nature, by no manner of means can you become free. Supposing you were free and in some way you lost that freedom, that shows that you were not free to begin with. Had you been free, what could have made you lose it? The independence can never be made dependent; if it is really dependent, its independence was a hallucination.
>
> Of the two sides, then, which will you take? If you say that the soul was by its nature pure and free, it naturally follows that there was nothing in this universe which could make it bound or limited. But if there was anything in nature which could bind the soul, it naturally follows that it was not free, and your statement that it was free is a delusion. So if it is possible for us to attain freedom, the conclusion is inevitable that the soul is by its nature free. It cannot be otherwise. Freedom means independence of anything outside, and that means that nothing outside itself could work upon it as a cause.[13]

With the concept of freedom of the soul as the backdrop in relation to social emancipation of man, Vivekananda elsewhere urges on realisation of the concept of freedom as a return of everything and every one of the society to the Source, which is Atman that inspires us to exercise free-will against any form of bondage:

> Everything we know is a compound, and all sense-knowledge comes through analysis. To think that mind is simple, or

> independent is dualism. Philosophy is not got by studying books; the more you read books, the more muddled becomes the mind. The idea of unthinking philosophers was that the mind was simple, and this led them to believe in free-will. Psychology, the analysis of the mind, shows the mind to be a compound, and every compound must be held together by some outside force; so the will is bound by the combination of outside forces. Man cannot even will to eat unless he is hungry. Will is subject to desire. But we are free; everyone feels it.
>
> The agnostic says this idea is a delusion. Then, how do you prove the world? Its only proof is that we all see it and feel it; so just as much we all feel freedom. If universal consensus affirms this world, then it must be accepted as affirming freedom; but freedom is not of the will as it is. The constitutional belief of man in freedom is the basis of all reasoning. Freedom is of the will as it was before it became bound. The very idea of free-will shows every moment man's struggle against bondage. The free can be only one, the Unconditioned, the Infinite, the Unlimited.[14]

Freedom to annihilate infatuation and ignorance is the hallmark of social enlightenment. It is freedom in man and society that shows the supreme path of concentration of the mind. If the mind is concentrated, the manifestation of Brahman in every one in the society becomes a reality. Universal synthesis by means of exercising freedom-in-life is the ideal pathway to deliver others in the society from all sorts of infatuation. It is a difficult task but it is always challenging. Only those having brave hearts can win over all lure of infatuation.

In his salutation to Bhagavan Ramakrishna, 'the Preacher of the gospel of universal synthesis' as written in a letter to Shri Sarat Chandra Chakravarti on 19th March,1897, Vivekananda opens out his in-depth socio-spiritual vision:

> I have already felt that yearning for Freedom— potent enough to put the heart into turmoil— which your letter suggests you

> are experiencing. It is this yearning that gradually brings on a concentration of the mind on the eternal Brahman. "There is no other way to go by." May this desire blaze up more and more in you, until all your past Karma and future tendencies are absolutely annihilated. Close upon the heels of that will follow, all on a sudden, the manifestation of Brahman, and with it the destruction of all craving for the sense-world. That this freedom-in-life is approaching for your welfare is easily to be inferred from the strength of your fervour. Now I pray to that world-teacher, Shri Ramakrishna, the Preacher of the gospel of universal synthesis, to manifest himself in the region of your heart, so that, having attained the consummation of your desires, you may with an undaunted heart try your best to deliver others from this dreadful ocean of infatuation. May you be ever possessed of valour! It is the hero alone, not the coward, who has liberation within his every reach. Gird up your loins, ye heroes, for before you are your enemies— the dire army of infatuation. It is undoubtedly true that "all great achievements are fraught with numerous impediments"; still you should exert your utmost for your end. Behold, how men are already in the jaws of the shark of infatuation! Oh, listen to their piteous heart-rending wails. Advance, forward, O ye brave souls, to set free those that are in fetters, to lessen the burden of woe of the miserable, and to illumine the abysmal darkness of ignorant hearts![15]

The yearning for freedom is a social reality and to respond to that reality by sacrificing self-interest is the new manifestation of freedom. It is that social freedom which turns a man into 'men' in the society. He no longer remains bound within himself but finds his world of endless expansion and boundless joy in the midst of a world society. The whole world becomes his most endearing one— *Vasudhaivakutumvakam*— that allows every individual to exercise freedom with all sanity and wisdom, peace and progress. The relation between society and truth as an eternal spiritual force in the light of the above becomes very close and meaningful. It turns life into a magnanimous essence of excellence and ascent. As a radical thinker of freedom in the light of truth and society, Vivekananda boldly points out:

> *Truth does not pay homage to any society, ancient or modern. Society has to pay homage to Truth or die.* Societies should be moulded upon truth, and truth has not to adjust itself to society. If such a noble truth as unselfishness cannot be practised in society, it is better for man to give up society and go into the forest. That is the daring man. There are two sorts of courage. One is the courage of facing the cannon. And the other is the courage of spiritual conviction. An Emperor who invaded India was told by his teacher to go and see some of the sages there. After a long search for one, he found a very old man sitting on a block of stone. The Emperor talked with him a little and became very much impressed by his wisdom. He asked the sage to go to his country with him. "No," said the sage, "I am quite satisfied with my forest here." Said the Emperor, "I will give you money, position, wealth. I am the Emperor of the world." "No," replied the man, "I don't care for those things." The Emperor replied, "If you do not go, I will kill you." The man smiled serenely and said, "That is the most foolish thing you ever said, Emperor. You cannot kill me. Me the sun cannot dry, fire cannot burn, sword cannot kill, for I am the birthless, the deathless, the ever-living omnipotent, omnipresent Spirit." This is spiritual boldness, while the other is the courage of a lion or a tiger... What good is it to talk of the strength of your muscles, of the superiority of your Western institutions, if you cannot make Truth square with your society, if you cannot build up a society into which the highest Truth will fit? What is the use of this boastful talk about your grandeur and greatness, if you stand up and say, "This courage is not practical." Is nothing practical but pounds, shillings, and pence? If so, why boast of your society? *That society is the greatest, where the highest truths become practical.* That is my opinion; and if society is not fit for the highest truths, make it so; and the sooner, the better. Stand up,

> men and women, in this spirit, dare to believe in the Truth, dare to practise the Truth! The world requires a few hundred bold men and women. Practise that boldness which dares know the Truth, which dares show the Truth in life, which does not quake before death, nay, welcomes death, makes a man know that he is the Spirit, that, in the whole universe, nothing can kill him. Then you will be free.[16]

Admittedly, freedom in the light of Truth becomes the hallmark of a sound and vibrant, radical and progressive society. It rebuilds the vision of the society where every human being is the indomitable Spirit. The quest for freedom of the individual in terms of Truth and morality as the pointers to a celebrated society is very important for excellence and ascent. The essence of everything in perfect tune with reality is a must for every society that looks forward to enriching the march for freedom. There is no scope for compromise with anything that stands in the way of advancement of society in and through freedom. This is Truth, and society cannot but endear it. This is religion, where freedom upholds Truth as the essence of the society. This is also freedom baptised in the symphony of science and religion, poetry and philosophy in an ambiance of ever-efflorescent spontaneity.

The quest for the radical society as above is hallowed with the spirit of the Ever-Free, Ever-Blissful, Ever-Existing. As Vivekananda poignantly states:

> In the old Upanishads we find sublime poetry; their authors were poets. Plato says, inspiration comes to people through poetry, and it seems as if these ancient Rishis, seers of Truth, were raised above humanity to show these truths through poetry. They never preached, nor philosophised, nor wrote. Music came out of their hearts. In Buddha, we had the great, universal heart and infinite patience, making religion practical and bringing it to everyone's door. In Shankaracharya, we saw tremendous intellectual power, throwing the scorching light of reason upon everything. We want today that bright sun of intellectuality joined with the heart of Buddha, the wonderful infinite heart

> of love and mercy. This union will give us the highest philosophy. Science and religion will meet and shake hands. Poetry and philosophy will become friends. This will be the religion of the future, and if we can work it out, we may be sure that it will be for all times and peoples. This is the one way that will prove acceptable to modern science, for it has almost come to it. When the scientific teacher asserts that all things are the manifestation of one force, does it not remind you of the God of whom you hear in the Upanishads: "As the one fire entering into the universe expresses itself in various forms, even so that One Soul is expressing Itself in every soul and yet is infinitely more besides?" Do you not see whither science is tending? The Hindu nation proceeded through the study of the mind, through metaphysics and logic. The European nations start from external nature, and now they too are coming to the same results. We find that searching through the mind we at last come to that Oneness, the Universal One, the Internal Soul of everything, the Essence and Reality of everything, the Ever-Free, the Ever-Blissful, the Ever-Existing. Through material science we come to the same Oneness. Science today is telling us that all things are but the manifestation of one energy which is the sum total of everything which exists, and the trend of humanity is towards freedom and not towards bondage.[17]

A radical society fired with the spirit of freedom to arise and awake from the hypnotism of diverse weaknesses and constraints is the need everywhere. It is particularly needed in our country where the people of the society are yet to learn and practise the infinite value of freedom. The Infinite Soul in every one must be given freedom to manifest. In explaining the mission of the Vedanta, Vivekananda boldly observes:

> Who is responsible? And the answer comes every time: Not the English; no, they are not responsible; it is we who are responsible for all our misery and all our degradation, and we alone are responsible. Our aristocratic ancestors went on treading the common masses of our country underfoot, till they became

> helpless, till under this torment the poor, poor people nearly forgot that they were human beings. They have been compelled to be merely hewers of wood and drawers of water for centuries, so much so, that they are made to believe that they are born as slaves, born as hewers of wood and drawers of water. With all our boasted education of modern times, if anybody says a kind word for them, I often find our men shrink at once from the duty of lifting them up, these poor downtrodden people. Not only so, but I also find that all sorts of most demonical and brutal arguments, culled from the crude ideas of hereditary transmission and other such gibberish from the Western world, are brought forward in order to brutalise and tyrannise over the poor all the more.[18]

A new society blessed with freedom is the only alternative to eliminate all superstitions and abstractions in the name of religion. The vast amount of progress that every society pines for becomes a reality in the event of its people always bold and free to adore and practice freedom in every affair of life. This also makes them idealise the true religion of man and society blessed with the true end-in-view of spirituality. Referring to the great saying of Manu on learning the way to freedom as the ideal of an individual for the progress of an altruistic society, Vivekananda, in his reply to the address of welcome at Ramnad on 25th January, 1897, extends the horizon of freedom and society towards an ever excellent efflorescence of spirituality:

> "Learn good knowledge with all devotion from the lowest caste. Learn the way to freedom, even if it comes from a Pariah, by serving him. If a woman is a jewel, take her in marriage even if she comes from a low family of the lowest caste." Such is the law laid down by our great and peerless legislator, the divine Manu. This is true. Stand on your feet, and assimilate what you can; learn from every nation, take what is of use to you. But remember that as Hindus everything else must be subordinated to our national ideals. Each man has a mission in life, which is the result of all his infinite past Karma. Each of

you was born with a splendid heritage, which is the whole of the infinite past life of your glorious nation. Millions of your ancestors are watching, as it were, every action of yours, so be alert. And what is the mission with which every Hindu child is born? Have you not read the proud declaration of Manu regarding the Brahmins where he says that the birth of the Brahmin is "for the protection of the treasury of religion"? I should say that *that* is the mission, not only of the Brahmin, but of every child, whether boy or girl, who is born in this blessed land "for the protection of the treasury of religion". And every other problem in life must be subordinated to that one principal theme. That is also the law of harmony in music. There may be a nation whose theme of life is political supremacy; religion and everything else must become sub-ordinate to that one great theme of its life. But here is another nation whose great theme of life is spirituality and renunciation, whose one watchword is that this world is all vanity and a delusion of three days, and everything else, whether science or knowledge, enjoyment or powers, wealth, name, or fame, must be subordinated to that one theme. The secret of a true Hindu's character lies in the subordination of his knowledge of European sciences and learning, of his wealth, position, and name, to that one principal theme which is inborn in every Hindu child— the spirituality and purity of the race. Therefore, between these two, the case of the orthodox man who has the whole of that life-spring of the race, spirituality, and the other man whose hands are full of Western imitation-jewels but has no hold on the life-giving principle, spirituality— of these, I do not doubt that every one here will agree that we should choose the first, the orthodox, because there is some hope in him— he has the national theme, something to hold to; so he will live, but the other will die. Just as in the case of individuals, if the principle of life is undisturbed, if the principal function of that individual life is present, any injuries received as regards other functions are not serious, do not kill the individual, so,

> as long as this principal function of our life is not disturbed, nothing can destroy our nation. But mark you, if you give up that spirituality, leaving it aside to go after the materialising civilisation of the West, the result will be that in three generations you will be an extinct race; because the backbone of the nation will be broken, the foundation upon which the national edifice has been built will be undermined, and the result will be annihilation all around.[19]

How should we become the true messengers of spirituality as the harbinger of a noble, magnanimous and serene global society? How to translate the great mission for universal freedom in terms of trans-social freedom of the mind: *Udaracharitanam tu vasudhaivakutumvakam?* Let all forms of social and allied superstitions be totally uprooted in the light of freedom of an enlightened mind. Let all be bold enough to uphold 'our religion, our national life, our spirituality'.

In a lecture delivered at the Triplicane Literary Society, Chennai, Vivekananda has forewarned us against the great menace inflicted by various types of superstitions writ large in the society almost everywhere and advised to be bold enough to be up and doing in upholding freedom to think and freedom to progress:

> We must go out, we must conquer the world through our spirituality and philosophy. There is no other alternative, we must do it or die. The only condition of national life, of awakened and vigorous national life, is the conquest of the world by Indian thought.
>
> At the same time we must not forget that what I mean by the conquest of the world by spiritual thought is the sending out of the life-giving principles, not the hundreds of superstitions that we have been hugging to our breasts for centuries. These have to be weeded out even on this soil, and thrown aside, so that they may die for ever. These are the causes of the degradation of the race and will lead to softening of the brain. That brain which cannot think high and noble thoughts, which has lost all

power of originality, which has lost all vigour, that brain which is always poisoning itself with all sorts of little superstitions passing under the name of religion, we must beware of. In our sight, here in India, there are several dangers. Of these, the two, Scylla and Cherybdis, rank materialism and its opposite arrant superstition, must be avoided. There is the man today who after drinking the cup of Western wisdom, thinks that he knows everything. He laughs at the ancient sages. All Hindu thought to him is arrant trash— philosophy mere child's prattle, and religion the superstition of fools. On the other hand, there is the man educated, but a sort of monomaniac, who runs to the other extreme, and wants to explain the omen of this and that. He has philosophical and metaphysical, and Lord knows what other puerile explanations for every superstition that belongs to this peculiar race, or his peculiar gods, or his peculiar village. Every little village superstition is to him a mandate of the Vedas, and upon this carrying out of it, according to him, depends the national life. You must beware of this. I would rather see every one of your rank atheists than superstitious fools, for the atheist is alive and you can make something out of him. But if superstition enters, the brain is gone, the brain is softening, degradation has seized upon the life. Avoid these two. Brave, bold men, these are what we want. What we want is vigour in the blood, strength in the nerves, iron muscles and nerves of steel, not softening namby-pamby ideas. Avoid all these. Avoid all mystery. There is no mystery in religion. Is there any mystery in the Vedanta, or in the Vedas, or in the Samhitas, or in the Puranas? What secret societies did the sages of yore establish to preach their religion? What sleight-of-hand tricks are there recorded as used by them to bring their grand truths to humanity? Mystery mongering and superstition are always signs of weakness. These are always signs of degradation and of death. Therefore, beware of them; be strong, and stand on your own feet. Great things are there, most marvellous things. We may call them supernatural things so far as our ideas of

> nature go, but not one of these things is a mystery. It was never preached on this soil that the truths of religion were mysteries or that they were the property of secret societies sitting on the snow-caps of the Himalayas. I have been in the Himalayas. You have not been there; it is several hundreds of miles from your homes. I am a Sannyasin, and I have been for the last fourteen years on my feet. These mysterious societies do not exist anywhere. Do not run after these superstitions. Better for you and for the race that you become rank atheists, because you would have strength, but these are degradation and death. Shame on humanity that strong men should spend their time on these superstitions, spend all their time in inventing allegories to explain the most rotten superstitions of the world. Be bold; do not try to explain everything that way. The fact is that we have many superstitions, many bad spots and sores on our body – these have to be excised, cut off, and destroyed— but these do not destroy our religion, our national life, our spirituality.[20]

What, then, should be the role of man in terms of freedom and society? How would he prove his worth best? How would he react against anything that comes in the way of freedom of mind and realisation of the Self? How to be self identified as the Self? How to be truly radical in every aspect of individual and, for that end-in-view, illumined social life?

In one of his inspired talks on *Avadhuta Gita* or *"Song of the Purified"* by Dattatreya, the son of Atri and Anasuya, and the incarnation of Brahma, Vishnu, and Maheswara, Vivekananda has made an unparalleled and radical exposition on the uniqueness of man the ever free contributor to an ever cherished evolving society:

> No thought, no word, no deed, creates a bondage for me. I am beyond the senses, I am knowledge and bliss.
>
> There is neither existence nor non-existence, all is Atman. Shake off all ideas of relativity; shake off all superstitions; let caste and birth and Devas and all else vanish. Why talk of being and becoming? Give up talking of dualism and Advaitism!

> When were you two, that you talk of two or one? The universe is this Holy One and He alone. Talk not of Yoga to make you pure; you are pure by your very nature. None can teach you.
>
> Men like him who wrote this song are what keep religion alive. They have actually realised; they care for nothing, feel nothing done to the body, care not for heat and cold or danger or anything. They sit still and enjoy the bliss of Atman, while red-hot coals burn their body, and they feel them not.
>
> When the threefold bondage of knower, knowledge, and known ceases, there is the Atman.
>
> What if you have controlled the mind, what if you have not? What if you have money, what if you have not? You are the Atman ever pure. Say, 'I am the Atman. No bondage ever came near me. I am the changeless sky; clouds of belief may pass over me, but they do not touch me.'
>
> Burn virtue, burn vice. Freedom is baby talk. I am that immortal Knowledge. I am that purity.
>
> No one was ever bound, none was ever free. There is none but me. I am the Infinite, the Ever-Free. Talk not to me! What can change me, the essence of knowledge! Who can teach, who can be taught?[21]

An altogether social iconoclast, Vivekananda rises above the self for the glory of the Self that cares not in isolation but for union of the whole global human society. Such an ideal preaches the vision of the social man yet to be discovered in his real identity in the social enrichment of divine reality. When he upgrades man as a social being of excellence, he throws the eternal challenge—*charaiveti,* march ahead. This march is not an easy one. It calls for unending preparation, unbiased decision of the mind, and unflinching devotion to uphold and empower freedom from all forms of socio-spiritual ukase.

When Vivekananda speaks about unending renunciation, we get the real concept of realisation in terms of the society. The sense organs need proper control. Not pleasure out of sense organs, but self-sacrifice is the foundation of an illumined society. Vivekananda characteristically unfolds this truth:

> The lower the organism, the greater is its pleasure in the senses. Think of the lowest animals and the power of touch... When you come to man, you will see that the lower the civilisation of the man, the greater is the power of the senses...The higher the organism, the lesser is the pleasure of the senses. A dog can eat a meal, but cannot understand the exquisite pleasure of thinking about metaphysics. He is deprived of the wonderful pleasure which you get through the intellect. The pleasures of the senses are great. Greater than those are the pleasures of the intellect. When you attend the fine fifty-course dinner in Paris, that is pleasure indeed. But in the observatory, looking at the stars, seeing...worlds coming and developing—think of that! It must be greater, for I know you forget all about eating. That pleasure must be greater than what you get from worldly things. You forget all about wives, children, husbands, and everything; you forget all about the sense-plane. That is intellectual pleasure. It is common sense that it must be greater than sense-pleasure. It is always for greater joy that you give up the lesser. This is practical religion— the attainment of freedom, renunciation. Renounce!
>
> Renounce the lower so that you may get the higher. What is the foundation of society? Morality, ethics, laws. Renounce. Renounce all temptation to take your neighbour's property, to put hands upon your neighbour, all the pleasure of tyrannising over the weak, all the pleasure of cheating others by telling lies. Is not morality the foundation of society? What is marriage but the renunciation of unchastity? The savage does not marry. Man marries because he renounces. So on and on. Renounce! Renounce! Sacrifice! Give up! Not for zero. Not for nothing. But to get the higher. But who can do this? You cannot, until you have got the higher. You may talk. You may struggle.

> You may try to do many things. But renunciation comes by itself when you have got the higher. Then the lesser falls by itself.[22]

A society with ever aspiring higher thoughts and nobler visions well flagged by a stream of radical perspectives is what Vivekananda has highlighted on different occasions. Unless the society makes a healthy climate of freedom to think and, accordingly, freedom to act, the progress of man becomes a myth. A transparent view of reincarnation as he puts forward shows how freedom to think afresh by means of frank askances gives an in-depth vision of an ever altruistic society:

> Here is one child born in the province of a just and merciful God, with every circumstance conducing to his becoming a good and useful member of the human race, and perhaps at the same instant and in the same city another child is born under circumstances every one of which is against his becoming good. We see children born to suffer, perhaps all their lives, and that owing to no fault of theirs. Why should it be so? What is the cause? Of whose ignorance is it the result? If not the child's, why should it suffer for its parents' actions?
>
> It is much better to confess ignorance than to try to evade the question by the allurements of future enjoyments in proportion to the evil here, or by posing "mysteries". Not only undeserved suffering forced upon us by any agent is immoral— not to say unjust— but even the future-making-up theory has no legs to stand upon.
>
> How many of the miserably born struggle towards a higher life, and how many more succumb to the circumstances they are placed under? Should those who grow worse and more wicked by being forced to be born under evil circumstances be rewarded in the future for the wickedness of their lives? In that case the more wicked the man is here, the better will be his deserts hereafter.
>
> There is no other way to vindicate the glory and the liberty of the human soul and reconcile the inequalities and the horrors

> of this world than by placing the whole burden upon the legitimate cause— our own independent actions or Karma. Not only so, but every theory of the creation of the soul from nothing inevitably leads to fatalism and preordination, and instead of a Merciful Father, places before us a hideous, cruel, and an ever-angry God to worship. And so far as the power of religion for good or evil is concerned, this theory of a created soul, leading to its corollaries of fatalism or preordination, is responsible for the horrible idea prevailing among some Christians and Mohammedans that the heathens are the lawful victims of their swords, and all the horrors that have followed and are following it still.[23]

Redirecting religion or anything whatsoever that stands in the way of proper and natural efflorescence of freedom to grow and develop for the manifestation inherent in every human being is never Vivekananda's cup of tea. He would rather forsake religion or anything to uphold liberty as the essence of excellence and ascent of man. His very solemn urge for becoming the God of the poor—*Daridradevo bhava*—is the life-blood of social and humane emancipation of man from all forms of orthodoxy or conservatism, all crudities, and, above all, all narrowness of vision.

Admittedly, Vivekananda's vision of man in the light of the above becomes clear and explicit from his radical statement:

> We believe that it is the duty of every *soul* to treat, think of, and behave to other *souls* as such, i.e. as *Gods,* and not hate or despise, or vilify, or try to injure them by any manner or means. This is the duty not only of the Sannyasin, but of all men and women.
>
> The soul has neither sex, nor caste, nor imperfection. We believe that nowhere throughout the Vedas, Darshanas, or Puranas, or Tantras, is it ever said that the soul has any sex, creed, or caste. Therefore, we agree with those who say, "What has religion to do with social reforms?" But they must also agree with us when we tell them that religion has no business to formulate social laws and insist on the difference between beings,

> because its aim and end is to obliterate all such fictions and monstrosities.
>
> If it be pleaded that through the difference we would reach the final equality and unity, we answer that the same religion has said over and over again that mud cannot be washed with mud. As if a man can be moral by being immoral!
>
> Social laws are created by economic conditions under the sanction of religion. The terrible mistake of religion was to interfere in social matters. But how hypocritically it says and thereby contradicts itself, "Social reform is not the business of religion"! True, what we want is that religion should not be a social reformer, but we insist at the same time that society has no right to become a religious law-giver.[24]

The dynamic role of man and society is the touchstone of advancement. It always calls forth a fruitful step towards a religion of consciousness that prompts every one to adjust in order to live in the society to which one belongs. Vivekananda is very transparent and radical on this point:

> What I say is not, "Reform", but, "Move on". Nothing is too bad to reform. Adaptability is the whole mystery of life— the principle underneath which serves to unfold it. Adjustment or adaptation is the outcome of the Self pitted against external forces tending to suppress It. He who adjusts himself best lives the longest. Even if I do not preach this, society is changing, it must change. It is not Christianity nor science, it is necessity, that is working underneath, the necessity that people must have to live or starve.[25]

What, then, are the pre-requisites for man in relation to society? These are love and freedom to exercise it by eliminating all forms of jealousy. His watchword is humility with constant feeling for others and work with unalloyed devotion to the welfare of the society. "First", as Vivekananda advises us:

> we must go out of the world and make ourselves fit instruments. Make yourself a dynamo. *Feel* first for the world. At a time

> when all men are ready to work, where is the man of *feeling* ? Where is the feeling that produced an Ignatius Loyola? Test your love and humility. That man is not humble or loving who is jealous. Jealousy is a terrible, horrible sin; it enters a man so mysteriously. Ask yourself, does your mind react in hatred or jealousy? Good works are continually being undone by tons of hatred and anger which are being poured out on the world. If you are pure, if you are strong, *you, one* man, are equal to the whole world.
>
> The brain to conceive the next condition of doing good works is only a dry Sahara after all; it cannot do anything alone unless it has the *feeling* behind it. Take love, which has never failed; and then the brain will conceive, and the hand will work righteousness.[26]

Do we really feel and act accordingly for the society in perfect tune with love and humility?

References

1. Swami Vivekananda: *The Complete Works of Swami Vivekananda,* Advaita Ashrama, Kolkata, Mayavati Memorial Edition, 1989, Vol. V, p. 241.
2. *Ibid.,* Vol. VIII, p. 307.
3. *Ibid.,* p. 248.
4. *Ibid.,* Vol. I, p. 502.
5. *Ibid.,* pp. 59-60.
6. *Ibid.,* Vol. V, pp. 145-146.
7. *Ibid.,* Vol. III, p. 291.
8. *Ibid.,* pp. 272-273.
9. *Ibid.,* Vol. V, pp. 215-216.
10. *Ibid.,* p. 249.
11. *Ibid.,* p. 250.
12. *Ibid.,* Vol. III, pp. 142-143.
13. *Ibid.,* Vol. II, pp. 195-196.
14. *Ibid.,* Vol. VII, p. 48.
15. *Ibid.,* p. 504.

16. *Ibid.*, Vol. II, pp. 84-85.
17. *Ibid.*, pp. 140-141.
18. *Ibid.*, Vol. III, p. 192.
19. *Ibid.*, pp. 151-153.
20. *Ibid.*, pp. 277-279.
21. *Ibid.*, Vol. VII, pp. 72-73.
22. *Ibid.*, Vol. IV, pp. 242-243.
23. *Ibid.*, pp. 269-270.
24. *Ibid.*, pp. 357-358.
25. *Ibid.*, Vol. VI, p. 110.
26. *Ibid.*, pp. 144-145.

3

Freedom and Education: Vivekananda's Introspection

Education holds the key to the being and becoming of man. For this, what is very important and essential is freedom. Freedom to be as one ought to be in order to justify one's being and becoming cannot for a single moment be averted. If one is not free, one is yet to learn how to arise and advance for self-respect, self-realisation and self-devotion. Again, if one is not free, the advancement of the society in which one lives becomes absolutely impossible.

A radical thinker par excellence in education, Swami Vivekananda, while explaining what true education stands for, strongly asserts:

> What is education? Is it book-learning? No. Is it diverse knowledge? Not even that. The training by which the current and expression of will are brought under control and become fruitful is called education. Now consider, is that education as a result of which the will, being continuously choked by force through generations, is well-nigh killed out; is that education under whose sway even the old ideas, let alone the new ones, are disappearing one by one; is that education which is slowly making man a machine? It is more blessed, in my opinion, even to go wrong, impelled by one's free will and intelligence than to be good as an automation. Again, can that be called

> society which is formed by an aggregate of men who are like lumps of clay, like lifeless machines, like heaped up pebbles? How can such society fare well?[1]

Freedom to nurse and enrich a positive mental attitude ensures a sound society. If education is geared towards training of the sense-organs by cultivating free-will for love and devotion, sacrifice and dedication, the whole purpose of manifestation of fulness inherent in every human being will be successful.

While delineating with social problems, Vivekananda categorically points out how freedom in education in the light of love, sacrifice, 'devotion to the universal Virat' becomes a serene reality:

> What glory is there in the renunciation of an eternal beggar? What virtue is there in the sense-control of one devoid of sense-power? What again is the self-sacrifice of one devoid of idea, devoid of heart, devoid of high ambition, and devoid of conception of what constitutes society? What expression of devotedness to a husband is there by forcing a widow to commit Sati? Why make people do virtuous deeds by teaching superstitions? I say, liberate, undo the shackles of people as much as you can. Can dirt be washed by dirt? Can bondage be removed by bondage? Where is the instance? When you would be able to sacrifice all desire for happiness for the sake of society, then you would be the Buddha, then you would be free: that is far off. Again, do you think the way to do it lies through expression?...The truth is that in this country parents and relatives can ruthlessly sacrifice the best interests of their children and others for their own selfish ends to save themselves by compromise to society; and the teaching of generations rendering the mind callous has made it perfectly easy. He, the brave alone, can deny self. The coward, afraid of the lash, with one hand wipes his eyes and gives with the other. Of what avail are such gifts? It is a far cry to love universal. The young plant should be hedged in and taken care of. One can hope gradually

> to attain to universal love if one can learn to love one object unselfishly.[2]

Freedom in education calls forth freedom to learn and know, ask and wonder, think and act positively. Unless a positive mental attitude is formed and exercised through freedom to create and think critically, the purpose of education becomes futile and meaningless. Reawakening of self-esteem and self-confidence through positive exercise of freedom as Vivekananda points out is the surest way of advancement in education and life:

> We have had a negative education all along from our boyhood. We have only learnt that we are nobodies. Seldom are we given to understand that great men were ever born in our country. Nothing positive has been taught to us. We do not even know how to use our hands and feet! We master all the facts and figures concerning the ancestors of the English, but we are sadly unmindful of our own. We have learnt only weakness. Being a conquered race, we have brought ourselves to believe that we are weak and have no independence in anything. So, how can it be but that the Shraddha is lost? The idea of true Shraddha must be brought back once more to us, the faith in our own self must be reawakened, and, then only, all the problems which face our country will gradually be solved by ourselves.[3]

As a radical thinker of education for social emancipation, Vivekananda prioritises the excellence of an individual in bringing about a positive and effective social change. He does not approve commonality or majority as such, because social advancement demands the role of the most intelligent ones who delve deep into the problems from which a society suffers, and suggest positive avenues of freedom to march ahead for all round social advancement. "What we call majority is," in the invaluable words of Vivekananda:

> mainly composed of fools and men of common intellect. Men who have brains to think for themselves are few, everywhere. These few men with brains are the real leaders in everything and every department of work; the majority are guided by them

as with a string, and that is good, for everything goes all right when they follow in the footsteps of these leaders. Those are only fools who think themselves too high to bend their heads to anyone, and they bring on their own ruin by acting on their own judgment. You talk of social reform? But what do you do? All that you mean by your social reform is either widow remarriage, or female emancipation, or something of that sort. Do you not? And these again are directed within the confines of a few castes only. Such a scheme of reform may do good to a few no doubt, but of what avail is that to the whole nation? Is that reform or only a form of selfishness— somehow to cleanse your own room and jeep it tidy and let others go from bad to worse!

** ** **

Most of what you talk of as social reform does not touch the poor masses; they have already those things— the widow remarriage, female emancipation, etc.— which you cry for. For this reason they will not think of those things as reforms at all. What I mean to say is that want of Shraddha has brought in all the evils among us, and is bringing in more and more. My method of treatment is to take out by the roots the very causes of the disease and not to keep them merely suppressed. Reform we should have in many ways; who will be so foolish as to deny it?[4]

The essence of freedom in terms of education and vice versa is the eternal thirst for the unknown and the infinite. That is education endearing marvels and adventure. For such education, one is always in quest of meanings free and diverse, unending and altogether interesting. Unless 'the eternal cry' in every one of us is appropriately responded, the blessings of freedom in education become an illusion. Vivekananda characteristically spells out this truth:

Have you marked the eternal cry going on through the ages in every breast? We are deceived by poverty. We become wealthy and are deceived by wealth. We are ignorant. We read and learn

> and are deceived with knowledge. No man is ever satisfied. That is the cause of misery, but it is also the cause of all blessing. That is the sure sign. How can you be satisfied with this world?... If tomorrow this world becomes heaven, we will say, "Take this away. Give us something else."
>
> The infinite soul can never be satisfied but by the Infinite itself... Infinite desire can only be satisfied by infinite knowledge—nothing short of that. Worlds will come and go. What of that? The soul lives and for ever expands. Worlds must come into the soul. Worlds must disappear in the soul like drops in the ocean. And this world to become the goal of the soul! If we have common sense, we cannot be satisfied, though this has been the theme of the poets in all the ages, always telling us to be satisfied. And nobody has been satisfied yet! Millions of prophets have told us, "Be satisfied with your lot"; poets sing. We have told ourselves to be quiet and satisfied, yet we are not. It is the design of the Eternal that there is nothing in this world to satisfy my soul, nothing in the heavens above, and nothing beneath. Before the desire of my soul, the stars and the worlds, upper and lower, the whole universe, is but a hateful disease, nothing but that. That is the meaning.[5]

Experience is the key to education and that education is crystallised by the exercise of freedom. If one is wholly dependent on books alone and does not exercise one's freedom to learn through challenging each and every point of learning throughly and independently, the purpose of real education is appallingly defeated. Hence, the importance of personal experience well applied to book-learning is undeniable. It makes ample room for exercise of curiosity as one of the great and incomparable blessings of freedom to learn and advance. As Vivekananda clearly observes:

> We may talk and reason all our lives, but we shall not understand a word of truth, until we experience it ourselves. You cannot hope to make a man a surgeon by simply giving him a few books. You cannot satisfy my curiosity by showing me a map; I must have actual experience. Maps can only create curiosity in

> us to get more perfect knowledge. Beyond that, they have no value whatever. Clinging to books only degenerates the human mind. Was there ever a more horrible blasphemy than the statement that all the knowledge of God is confined to this or that book? How dare men call God infinite, and yet try to compress Him within the covers of a little book! Millions of people have been killed because they did not believe what the books said, because they would not see all the knowledge of God within the covers of a book.[6]

Man's thirst for knowing the unknown by challenging every item of knowledge and experience is one of the surest signs of devotion to radical education.

That real and radical education is always innovative, self-sourced, creative, critical and self-dependent and never parasitical is yet to be taken into serious consideration in the arena of education. This is evident in case of child education where the educational process very often starts with the firm belief that it is entirely dependent on teachers. This simply kills the very essence of education and makes it artificial and parasitical. Moreover, it dishonours a child in disregarding its own possibilities and potentialities where radical thoughts and visions exist, as it were, in the form of a cocoon. As Vivekananda with his own childhood experience forewarns:

> You scarcely meet any man or woman who is not struggling for some sort of religion; and how many are satisfied, or rather how few are satisfied! How few find anything! And why? Simply because most of them go after impossible tasks. They are forced into these by the dictation of others. For instance, when I am a child, my father puts a book into my hand which says God is such and such. What business has he to put that into my mind? How does he know what way I would develop? And being ignorant of my constitutional development, he wants to force his ideas on my brain, with the result that my growth is stunted. You cannot make a plant grow in soil unsuited to it. A child teaches itself. But you can *help* it to go forward in its own way. What you can do is not of the positive nature, but of the

> negative. You can take away the obstacles, but knowledge comes out of its own nature. Loosen the soil a little, so that it may come out easily. Put a hedge round it; see that it is not killed by anything, and there your work stops. You cannot do anything else. The rest is a manifestation from *within* its own nature. So with the education of a child; a child educates itself. You come to hear me, and when you go home, compare what you have learnt, and you will find you have thought out the same thing; I have only given it expression. I can never teach you anything; you will have to teach yourself, but I can help you perhaps in giving expression to that thought.
>
> So in religion— more so— I must teach myself religion. What right has my father to put all sorts of nonsense into my head? What right has my master or society to put things into my head? Perhaps they are good, but they may not be *my* way. Think of the appalling evil that is in the world today, of the millions and millions of innocent children perverted by wrong ways of teaching. How many beautiful things which would have become wonderful spiritual truths have been nipped in the bud by this horrible idea of a family religion, a social religion, a national religion, and so forth. Think of what a mass of superstition is in your head just now about your childhood's religion, or your country's religion, and what an amount of evil it does, or can do. Man does not know what a potent power lies behind each thought and action.[7]

Modification in teaching in accordance with the trends and tendencies of the learner's way of learning acts as an enzyme to radical education. Her/His needs must be prioritised. In one of his inspired talks delivered on 5th August 1895, Vivekananda clearly describes:

> The teaching must be modified according to the needs of the taught. The consuming fire is ready for all, even water and chunks of ice quickly consume. Fire a mass of bird-shot, one at least will strike; give a man a whole museum of truths, he will at once take what is suited to him. Past lives have moulded our

> tendencies; give to the taught in accordance with his tendency. Intellectual, mystical, devotional, practical— make one the basis, but teach the others with it. Intellect must be balanced with love, the mystical nature with reason, while practice must form part of every method. Take every one where he stands and push him forward. Religious teaching must always be constructive, not destructive.
>
> Each tendency shows the life-work of the past, the line or radius along which that man must move. All radii lead to the centre. Never even attempt to disturb anyone's tendencies; to do that puts back both teacher and taught. When you teach Jnana, you must become a Jnani and stand mentally exactly where the taught stands. Similarly, in every other Yoga. Develop every faculty as if it were the only one possessed, this is the true secret of so-called harmonious development. That is get extensity with intensity, but not at its expense. We are infinite. There is no limitation in us, we can be as intense as the most devoted Mohammedan and as broad as the most roaring atheist.[8]

How, then, should be the quest of a true teacher? He must teach with sympathy and love, adoration and optimism. Nothing should be kept secret from the learner. Nothing, again, should be presented in ambiguity and abstraction. The world of right introspection of the learner should be ignited. And the rest would follow automatically, allowing freedom to learn is more important than anything in teaching.

In defining and explaining the role of a true teacher, Vivekananda emphasises on freedom as the hallmark of meaningful and purposeful education that cares for 'the tendency of the taught':

> The true teacher is one who can throw his whole force into the tendency of the taught. Without real sympathy we can never teach well. Give up the notion that man is a responsible being, only the perfect man is responsible. The ignorant have drunk deep of the cup of delusion and are not sane. You, who *know,* must have infinite patience with these. Have nothing but love

> for them and find out the disease that has made them see the world in a wrong light, then help them to cure it and see aright. Remember always that only the free have free will; all the rest are in bondage and are not responsible for what they do. Will as well is bound. The water when melting on the top of the Himalayas is free, but becoming the river, it is bound by the banks; yet the original impetus carries it to the sea, and it regains its freedom. The first is the "fall of man", the second is the "resurrection". Not one atom can rest until it finds its freedom.[9]

The quest for the new and the unknown is the unique blessing of freedom. It makes education living and thrilling. It prepares the mind to make newer and finer inroads to success and fulness. Indeed, freedom in education stands for and strengthens the power of finding out the new and the unknown. It presents the mind with two invaluable components. The first is to think and the second, to do. This is not all. There is not the end. It is an endless endeavour to refine the power to think and act accordingly. Strength, agility, alertness and perseverance in particular act as a unit of added impetus in education in the exercise of freedom where failure is never a curse but an ever inspiring fountain of success. In the inspiring and radical words of Vivekananda:

> Let us think something new, even it be wrong. It is better to do that. Why should you not try to hit the mark? We become wiser through failures. Time is infinite. Look at the wall. Did the wall ever tell a lie? It is always the wall. Man tells a lie—and becomes a god too. It is better to do something; never mind even if it proves to be wrong; it is better than doing nothing. The cow never tells a lie, but she remains a cow, all the time. Do something! Think some thought; it doesn't matter whether you are right or wrong. But think something! Because my forefathers did not think this way, shall I sit down quietly and gradually lose my sense of feeling and my own thinking faculties? I may as well be dead! And what is life worth if we have no living ideas, no convictions of our own about religion? There is some hope for the atheists, because though they differ from

> others, they think for themselves. The people who never think anything for themselves are not yet born into the world of religion; they have a mere jelly-fish existence. They will not think; they do not care for religion. But the disbeliever, the atheist, cares, and he is struggling. So think something! Struggle Godward! Never mind if you fail, never mind if you get hold of a queer theory. If you are afraid to be called queer, keep it in your own mind— you need not go and preach it to others. But do something! Struggle Godward! Light must come. If a man feeds me every day of my life, in the long run I shall lose the use of my hands. Spiritual death is the result of following each other like a flock of sheep. Death is the result of inaction. Be active; and wherever there is activity, there must be difference. Difference is the sauce of life; it is the beauty, it is the art of everything. Difference makes all beautiful here. It is variety that is the source of life, the sign of life.[10]

Freedom in education means freedom to reveal one's true identity. Unless that freedom is exercised in and through education, the identity of an individual learner is in peril. The newer avenues radical and revolutionary must be honoured for the best efflorescence of knowledge; otherwise, knowledge acts like a dead instrument of learning and teaching in a dull and mechanical ambiance of passivity and artificiality.

The diversity in quest of knowledge of the right kind and of the right mind in a right citadel of culture signifies true education. It is freedom and freedom alone that can guarantee such a platform of radical thinking. As Vivekananda introspects:

> If every act in a man's life has been all previously determined, then what need is there for the culture of the faculty of thought— where is the field for the free play of independent thought and action? In course of time, for want of proper use, all activity is given up, all originality is lost, a sort of Tamasika dreamy lifelessness hovers over the whole nation, and headlong it goes down and down…

Considering all these points, it must be admitted that, though the presence of knowledge everywhere in every individual is an eternal truism, yet the path pointed out by the great ones of the earth has the glory peculiar to it, and that there is a peculiar interest attached to the transmission of knowledge through the seccession of teachers and their disciples. Each of them has its place in the development of the sum total of knowledge; and we must learn to estimate them according to their respective merits. But, perhaps, being carried away by their over-zealous and blind devotion to their Masters, the successors and followers of these great ones sacrifice truth before the altar of devotion and worship to them, and misrepresent the true meaning of the purpose of those great lives by insisting on personal worship, that is they kill the principle for the person.

This is also a fact of common experience that when man himself has lost all his own strength, he naturally likes to pass his days in idle remembrance of his forefathers' greatness. The devoted heart gradually becomes the weakest in its constant attempt to resign itself in every respect to the feet of its ancestors, and at last a time comes when this weakness teaches the disabled yet proud heart to make the vain glory of its ancestors' greatness as the only support of its life. Even if it be true that your ancestors possessed all knowledge, which has in the efflux of time been lost to you, it follows that you, their descendants, must have been instrumental in this disappearance of knowledge, and now it is all the same to you whether you have it or not. To talk of losing or having this already lost knowledge serves no useful purpose at present. You will have to make new efforts, to undergo troubles over again, if you want to recover it.[11]

From the above, it is transparent that the education that makes room for newer visions, greater principles and stronger challenges than what has already been done comes under the purview of radicalism which is never a cup of tea for the indolent and passive, imitative and irresponsible. It will be simply inviting death to one's creative thinking and critical awareness which are vitalised in the womb of freedom in education.

The inner light with which we are blessed is actually the blessing of freedom. When we appreciate this freedom, learning becomes meaningful. Books then become suggestive. It is freedom that strengthens faith in ourselves. It is freedom that upholds and protects our inner light. It is more important than religion as such. It is religion that replaces the so-called religion that we adore and accept as the guide and sacred pathfinder or emancipator of life. Vivekananda's radical introspection on this point is very relevant and down-to-earth:

> Books suggest the inner light and the method of bringing that out, but we can only understand them when we have earned the knowledge ourselves. When the inner light has flashed for you, let books go, and look only within. You have in you all and a thousand times more than is in all the books. Never lose faith in yourself, you can do anything in this universe. Never weaken, all power is yours.
>
> If religion and life depend upon books or upon the existence of any prophet whatsoever, then perish all religion and books! Religion is in us. No books or teachers can do more than help us to find it, and even without them we can get all truth within. You have gratitude for books and teachers without bondage to them and worship your Guru as God, but do not obey him blindly; love him all you will, but think for yourself. No blind belief can save you, work out your own salvation. Have only one idea of God— that He is an eternal help.[12]

For the advancement of freedom in education, man must have self-belief, self-power and self-activity. Nobody is there to teach him. He teaches himself, and if he teaches himself so with the exercise of his own freedom of advancement, his success is assured. He must go beyond knowledge and differentiation. As Vivekananda introspects:

> Knowledge is mere classification. When we find many things of the same kind we call the sum of them by a certain name and

> are satisfied; we discover "facts", never "why". We take a circuit in a wider field of darkness and think we know something! No "why" can be answered in this world; for that we must go to God. The Knower can never be expressed; it is as when a grain of salt drops into the ocean, it is at once merged in the ocean.
>
> Differentiation creates; homogeneity or sameness is God. Get beyond differentiation; then you conquer life and death and reach eternal sameness and are in God, are God. Get freedom, even at the cost of life. All lives belong to us as leaves to a book; but we are unchanged, the Witness, the Soul, upon whom the impression is made, as when the impression of a circle is made upon the eyes when a firebrand is rapidly whirled round and round.[13]

In the arena of education, the most important position is held by the teacher. Is every teacher true to his teaching? If true, then surely he must be radical as the learner. If not, let there be no teacher and teaching. By being radical, both the learner and the teacher must be guided by the spirit of freedom. This freedom primarily means freedom to accept or reject any component of teaching-learning in terms of transparency and universality, besides reliability, validity, objectivity, relevance and so on. Now if it so happens that education under any circumstances loses sight of the importance and role of freedom, it ceases to be education and stands for ignorance of or betrayal to the real spirit of education.

To be blessed with the radical teacher devoted to imparting teaching in fusion with freedom to exercise love, sympathy, and goodness as the real spirit of education is to be on the right track of ascent and excellence. The real teacher as such opens all avenues of efflorescence wide open and free to the learner. Only then education becomes a means of living and joyous relationship between the teacher and the learner.

What, then, should be the real motive of the teacher? In the invaluable words of Vivekananda:

> The teacher must not teach with any ulterior selfish motive—for money, name, or fame; his work must be simply out of love,

out of pure love for mankind at large. The only means through which spiritual force can be transmitted is love. Any selfish motive, such as the desire for gain or for name, will immediately destroy this conveying medium. God is love, and he who has known God, as love can be a teacher of godliness and God to man.

When you see that in your teacher these conditions are all fulfilled, you are safe; if they are not, it is unsafe to allow yourself to be taught by him, for there is the great danger that, if he cannot convey goodness to your heart, he may convey wickedness. This danger must by all means be guarded against. *Shrotriyoavrijinokamahato yo Brahmavittamah*—"He who is learned in the scriptures, sinless, unpolluted by lust, and is the greatest knower of the Brahman" is the real teacher.

From what has been said, it naturally follows that we cannot be taught to love, appreciate, and assimilate religion everywhere and by everybody. The "books in the running brooks, sermons in stones, and good in everything" is all very true as a poetical figure; but nothing can impart to a man a single grain of truth unless he has the undeveloped germs of it in himself. To whom do the stones and brooks preach sermons? To the human soul, the lotus of whose inner holy shrine is already quick with life. And the light which causes the beautiful opening out of this lotus comes always from the good and wise teacher. When the heart has thus been opened, it becomes fit to receive teaching from the stones or the brooks, the stars, or the sun, or the moon, or from anything which has its existence in our divine universe; but the unopened heart will see in them nothing but mere stones or mere brooks. A blind man may go to a museum, but he will not profit by it in any way; his eyes must be opened first, and then alone he will be able to learn what the things in the museum can teach.[14]

One of the most important components of radical education is to broaden our mind and widen our outlook. Narrowness dwarfs the spirit of freedom. It kills the vision of dissemination of thoughts and feelings, ideas and ideals. It also kills the spirit of tendering what is best to others in and around us. In his reply to the address of welcome accorded to him in Kolkata after his return from the Parliament of Religions, Vivekananda reminds us:

> One of the great causes of India's misery and downfall has been that she has narrowed herself, went into her shell as the oyster does, and refused to give her jewels and her treasures to the other races of mankind, refused to give the life-giving truths to existing nations outside the Aryan fold. That has been the one great cause; that we did not go out, that we did not compare notes with other nations— that has been the one great cause of our downfall, and every one of you knows that that little stir, the little life that you see in India, begins from the day when Raja Rammohan Roy broke through the walls of that exclusiveness. Since that day, history in India has taken another turn, and now it is growing with accelerated motion. If we have had little rivulets in the past, deluges are coming, and none can resist them. Therefore, we must go out, and the secret of life is to give and take. Are we to take always, to sit at the feet of the Westerners to learn everything, even religion? We can learn mechanism from them. We can learn many other things. But we have to teach them something, and that is our religion, that is our spirituality. For a complete civilisation the world is waiting, waiting for the treasures to come out of India, waiting for the marvellous inheritance of the race, which, through decades of degradation and misery, the nation has still clutched to her breast. The world is waiting for that treasure; little do you know how much of hunger and of thirst there outside of India for these wonderful treasures of our forefathers. We talk here, and quarrel with each other, we laugh at and we ridicule everything sacred, till it has become almost a national vice to ridicule everything holy. Little do we understand the heart-pangs of millions waiting outside the walls, stretching forth their hands for a little sip of that nectar which our forefathers have preserved in this land of India. Therefore, we must go

> out, exchange our spirituality for anything they have to give us; for the marvels of the religion of spirit we will exchange the marvels of the religion of matter. We will not be students always, but teachers also. There cannot be friendship without equality, and there cannot be equality when one party is always the teacher and the other party sits always at his feet. If you want to become equal with the Englishman or the American, you will have to teach as well as to learn, and you have plenty yet to teach to the world for centuries to come. This has to be done. Fire and enthusiasm must be in our blood.[15]

Admittedly, to rise above all forms of narrowness and welcome new platforms for exchange of ideas and ideals are the positive pointers for education for advancement and culture of radical thoughts. This also allows us to be free from all dogmas and superstitions that affect free and fair thinking. A new world of radical thinking welcomes us. This thinking incorporates one of the most important and essential components of radical humanism. It is reverence— shraddha. It unfolds man to honour others to honour himself. It accelerates the finer qualities of the head and the heart of everyone devoted to life and education as an eternal challenge for excellence and ascent. Referring to the great sayings of the Katha Upanishad, Vivekananda elegantly submits to his listeners:

> Think not that you are poor, that you have no friends. Ay, who ever saw money make the man? It is man that always makes money. The whole world has been made by the energy of man, by the power of enthusiasm, by the power of faith.
>
> Those of you who have studied that most beautiful of all the Upanishads, the Katha, will remember how the king was going to make a great sacrifice, and, instead of giving away things that were of any worth, he was giving away cows and horses that were not of any use, and the book says that at that time Shraddha entered into the heart of his son Nachiketa. I would not translate this word Shraddha to you, it would be a mistake; it is a wonderful word to understand, and much depends on it; we will see how it works, for immediately we find Nachiketa

> telling himself, "I am superior to many, I am inferior to few, but nowhere am I the last, I can also do something" and this boldness increased, and the boy wanted to solve the problem which was in his mind, the problem of death. The solution could only be got by going to the house of Death, and the boy went. There he was, brave Nachiketa, waiting at the house of Death for three days, and you know how he obtained what he desired. What we want is this Shraddha. Unfortunately, it is nearly vanished from India, and this is why we are in our present state. What makes the difference between man and man is the difference in this Shraddha and nothing else. What makes one man great and another weak and low is this Shraddha. My Master used to say, he who thinks himself weak will become weak, and that is true. This Shraddha must enter into you. Whatever of material power you see manifested by the Western races is the outcome of this Shraddha, because they believe in their muscles and if you believe in your spirit, how much more will it work! Believe in that infinite soul, the infinite power, which, with consensus of opinion, your books and sages preach. That Atman which nothing can destroy, in It is infinite power only waiting to be called out. For here is the great difference between all other philosophies and the Indian philosophy. Whether dualistic, qualified monistic, or monistic, they all firmly believe that everything is in the soul itself; it has only to come out and manifest itself; therefore, this Shraddha is what I want, and what all of us here want, this faith in ourselves, and before you is the great task to get back that faith. Give up the awful desire that is creeping into our national blood, that idea of ridiculing everything, that loss of seriousness. Give that up. Be strong and have this Shraddha, and everything else is bound to follow.[16]

The education of Shraddha which is the outcome of freedom nursed and manifested in all purity and serenity is the representation and idealisation of Truth. In our contemplation and action the spirit of Shraddha is manifested in terms of truth. How to be christened with the spirit of truth that calls for respect for work is the eternal lesson of man.

Referring to Karma-Yoga, Vivekananda reminds us of the truth that we must cultivate the power to think and know— the power that is within every one of us to be nurtured and respected with all adoration and sincerity. In his words:

> No one can get anything unless he earns it. This is an eternal law. We may sometimes think it is not so, but in the long run we become convinced of it. A man may struggle all his life for riches; he may cheat thousands, but he finds at last that he did not deserve to become rich, and his life becomes a trouble and a nuisance to him. We may go on accumulating things for our physical enjoyment, but only what we earn is really ours. A fool may buy all the books in the world, and they will be in his library; but he will be able to read only those that he deserves to; and this deserving is produced by Karma. Our Karma determines what we deserve and what we can assimilate. We are responsible for what we are; and whatever we wish ourselves to be, we have the power to make ourselves. If what we are now has been the result of our own past actions, it certainly follows that whatever we wish to be in future can be produced by our present actions; so we have to know how to act. You will say, "What is the use of learning how to work? Everyone works in some way or other in this world." But there is such a thing such as fritting away our energies. With regard to Karma-Yoga, the Gita says that it is doing work with cleverness and as a science; by knowing how to work, one can obtain the greatest results. You must remember that all work is simply to bring out the power of the mind which is already there, to wake up the soul. The power is inside every man, so is knowing; the different works are like blows to bring them out, to cause these giants to wake up.[17]

The real freedom to work in order to educate oneself begins with the learning of the lesson of self-identity and self-respect. Unless one respects oneself and establishes one's own identity, there is every possibility of education devoid of its true nature. Freedom to think and enrich our identity in terms of the self and those of others presents us with manifold experiences.

In elucidating the spirit of man exercising dynamic personality as the outcome of true education, Vivekananda adroitly observes:

> What is the use of polishing up the outside when there is no inside? The end and aim of all training is to make the man grow. The man who influences, who throws his magic, as it were, upon his fellow-beings, is a dynamo of power, and when that man is ready, he can do anything and everything he likes; that personality put upon anything will make it work.
>
> Now, we see that though this is a fact, no physical laws that we know of will explain this. How can we explain it by chemical and physical knowledge? How much of oxygen, hydrogen, carbon, how many molecules in different positions, and how many cells, etc., etc. can explain this mysterious personality? And we still see, it is a fact, and not only that, it is the real man; and it is that man that lives and moves and works, it is that man that influences, moves his fellow-beings, and passes out, and his intellect and books and works are but traces left behind. Think of this. Compare the great teachers of religion with the great philosophers. The philosophers scarcely influenced anybody's inner man, and yet they wrote most marvellous books. The religious teachers, on the other hand, moved countries in their lifetime. The difference was made by personality. In the philosopher it is a faint personality that influences; in the great prophets it is tremendous. In the former we touch the intellect, in the latter we touch life. In the one case, it is simply a chemical process, putting certain chemical ingredients together which may gradually combine and under proper circumstances bring out a flash of light or may fail. In the other, it is like a torch that goes round quickly, lighting others.[18]

Continuous and careful crystallisation of the self is what true education stands for, and for this end in view, freedom in education shows the most interesting and innovative avenue of excellence in every direction. For example, the lesson on patriotism is best learnt through exercise of the spirit of freedom to think, feel and love in all sincerity of purpose of contemplation. The more sincerely we feel, think and love everyone near or far, the more is the experience in coming closest to the great vision of altruism which is one of the most poignant characteristics of education.

As a matchless admirer and exponent of freedom in education for practical exercise of patriotism, Vivekananda characteristically highlights the fact as above:

> I believe in patriotism, and I have my own ideal of patriotism. Three things are necessary for great achievements. First, feel from the heart. What is in the intellect or reason? It goes a few steps and there it stops. But through the heart comes inspiration. Love opens the most impossible gates; love is the gate to all the secrets of the universe. Feel, therefore, my would-be reformers, my would-be patriots! Do you feel? Do you feel that millions and millions of the descendants of gods and of sages have become next-door neighbours to brutes? Do you feel that millions are starving today, and millions have been starving for ages? Do you feel that ignorance has come over the land as a dark cloud? Does it make you restless? Does it make you sleepless? Has it gone into your blood, coursing through your veins, becoming consonant with your heartbeats? Has it made you almost mad? Are you seized with that one idea of the misery of ruin, and have you forgotten all about your name, your fame, your wives, your children, your property, even your own bodies? Have you done that? That is the first step to become a patriot, the very first step. I did not go to America, as most of you know, for the Parliament of Religions, but this demon of a feeling was in me and within my soul. I travelled twelve years all over India, finding no way to work for my countrymen, and that is why I went to America. Most of you know that, who knew me then. Who cared about this Parliament of Religions? Here was my own flesh and blood sinking every day, and who cared for them? This was my first step.

> You may feel, then; but instead of spending your energies in frothy talk, have you found any way out, any practical solution, some help instead of condemnation, some sweet words to soothe their miseries, to bring them out of this living death?
>
> Yet that is not all. Have you got the will to surmount mountain-high obstructions? If the whole world stands against you sword in hand, would you still dare to do what you think is right? If your wives and children are against you, if all your money goes, your name dies, your wealth vanishes, would you still stick to it? Would you still pursue it and go on steadily towards your own goal? As the great King Bhartrihari says, "Let the sages blame or let them praise; let the goddess of fortune come or let her go wherever she likes; let death come today, or let it come in hundreds of years; he indeed is the steady man who does not move one inch from the way of truth." Have you got that steadfastness? If you have these three things, each one of you will work miracles. You need not write in the newspapers, you need not go about lecturing; your very face will shine. If you live in a cave, your thoughts will permeate even through the rock walls, will go vibrating all over the world for hundreds of years, may be, until they will fasten on to some brain and work out there. Such is the power of thought, of sincerity, of purity of purpose.[19]

With the enrichment of thought, sincerity and purity as the finer components of freedom well exercised in education, the formation and cultivation of character becomes normal and obvious. Indeed, character, "the sum total of the bent" of one's mind as Vivekananda expresses, is the true outcome of the best exercise of freedom in education. It indicates how one should be prepared to exercise the inner power to discover or unveil oneself in terms of knowledge which is inherent in oneself. As Vivekananda significantly observes:

> The goal of mankind is knowledge. That is the one ideal placed before us by Eastern philosophy. Pleasure is not the goal of man, but knowledge. Pleasure and happiness come to an end.

> It is a mistake to suppose that pleasure is the goal. The cause of all the miseries we have in the world is that men foolishly think pleasure to be the ideal to strive for. After a time man finds that it is not happiness, but knowledge, towards which he is going, and that both pleasure and pain are great teachers, and that he learns as much from evil as from good. As pleasure and pain pass before his soul they have upon it different pictures, and the result of these combined impressions is what is called man's "character". If you take the character of any man, it really is but the aggregate of tendencies, the sum total of the bent of his mind; you will find that misery and happiness are equal factors in the formation of that character. Good and evil have an equal share in moulding character, and in some instances misery is a greater teacher than happiness. In studying the great characters the world has produced, I dare say, in the vast majority of cases, it would be found that it was misery that taught more than happiness, it was poverty that taught more than wealth, it was blows that brought out their inner fire more than praise.
>
> Now this knowledge, again, is inherent in man. No knowledge comes from outside; it is all inside. What we say a man "knows", should, in strict psychological language, be what he "discovers" or "unveils"; what a man "learns" is really what he "discovers", by taking the cover off his own soul, which is a mine of infinite knowledge.[20]

Freedom to exercise one's inherent knowledge is the key to real education. When we forget this, education becomes mechanical, artificial, dull, drab and non-functional. The secular or spiritual purpose of education becomes a total abstraction in the absence of one's own involvement in the discovery or manifestation. From the standpoint of Karma-Yoga, Vivekananda elucidates:

> All knowledge, therefore, secular or spiritual, is in the human mind. In many cases it is not discovered, but remains covered, and when the covering is being slowly taken off, we say, "We are learning," and the advance of knowledge is made by the advance of this process of uncovering. The man from whom

this veil is being lifted is the more knowing man, the man upon whom it lies thick is ignorant, and the man from whom it has entirely gone is all-knowing, omniscient. There have been omniscient men, and, I believe, there will be yet; and that there will be myriads of the mind the cycles to come. Like fire in a piece of flint, knowledge exists in the mind; suggestion is the friction which brings it out. So with all our feelings and action— our tears and our smiles, our joys and our griefs, our weeping and our laughter, our curses and our blessings, our praises and our blames— every one of these we may find, if we calmly study our own selves, to have been brought out from within ourselves by so many blows. The result is what we are. All these blows taken together are called Karma—work, action. Every mental and physical blow that is given to the soul, by which, as it were, fire is struck from it, and by which its own power and knowledge are discovered, is Karma, this word being used in its widest sense. Thus, we are all doing Karma all the time.[21]

In doing Karma all the time, we explore ourselves. This exploration needs freedom to introspect with unalloyed vision. Vivekananda makes this ardent introspection where his Master is the living example of how to exercise freedom as an unparalleled means of education for fullness. In reply to the address of welcome delivered at Calcutta, he frankly proves this point by referring to the immense role of Shri Ramakrishna in the exercise of freedom in education:

> If there has been anything achieved by me, by thoughts, or words, or deeds, if from my lips has ever fallen one word that has helped any one in the world, I lay no claim to it, it was his. But if there have been curses falling from my lips, if there has been hatred coming out of me, it is all mine and not his. All that has been weak has been mine, and all that has been life-giving, strengthening, pure, and holy, has been his inspiration, his words, and he himself. Yes, my friends, the world has yet to know that man. We read in the history of the world about prophets and their lives, and these come down to us through

> centuries of writings and workings by their disciples. Through thousands of years of chiselling and modelling, the lives of the great prophets of yore come down to us ; and yet, in my opinion, not one stands so high in brilliance as that life which I saw with my own eyes, under whose shadow I have lived, at whose feet I have learnt everything— the life of Paramahamsa.[22]

The humility that is expressed in these words not only upholds the unique contribution of freedom to education but also shows the deep sense of reverence for the apostle of real learning where the teacher never claims for his proficiency in teaching and the learner, too, disclaims his power of learning. Indeed, when we introspect in freedom, we learn best. And this best learning is everlasting.

The power to learn is in the very womb of freedom. It ignites introspection which is the heart of true education. And when true education is functional, it guarantees efflorescence of individuality. The individual suffers from absence of exercise of freedom, and so education becomes a parasitical affair. It also loses force which is the invaluable gift of freedom. It also loses its power to identify the components of liking and disliking. The result is disastrous.

Pointing out the three states of the mind, Vivekananda instructs us to exercise freedom for the best manifestation of the self in order to have freedom to find out and appreciate the joy of living in a serene way:

> There are three states of mind: the active, the passive, and the serene. The passive state is characterised by slow vibrations; the active by quick vibrations, and the serene by the most intense vibrations of all. Know that the soul is sitting in the chariot. The body is the chariot; the outer senses are the horses; and the mind the reins; and the intellect the charioteer. So man crosses the ocean of Maya. He goes beyond. He reaches God. When a man is under the control of his senses, he is of this world. When he has controlled the senses, he has renounced.

** ** **

> We must learn to control all our brain-centres consciously. The first step is the joy of living. Asceticism is fiendish. To laugh is better than to pray. Sing. Get rid of misery. Do not for heaven's sake infect others with it. Never think God sells a little happiness and a little unhappiness. Surround yourself with flowers and pictures and incense.[23]

A new spirit of optimism that Vivekananda has introduced in his education in and through freedom ignites us to learn the great lesson that we are infinite like the open blue sky. He also teaches the lesson that we are endless dreamers. Whatever we dream turns into reality only when we understand and appreciate the spirit of freedom that plays the most vital role in manifesting personality.

From the notes of a lecture which Vivekananda delivered at the Vedanta Society, New York, in June 1900, his poignant introspection on the interrelationship between freedom and education becomes very transparent:

> What then can satisfy man? Not gold. Not enjoyment. Not beauty. One Infinite alone can satisfy him, and that Infinite is Himself. When he realises this, then alone comes freedom.
>
> "This flute, with the sense-organs as its keyholes,
>
> With all its sensations, perceptions, and song,
>
> Is singing only one thing. It longs to go back to the
>
> wood whence it was cut!"
>
> "Deliver thou thyself by thyself!
>
> Ah, do not let thyself sink! For thou art thyself thy greatest friend.
>
> And thou thyself thy greatest enemy."
>
> Who can help the Infinite? Even the hand that comes to you through the darkness will have to be your own.
>
> Fear and desire are the two causes of all this, and who creates them? We ourselves. Our lives are but a passing from dream to dream. Man the infinite dreamer, dreaming finite dreams!

> Oh, the blessedness of it, that nothing external can be eternal! They little know what they mean, whose hearts quake when they hear that nothing in this relative world can be eternal.
>
> I am the infinite blue sky. Over me pass these clouds of various colours, remain a moment, and vanish. I am the same eternal blue. I am the witness, the same eternal witness of all. I see, therefore nature exists. I do not see, therefore she does not. Not one of us could see or speak if this infinite unity were broken for a moment.[24]

The indomitable spirit of man upholds freedom as the sine qua non in the upbringing that stands for education. The more refined through exercise of freedom in right earnest, the more is the perfection aimed at. True education never waits but rolls eternally like the spontaneous current of a river awaiting the encounter with the eternity. This is the blessing of freedom to be translated in education by means of exercise of individuality.

The concept of individuality when exercised as one of the most characteristic components of education in terms of freedom serves best under any circumstances. Poverty becomes a boon for progress. Conflicts then become a password for ascent and excellence. Sorrows and sufferings then become the positive fruits of education under the banner of freedom. No help, no success, no failure, but a strong will to perform, an unyielding power to nurture freedom first and freedom for ever –that is the right direction towards which education is to be organised and pursued, practised and disseminated.

In a letter written to Alasinga, Vivekananda refers to this introspective vision of freedom and education:

> We have no organisation, nor want to build any. Each one is quite independent to teach, quite free to preach whatever he or she likes.
>
> If you have the spirit within, you will never fail to attract others. Theosophists' method can never be ours, for the very simple reason that they are an organised sect, we are not.

> Individuality is my motto. I have no ambition beyond training individuals up. I know very little; that little I teach without reserve; where I am ignorant, I confess it as such, and never am I so glad as when I find people being helped by Theosophists, Christians, Mohammedans. Or anybody in the world. I am a Sannyasin; as such I consider myself a servant, not as a master in the world…If people love me, they are welcome, if they hate, they are also welcome.
>
> Each one will have to save himself, each one to do his own work. I seek no help, I reject none. Nor have I any right in the world to be helped. Whoever has helped me or will help, it will be their mercy to me, not my right, and as such I am eternally grateful.[25]

The education of the spirit of toleration and sympathy to which India has no parallel in the whole history of humanism throughout the world is due to the fact that true education always welcomes integration and totally makes a departure from aggression or retaliation. This is a unique lesson of religion born of and bred in the harmonious warmth of freedom to think, act and progress in peace, amity and co-operation. In fact, the education of religion cannot but be altruistic, for it believes in the quality and excellence in human growth and development. It averts conflict and intolerance because it focuses on negative freedom where education loses depth of vision of the mind for freedom and welfare of all.

Pointing out the ideal and universal role of religion in terms of education and freedom, Vivekananda observes in his speech delivered at the Triplicane Literary Society in Madras:

> Each nation must give in order to live. When you give life, you will have life; when you receive, you must pay for it by giving to all others; and that we have been living for so many thousands of years is a fact that stares us in the face, and the solution that remains is that we have been always giving to the outside world, whatever the ignorant may think. But the gift of India is the gift of religion and philosophy, and wisdom and spirituality. And religion does not want cohorts to march before its path

> and clears its way. Wisdom and philosophy do not march upon bleeding human bodies, do not march with violence but come on the wings of peace and love, and that has always been so. Therefore we had to give. I was asked by a young lady in London, "What have you Hindus done? You have never even conquered a single nation." This is true from the point of view of the Englishman, the brave, the heroic, the Kshatriya— conquest is the greatest glory that one man can have over another. That is true from his point of view, but from ours it is quite opposite. If I ask myself what has been the cause of India's greatness, I answer, because we have never conquered. That is our glory. You are hearing every day, and sometimes, I am sorry to say, from men who ought to know better, denunciations of our religion, because it is not at all a conquering religion. To my mind that is the argument why our religion is truer than any other religion, because it never conquered, because it never shed blood, because its mouth always shed on all, words of blessing, of peace, words of love and sympathy. It is here and here alone that the ideals of toleration were first preached. And it is here and here alone that toleration and sympathy have become practical; it is theoretical in every other country; it is here and here alone, that the Hindu builds mosques for the Mohammedans and churches for the Christians.[26]

The education of toleration and sympathy in fusion with freedom shows the surest way to quality and excellence. The process of exercising toleration in and through education takes recourse to crystallisation by means of exercise of freedom. The more the avenue of freedom is assured in education, the better is the span of quality dissemination which allows sympathy and cooperation a natural and spontaneous educational endeavour.

For a newer world of education with a magical touch of freedom to work and succeed in bringing about a radical change in national advancement, Vivekananda appeals to the young men of Madras:

> Money is not needed. Money is nothing. For the last twelve years of my life, I did not know where the next meal would

come from; but money and everything else I want must come, because they are my slaves, and not I theirs; money and everything else must come. Must— that is the word. Where are the men? That is the question. Young men of Madras, my hope is in you. Will you respond to the call of your nation? Each one of you has a glorious future if you dare believe me. Have a tremendous faith in yourselves, like the faith I had when I was a child, and which I am working out now. Have that faith, each one of you, in yourself— that eternal power is lodged in every soul— and you will revive the whole of India. Ay, we will then go to every country under the sun, and our ideas will before long be a component of the many forces that are working to make up every nation in the world. We must enter into the life of every race in India and abroad; we shall have to work to bring this about.[27]

Education is an endless pursuit for altruism. It always necessitates freedom of the mind as well as of the heart. If the mind is free from all narrowness and abstractions, the heart becomes a treasureland of wisdom and poignance, serenity and cadence. Only then we can have the truest idea of freedom and education. Then alone every one of us can boldly assert:

I am present! At Pralaya time,
When this vast universe is swallowed up,
Knowledge, and knower, and the known
Merged into one.[28]

When would we be blessed with the spirit of freedom and fulfilment in education as above?

References

1. Swami Vivekananda: *The Complete Works of Swami Vivekananda,* Advaita Ashrama, Kolkata, Mayavati Memorial Edition, 1989, Vol. IV, p. 490.
2. *Ibid.,* pp. 490-491.
3. *Ibid.,* Vol. V, p. 332.
4. *Ibid.,* pp. 333-334.

5. *Ibid.*, Vol. IV, pp. 240-241.
6. *Ibid.*, Vol. I, pp. 185-186.
7. *Ibid.*, Vol. IV, pp. 54-56.
8. *Ibid.*, Vol. VII, p. 98.
9. *Ibid.*, p. 99.
10. *Ibid.*, Vol. IV, pp. 126-127.
11. *Ibid.*, pp. 435-436.
12. *Ibid.*, Vol. VII, pp. 85-86.
13. *Ibid.*, pp. 18.
14. *Ibid.*, Vol. III, pp. 51-52.
15. *Ibid.*, pp. 317-318.
16. *Ibid.*, pp. 319-320.
17. *Ibid.*, Vol. I, p. 30.
18. *Ibid.*, Vol.II, pp. 15-16.
19. *Ibid.*, Vol. III, pp. 225-227.
20. *Ibid.*, Vol. I, pp. 27-28.
21. *Ibid.*, pp. 28-29.
22. *Ibid.*, Vol. III, pp. 312-313.
23. *Ibid.*, Vol. VIII, p. 227.
24. *Ibid.*, 250-251.
25. *Ibid.*,Vol. VII, p. 487.
26. *Ibid.*, Vol. III, pp. 273-274.
27. *Ibid.*, pp. 303-304.
28. *Ibid.*, Vol. IV, p. 515.

4

Freedom and Religion: Vivekananda's Points of Cohesion

Religion is freedom of the mind and the spirit. It is best exercised in terms of the divinity inherent in man. In the words of Swami Vivekananda, it is "the manifestation of divinity already in man". Every human being wants to be free from the little self in order to be hallowed with the inherent spirit of divinity that works wonders of all wonders and the beyond. It is this freedom that elevates man from what he apparently is to what his inherent spirit of divinity leads him to arrive at the great truth: I am Existence Absolute, Knowledge Absolute, Bliss Absolute.

The relation between freedom and religion is inseparable and unique. It is inseparable because it never allows confusion between the two. It is unique because it is in absolute fusion that upholds the image of man and freedom as one and the same from the point of perfection. Vivekananda expands this relation between freedom and religion in terms of man and 'oneness of human life':

> A man may be the greatest philosopher in the world, but a child in religion. When a man has developed a high state of spirituality he can understand that the kingdom of heaven is within him. That is the real kingdom of the mind. Thus, we see that the apparent contradictions and perplexities in every religion mark but different stages of growth. And, as such, we

have no right to blame anyone for his religion. There are stages of growth in which forms and symbols are necessary; they are the language that the souls in that stage can understand.

** ** **

"Blessed are the pure in heart, for they shall see God", yea, in this life. And that is salvation. There are those who teach that this can be gained by the mumbling of words. But no great Master ever taught that external forms were necessary for salvation. The power of attaining it is within ourselves. We live and move in God. Creeds and sects have their parts to play, but they are for children, they last but temporarily. Books never make religions, but religions make books. We must not forget that. No book ever created God, but God inspired all the great books. And no book ever created a soul. We must never forget that. The end of all religions is the realising of God in the soul. That is the one universal religion. If there is one universal truth in all religions, I place it here— in realising God. Ideals and be a thousand different radii, but they all converge to the one centre, and that is the realisation of God: something behind this world of sense, this world of eternal eating and drinking and talking nonsense, this world of false shadows and selfishness. There is that beyond all books, beyond all creeds, beyond the vanities of this world, and it is the realisation of God within yourself. A man may believe in all the churches in the world, he may carry in his head all the sacred books ever written, he may baptise himself in all the rivers of the earth, still, if he has no perception of God, I would class him with the rankest atheist, and a man may have never entered a church or a mosque, nor performed any ceremony, but if he feels God within himself and is thereby lifted above the vanities of the world, that man is a holy man, a saint, call him what you will. As soon as a man stands up and says he is right or his church is right, and all others are wrong, he is himself all wrong. He does not know that upon the proof of all the others depends the proof of his own. Love and charity for the whole human race, that is the test of true religiousness."[1]

The new concept of religion nurtured in freedom as Vivekananda presents us is not only transparent but also radical:

> The embodiment of freedom, the Master of nature, is what we call God. You cannot deny Him. No, because you cannot move or live without the idea of freedom. Would you come here if you did not believe you were free? It is quite possible that the biologist can and will give some explanation of this perpetual effort to be free. Take all that for granted, still the idea of freedom is there. It is a fact, as much so as the other fact that you cannot apparently get over, the fact of being under nature.
>
> Bondage and liberty, light and shadow, good and evil must be there, but the very fact of the bondage shows also this freedom hidden there. If one is a fact, the other is equally a fact. There must be this idea of freedom. While now we cannot see that this idea of bondage, in uncultivated man, is his struggle for freedom, yet the idea of freedom is there. The bondage of sin and impurity in the uncultivated savage is to his consciousness very small, for his nature is only a little higher than the animal's. What he struggles against is the bondage of physical nature, the lack of physical gratification, but out of this lower consciousness grows and broadens the higher conception of a mental or moral bondage and a longing for spiritual freedom. Here we see the divine dimly shining through the veil of ignorance. The veil is very dense at first and the light may be almost obscured, but it is there, ever pure and undimmed—the radiant fire of freedom and perfection. Man personifies this as the Ruler of the Universe, the One Free Being. He does not yet know that the universe is all one, that the difference is only in degree, in the concept."[2]

The vision of freedom in terms of religion and vice versa becomes more radiant in the exercise of unalloyed rationality. This means radicalism. This radical approach makes both religion and freedom pragmatic. As freedom does not allow dogmatism to remain static and above criticism, religion gets a favourable atmosphere to come out of ignorance and conservatism, darkness and blurred vision. As a matter of fact, all religious beliefs and ideas cannot but avert crystallisation by means of freedom exercised in an open and unbiased mind and an abiding vision of consciousness. The more conscious we are about the role of freedom in religion, the more is the freshness of conceptualisation of religion as a spontaneous and natural efflorescence of realisation of the self from diverse and challenging perspectives.

When we speak of religion, freedom generally suffers from absence of identification and authority. Obviously, this stands in the way of the true role of freedom in religion. As religion is a habit, natural and, of course, spontaneous, freedom cannot be isolated from this habit. The latter takes all responsibilities as the guide to religious ideas and practices. Indeed, when one is exercising any religion, one cannot dissociate oneself from the clear stream of reason as the appropriate exercise of freedom to think and act. This freedom to think and act further energises the concept of reasoning and arguments, principles and precepts that are best suited to the understanding and appreciation of any particular religion as the science of self-realisation.

In the light of the vision of freedom and religion as above, Vivekananda exquisitely portrays the unparalleled concept of the religion of man:

> There is but One— The Free— The Knower— Self!
> Without a name, without a form or stain.
> In Him is Maya dreaming all this dream.
> The witness, He appears as nature, soul.
> Know thou art That, Sannyasin bold! Say—
> "Om Tat Sat, Om!"
>
> Where seekest thou? That freedom, friend, this world
> Nor that can give. In books and temples vain
> The search. Thine only is the hand that holds

The rope that drags thee on. Then cease lament,
Let go thy hold, Sannyasin bold! Say—
"Om Tat Sat, Om!"

Say, "Peace to all: From me no danger be
To aught that lives. In those that dwell on high.
In those that lowly creep, I am the Self in all!
All life both here and there, do I renounce,
All heavens and earths and hells, all hopes and fears."
Thus cut thy bonds, Sannyasin bold! Say—
"Om Tat Sat, Om!"[3]

The new religion that is blessed by the spirit of freedom as Vivekananda highlights above takes us to a higher plane of human consciousness where anger, fear, greed, enmity and all other external forces of human emotions and sensibilities are soothed in the blessings of calmness of mind. Actually, what happens in case of a man who is free in religion is that he considers nothing more important than love which is the most powerful guiding force of the religion of man. Like a dualist, we begin ourselves as separate from God, and when we realise that divinity is already inherent in every one of us, we find that there is no difference in Love, Lover and the Beloved because they are always one and the same in terms of religion.

In explaining freedom from the standpoint of the religion of love as above, Vivekananda characteristically reminds us:

> We all have to begin as dualists in the religion of love. God is to us a separate Being, and we feel ourselves to be separate beings also. Love then comes in the middle, and man begins to approach God, and God also comes nearer and nearer to man. Man takes up all the various relationships of life as father, as mother, as son, as friend, as master, as lover, and projects them on his ideal of love, on his God. To him God exists as all these, and the last point of his progress is reached when he feels that he has become absolutely merged in the object of his worship.

> We all begin with love for ourselves, and the unfair claims of the little self make even love selfish. At last, however, comes the full blaze of light, in which this little self is seen to have become one with the Infinite. Man himself is transfigured in the presence of this Light of Love, and he realises at last the beautiful and inspiring truth that Love, the Lover, and the Beloved are One.[4]

The realisation of the vision of Love, Lover and the Beloved in terms of true religion also requires the practice of absolute freedom under self-abnegation and self-sacrifice. This is a very tough but challenging task— the task that translates renunciation into a true reality. The right to work brings forth the prize of freedom in the form of absolute self-sacrifice leading to the religion as 'the science of the human soul'. It never denies the identity of each man more or less striving endlessly to manifest the inherent divinity. As Vivekananda significantly observes:

> The world is not for cowards. Do not try to fly. Look not for success or failure. Join yourself to the perfectly unselfish will and work on. Know that the mind which is born to succeed join itself to a determined will and perseveres. You have the right to work, but do not become so degenerate as to look for results. Work incessantly, but see something behind the work. Even good deeds can find a man in great bondage. Therefore, be not bound by good deeds or desire for name or fame. Those who know this secret pass beyond this round of birth and death and become immortal.[5]

To enjoy liberty in contemplation is to enjoy religion as one's own, very much own. Religion then becomes a part and parcel of life. It becomes meaningful and life supportive. It then becomes living and sustaining also. It then transcends and becomes transparent with the religion of all religions because it triumphantly upholds the true meaning of freedom as the endless force of self-sacrifice and self-abnegation for the welfare of all.

The philosophy of freedom and religion in the light of self-sacrifice for the devotion to the welfare of all has its efflorescence in the ideals of love. When we think and act upon the true vision of freedom and religion from the perspective of perfection, the concept of love as the all-pervading force of the All Love becomes most illuminating and admirable. Vivekananda significantly spells out in this connection:

> All the ideals of love – [God] as [our] father, mother, friend, child— [are conceived in order to strengthen devotion in us and make us feel nearer and dearer to God]. The intensest love is that between the sexes. God must be loved with that sort of love. The woman loves her father; she loves her mother; she loves her child; she loves her friend. But she cannot express herself all to the father, nor to the mother, nor to the child, nor to the friend. There is only one person from whom she does not hide anything. So with the man...The [husband] wife relationship is the all-rounded relationship. The relationship of the sexes [has] all the other loves concentrated into one. In the husband, the woman has the father, the friend, the child. In the wife, the husband has mother, daughter, and something else. That tremendous complete love of the sexes must come [for God]— that same love with which a woman opens herself to a man without any bond of blood— perfectly, fearlessly, and shamelessly. No darkness! She would no more hide anything from her lover than she would from her own self. That very love must come [for God]. These things are hard and difficult to understand. You will begin to understand by and by, and all idea of sex will fall away. Like the water drop on the sand of the river bank on a summer day, even so is this life and all its relations.[6]

The concept of God as love as Vivekananda adroitly explains is not only natural and practical from the point of religion and freedom but also radical because it discards the sham and childish idea that God is the creator of this world. If religion, in perfect tune with freedom, does not stand for a real fusion between the differentiated and the undifferentiated, it fails to stand for true religion. There must be finally and simply a religion strengthened by the spirit of freedom which is the efflorescence of the higher Self. As Vivekananda characteristically analyses:

> What makes the undifferentiated appear differentiated to mind? This is the same kind of question as what is the origin of evil and free will? The question itself is contradictory and impossible, because the question takes for granted cause and effect. There is no cause and effect in the undifferentiated; the question assumes that the undifferentiated is in the same condition as the differentiated. "Whys" and "wherefors" are in mind only. The Self is beyond causation, and It alone is free. Its light it is which percolates through every form of mind. With every action I assert I am free, and yet every action proves that I am bound. The real Self is free, yet when mixed with mind and body, It is not free. The will is the first manifestation of the real Self; the first limitation therefore of this real Self is the will. Will is a compound of Self and mind. Now, no compound can be permanent so that when we will to live, we must die. Immortal life is a contradiction in terms, for life, being a compound, cannot be immortal. True being is undifferentiated and *eternal.* How does this Perfect Being become mixed up with will, mind, thought— all defective things? It never has become mixed. You are the real you; you never were will; you never have changed; you as a person never existed; It is illusion. Then on what, you will say, do the phenomena of illusion rest? This is a bad question. Illusion never rests on Truth, but only on illusion. Everything struggles to go back to what was before these illusions, to be free in fact. What then is the value of life? It is to give us experience. Does this view do away with evolution? On the contrary, it explains it. It is really the process of refinement of matter allowing the real Self to manifest Itself. It is as if a screen or a veil were between us and some other object. The object becomes clear as the screen is gradually withdrawn. The question is simply one of manifestation of the higher Self.[7]

The manifestation of the higher Self in terms of religion and freedom as Vivekananda upholds also attunes to the spirit of the

Vedanta which is the eternal spirit of man and religion. It is the spirit that is strengthened by the spirit of freedom. To become truly religious is to have a strong determination well supported by freedom for reconciliation of religion and the world. As he spells out the advancement of freedom through the practice of religion, truth and victory of man:

> I will hew out a way for myself. I will know the truth or give up my life in the attempt. For on this side it is nothing, it is gone, it is vanishing every day. The beautiful, hopeful, young person of today is the veteran of tomorrow. Hopes and joys and pleasures will die like blossoms with tomorrow's frost. That is one side; on the other, there are the great charms of conquest, victories over all the ills of life, victory over life itself, the conquest of the universe. On that side men can stand. Those who dare, therefore, to struggle for victory, for truth, for religion, are in the right way; and that is what the Vedas preach: Be not in despair; the way is very difficult, like walking on the edge of a razor; yet despair not, arise, awake, and find the ideal, the goal.
>
> Now all these various manifestations of religion, in whatever shape and form they have come to mankind, have this one common central basis. It is the preaching of freedom, the way out of this world. They never came to reconcile the world and religion, but to cut the Gordian knot, to establish religion in its own ideal, and not to compromise with the world. That is what every religion preaches, and the duty of the Vedanta is to harmonise all these aspirations, to make manifest the common ground between all the religions of the world, the highest as well as the lowest. What we call the most arrant superstition and the highest philosophy really have a common aim in that they both try to show the way out of the same difficulty, and in most cases this way is through the help of someone who is not himself bound by the laws of nature, in one word, someone who is free. In spite of all the difficulties and differences of opinion about the nature of the one free agent, whether he is a Personal God, or a sentient being like man, whether masculine,

> faminine, or neuter— and the discussions have been endless— the fundamental idea is the same. In spite of the almost hopeless contradictions of the different systems, we find the golden thread of unity running through them all, and in this philosophy, the golden thread has been traced, revealed little by little to our view, and the first step to this revelation is the common ground that all are advancing towards freedom.[8]

The spirit of freedom is one of the most important components of religion that promotes religion to spirituality and the beyond. Vivekananda idealises this spirit of freedom and calls upon the world to follow Indian religion and spirituality that leads to the Infinite. In his reply to the address of welcome at Ramnad on 25th February, 1897, he strongly asserts:

> In this land are, still, religion and spirituality, the fountains which will have to overflow and flood the world to bring in new life and new vitality to the Western and other nations, which are now almost borne down, half-killed and degraded by political ambitions and social scheming. From out of many voices, consonant and dissentient, from out of the medley of sounds filling the Indian atmosphere, rises up supreme, striking, and full, one note, and that is renunciation. Give up! That is the watchword of the Indian religions. This world is a delusion of two days. The present life is of five minutes. Beyond is the Infinite, beyond this world of delusion; let us seek that. This continent is illumined with brave and gigantic minds and intelligences which even think of this so-called infinite universe as only a mud-puddle; beyond and still beyond they go. Time, even infinite time, is to them but non-existence. Beyond and beyond time they go. Space is nothing to them; beyond that they want to go, and this going beyond the phenomenal is the very soul of religion. The characteristic of my nation is this transcendentalism, this struggle to go beyond, this daring to tear the veil off the face of nature and have at any risk, at any price, a glimpse of the beyond. That is our ideal, but of course all the people in a country cannot give up entirely. Do you

> want to enthuse them, then here is the way to do so. Your talks of politics, of social regeneration, your talks of money-making and commercialism— all these will roll off like water from a duck's back. This spirituality, then, is what you have to teach the world. Have we to learn anything else, have we to learn anything from the world? We have, perhaps, to gain a little in material knowledge, in the power of organisation, in the ability to handle powers, organising powers, in bringing the best results out of the smallest of causes. This perhaps to a certain extent we may learn from the West. But if any one preaches in India the ideal of eating and drinking and making merry, if any one wants to apotheosise the material world into a God, that man is a liar; he has no place in this holy land, the Indian mind does not want to listen to him. Ay, in spite of the sparkle and glitter of Western civilisation, in spite of all its polish and marvellous manifestation of power, standing upon this platform, I tell them to their face that it is all vain. It is vanity of vanities. God alone lives. The soul alone lives. Spirituality alone lives. Hold on to that.[9]

The invaluable role of spirituality as the pointer to the avenue of the beyond and still more beyond is the genesis of freedom that stands for true religion. A call for the Infinite in the endless warmth and care of freedom well crystallised in the discipline of a higher spirit of vision and a greater mission for celebration of consciousness makes religion an inseparable exponent of ascent and excellence. Deliberating on the nature of the soul in terms of infinity and oneness and introducing the story of the two birds on the same tree— the one majestic and calm, and the other afflicted with sense-enjoyments proving finally the fact that the latter is nothing but the reflection of the former— Vivekananda upholds the spirit of freedom and religion in perfect efflorescence of cohesion:

> If the soul is pure and perfect in its essence and nature, and if every soul is infinite and omnipotent, how is it that there can be many souls? There cannot be many infinites. There cannot be two even, not to speak of many. If there were two infinites,

> one would limit the other, and both become finite. The infinite can only be one, and boldly the last conclusion is approached—that it is but one and not two.
>
> ** ** **
>
> Such is the nature of the soul. This human soul goes after sense-enjoyments, vanities of the world; like animals it lives only in the senses, lives only in momentary titillations of the nerves. When there comes a blow, for a moment the head reels, and everything begins to vanish, and it finds that the world was not what it thought it to be, that life was not so smooth. It looks upward and sees the infinite Lord a moment, catches a glimpse of the majestic One, comes a little nearer, but is dragged away by its past actions. Another blow comes, and sends it back again. It catches another glimpse of the infinite Presence, comes nearer, and as it approaches nearer and nearer, it begins to find out that its individuality— its low, vulgar, intensely selfish individuality— is melting away; the desire to sacrifice the whole world to make that little thing happy is melting away; and as it gets gradually nearer and nearer, nature begins to melt away. When it has come sufficiently near, the whole vision changes, and it finds that it was the other bird, that this infinity which it had viewed as from a distance was its own Self, this wonderful glimpse that it had got of the glory and majesty was its own Self, and it indeed was that reality. The soul then finds That which is true in everything. That which is in every atom, everywhere present, the essence of all things, the God of the universe—know that thou art He, know that thou art free.[10]

That the soul of religion is freedom and the soul that upholds the Infinite in everyone and above everything is what Vivekananda time and again points out. The power of the Spirit and the force of the Infinite remain everlasting, all-pervading and self-existent, where freedom plays a very significant role in the manifestation of divinity. Referring to the Vedas, he characteristically delineates:

> Innumerable have been the manifestations of the power of the Spirit in the realm of matter, of the force of the Infinite in the

> domain of the finite, but the Infinite Itself is self-existent, eternal, and unchangeable. The passage of time makes no mark whatever on the dial of eternity. In its supersensuous region, which cannot be comprehended at all by the human understanding, there is no past and there is no future.
>
> The Vedas teach that the soul of man is immortal. The body is subject to the law of growth and decay; what grows must of necessity decay. But the indwelling spirit is related to the infinite and eternal life; it never had a beginning, and it will never have an end. One of the chief distinctions between the Vedic and the Christian religion is that the Christian religion teaches that each human soul had its beginning at its birth into this world; whereas the Vedic religion asserts that the spirit of man is an emanation of the Eternal Being and had no more a beginning than God Himself. Innumerable have been and will be its manifestations in its passage from one personality to another, subject to the great law of spiritual evolution, until it reaches perfection, when there is no more change.[11]

The relation between man and soul as the truest representative of religion is based on freedom. The soul, and not the mind, is ever free. Our identification with the mind is our bondage. The mind by itself fails to manifest in bondage but the soul with mind as its instrument is manifesting itself because it is ever free. Man evolves as the soul evolves through the exercise of freedom which stands for, manifests itself through nature and accelerates through excellence and the beyond. As Vivekananda categorically observes:

> Man is not mind, he is soul. The soul is ever free, boundless, and eternal. Herein is man's freedom, in the soul. The soul is always free, but the mind identifying itself with its own ephemeral waves, loses sight of the soul and becomes lost in the maze of time, space, and causation- Maya.
>
> This is the cause of our bondage. We are always identifying ourselves with the mind, and the mind's phenomenal changes.
>
> Man's free agency is established in the soul, and the soul, revealing itself to be free, is always asserting the fact in spite of

> the mind's bondage: "I am free! I am what I am! I am what I am!" this is our freedom. The soul— ever free, boundless, eternal— through actions and aeons is manifesting itself more and more through its instrument, the mind.
>
> What relation then does man bear to nature? From the lowest form of life to man, the soul is manifesting itself through nature. The highest manifestation of the soul is involved in the lowest form of manifest life and is working itself outward through the process called evolution.
>
> The whole process of evolution is the soul's struggle to manifest itself. It is a constant struggle against nature. It is a struggle against nature, and not conformity to nature, that makes man what he is.[12]

Non-attachment as one of the finest and most potent forces of religion is the true identity of freedom because true freedom in terms of religion always stands for self-abnegation and self-identity as a mere witness to everything that takes place in and around the world. In the ever aggravating problem of permanence of body-mind relationship, freedom as the way of life par excellence suffers from ambiguity. We fail to accept the fact that it *is* religion. It is the only pathfinder of harmony that exists in every human being. The more we are devoted to the religion of freedom from the standpoint of the true Self liberated from apparent constraints by means of the spirit and exercise of non-attachment, the better is the possibility of transparency and excellence.

In the quest for freedom and religion which should always be assured by a true scientific approach to the study of the human mind, Vivekananda's introspection on freedom and man is significant:

> The limited always requires a higher generalisation of the unlimited to explain itself. The bound can only be explained by the free, the caused by the uncaused. But again, the same difficulty is also here. What is free? The body or the mind? It is

apparent to all that they are as much bound by law as anything else in the universe.

Now the problem resolves itself into this dilemma: either the whole universe is a mass of never-ceasing change and nothing more, irrecoverably bound by the law of causation, not one particle having a unity of itself, yet is curiously producing an ineradicable delusion of permanence and freedom, or there is in us and in the universe something which is permanent and free, showing that the basal constitutional belief of the human mind is not a delusion. It is the duty of science to explain facts by bringing them to a higher generalisation. Any explanation, therefore, that first wants to destroy a part of the fact given to be explained, in order to fit itself to the remainder, is not scientific, whatever else it may be.

So any explanation that wants to overlook the fact of this persistent and all-necessary idea of freedom commits the above-mentioned mistake of denying a portion of fact in order to explain the rest, and is, therefore, wrong. The only other alternative possible, then, is to acknowledge, in harmony with our nature, that there is something in us which is free and permanent.

But it is not body; neither is it the mind. The body is dying every minute. The mind is constantly changing. The body is a combination, and so is the mind, and as such can never reach to a state beyond all change. But beyond this momentary sheathing of gross matter, beyond even the finer covering of the mind is the Atman, the true Self of man, the permanent, the ever free. It is his freedom that is percolating through layers of thought and matter, and, in spite of the colourings of name and form, is ever asserting its unshackled existence. It is his deathlessness, his bliss, his peace, his divinity that shines out and makes itself felt in spite of the thickest layers of ignorance. He is the real man, the fearless one, the deathless one, the free.[13]

Renunciation is the right road to religion that stands for the true exercise of freedom. This freedom teaches the great lesson of honouring and visualising God within each and every human being. All desires are constraints of freedom. All constraints of freedom must be eliminated by the religion of renunciation. As Vivekananda distinctly asserts:

> Give up all desire for enjoyment in earth or heaven. Control the organs of the senses and control the mind. Bear every misery without even knowing that you are miserable. Think of nothing but liberation. Have faith in Guru, in his teachings, and in the surety that you can get free. Say "Soham, Soham" whatever comes. Tell yourself this even in eating, walking, suffering; tell the mind this incessantly— that what we see never existed, that there is only "I". Flash—the dream will break! Think day and night, this universe is zero, only God is. Have intense desire to get free.
>
> All relatives and friends are but "old dry wells"; we fall into them and get dreams of duty and bondage, and there is no end. Do not create illusion by *helping* anyone. It is like a banyan tree, that spreads on and on. If you are a dualist, you are a fool to try to help God. If you are a monist, you know that you are God; where find duty? You have no duty to husband, child, friend. Take things as they come, lie still, and when your body floats, go; rise with the rising tide, fall with falling tide. Let the body die; this idea of body is but a worn-out fable. 'Be still and know that you are God.'[14]

A radical visionary of religion in terms of freedom, Vivekananda upholds the inherent divinity in man. This divinity prepares us to be totally detached from lust, greed or any other forms of vagaries of life. These only reward us with bondage and selfishness. These only act as barriers to visualise the Atman and realise religion in and through freedom.

In course of a conversation with a disciple, Vivekananda observes:

> When the mind is purified, when one is free from the attachment for lust and gold, one sees lots of visions, most wonderful ones!

> But one should not pay heed to them. The aspirant cannot advance further if he sets his mind constantly on them. Haven't you heard that Shri Ramakrishna used to say, 'Countless jewels lie uncared for in the outer courts of my beloved Lord's sanctum'? We must come face to face with the Atman; what is the use of setting one's mind on vagaries like those?[15]

To have a fresh look at religion is to characterise it in terms of thought and action. But every thought and action must be enriched by the glory of one's own religion. That serves as a pointer to freedom towards a refined vision of religion. At the same time, the cultivation of religion gets a newer spurt of advancement in excellence and ascent by means of manipulating the rich fruits of experience received from tradition and culture of the religion of one's own being. In an address entitled "The Future of India", Vivekananda poignantly reminds us:

> Many times have I been told that looking into the past only degenerates and leads to nothing, and that we should look to the future.This is true. But out of the past is built the future. Look back, therefore, as far as you can, drink deep of the eternal fountain that are behind, and after that, look forward, march forward and make India brighter, greater, much higher than she ever was. Our ancestors were great. We must first recall that. We must learn the elements of our being, the blood that courses in our veins; we must have faith in that blood and what it did in the past; and out of that faith and consciousness of past greatness, we must build India yet greater than what she has been. There have been periods of decay and degradation. I do not attach much importance to them; we all know that. Such periods have been necessary. A mighty tree produces a beautiful ripe fruit. That fruit falls on the ground, it decays and rots, and out of that decay springs the root and the future tree, perhaps mightier than the first one. This period of decay through which we have passed was all the more necessary. Out of this decay is coming the India of the future; it is sprouting, its first

> leaves are already out; and a mighty, gigantic tree, the Urdhvamula, is here, already beginning to appear.[16]

A foreseer in integrating man and religion, Vivekananda has highlighted the role of freedom as the spirit of progress through cultivation of the common ground of tradition. This enlarges the positive role of religion and freedom. This also encourages the spirit of generosity and cordial relationship between man and man in the society and strengthens the bond of free and unbiased human relationship. In his classic words:

> Race, religion, language, government— all these together make a nation. The elements which compose the nations of the world are indeed very few, taking race after race compared to this country. Here have been the Aryan, the Dravidian, the Tartar, the Turk, the Moghul, the European— all the nations of the world, as it were, pouring their blood into this land. Of languages the most wonderful conglomeration is here; of manners and customs there is more difference between two Indian races than between the European and the Indian races.
>
> The one common ground that we have is our sacred tradition, our religion. That is the only common ground, and upon that we shall have to build. In Europe, political ideas form the traditional unity. In Asia, religious ideals form the national unity. The unity in religion, therefore, is absolutely necessary as the first condition of the future of India. There must be the recognition of one religion throughout the length and breadth of this land. What do I mean by one religion? Not in the sense of one religion as held among the Christians, or the Mohammedans, or the Buddhists. We know that our religion has certain common grounds, common to all sects, however varying their conclusions may be, however different their claims may be. So there are certain common grounds; and within their limitation this religion of ours admits of a marvellous variation, an infinite amount of liberty to think and live our own lives. We all know that, at least those of us who have thought; and what we want is to bring out these life-giving common principles

> of our religion, and let every man, woman, and child, throughout the length and breadth of this country, understand them, know them, and try to bring them out in their lives. This is the first step, and, therefore, it has to be taken.[17]

The concept of Bhakti as a form of practice in religion as Vivekananda explains is also based on the spirit of religion. In fact, he has practically no parallel in this radical vision. He has made religion wide open in terms of freedom that ensures the enlightened and all-embracing vision of altruism. Referring to the Puranas, he serenely observes:

> The germs of Bhakti are there already; the germs are even in the Samhita; the germs a little more developed are in the Upanishads; but they are worked out in their details in the Puranas.
>
> To understand Bhakti, therefore, we have got to understand these Puranas of ours. There have been great discussions of late as to their authenticity. Many a passage of uncertain meaning has been taken up and criticised. In many places it has been pointed that the passages cannot stand the light of modern science and so forth. But, apart from all these discussions, apart from the scientific validity of the statements of the Puranas, apart from their valid or invalid geography, apart from their valid or invalid astronomy, and so forth, what we find for a certainty, traced out bit by bit almost in every one of these volumes, is this docreine of Bhakti, illustrated, reillustrated, stated and restated, in the lives of saints and in the lives of kings. It seems to have been the duty of the Puranas to stand as illustrations for that great ideal of the beautiful, the ideal of Bhakti, and this, as I have stated, is so much nearer to the ordinary man. Very few indeed are there who can understand and appreciate, far less live and move, in the grandeur of the full blaze of the light of the Vedanta, because the first step for the pure Vedantist is to be Abhih, fearless. Weakness has got to go because a man dares to become a Vedantist, and we know how difficult that is. Even those who have given up all

> connection with the world, and have very few bondages to make them cowards, feel in the heart of their hearts how weak they are at moments, at times how soft they become, how cowed down; much more so is it with men who have so many bondages, and have to remain as slaves to so many hundred and thousand things, inside of themselves and outside of themselves, men every moment of whose life is dragging-down slavery. To them the Puranas come with the most beautiful message of Bhakti.[18]

The deliverance of man as one of the finest ideals of religion is Bhakti. It is devotion which is the manifestation of serene love. Freedom and religion synchronised in love finds its true meaning not in theory but in endless pursuit for fullness of vision. It must be human love. Otherwise, religion turns into a dead practice of rites and rituals.

In explaining the spirit of Bhakti-Yoga as a way of understanding and appreciating the true fusion of man and God in terms of deliverance, Vivekananda upholds:

> Bhakti or worship or love in some form or other is the easiest, pleasantest, and most natural way of man. The natural state of this universe is attraction; and that is surely followed by an ultimate disunion. Even so, love is the natural impetus of union in the human heart; and though itself a great cause of misery, properly directed towards the proper object, it brings deliverance. The object of Bhakti is God. Love cannot be without a subject and an object. The object of love again must be at first a being who can reciprocate our love. Therefore, the God of love must be in some sense a human God. He must be a God of love. Aside from the question whether such a God exists or not, it is a fact that to those who have love in their heart this Absolute appears as a God of love, as personal.
>
> The lower forms of worship, which embody the idea of God as a judge or punisher or some -one to be obeyed through fear, do not deserve to be called love, although they are forms of worship gradually expanding into higher forms. We pass on to the

> consideration of love itself. We will illustrate love by a triangle, of which the first angle at the base is fearlessness. So long as there is fear, it is not love. Love banishes all fear. A mother with her baby will face a tiger to save her child. The second angle is that love never asks, never begs. The third or the apex is that love loves for the sake of love itself. Even the idea of object vanishes. Love is the only form in which love is loved.[19]

Religion as the exponent of love well substantiated by freedom is the eternal quest for perfection. It is devotion in its most ideal and purest form both in contemplation as well as in perfection. Love for love's sake is the religion that culminates in freedom. Tracing the history of religion in India, Vivekananda presents us with the fact that religion is freedom of love in any form whatsoever strengthened by the spirit of freedom:

> At first we think of a Personal God, and call Him Creator, Omnipotent, Omniscient, and so forth. But when love comes, God is only love. The loving worshipper does not care *what* God is, because he wants nothing from Him. Says an Indian saint, "I am no beggar!" neither does he fear. God is loved as a human being.
>
> Here are some of the systems founded on love: (1) Shanta, common, peaceful love, with such thoughts as those of fatherhood and help; (2) Dasya, the ideal of service; God as master or general or sovereign, giving punishments and rewards; (3) Vatsalya, God as mother or child. In India, the mother never punishes. In each of these stages, the worshipper forms an ideal of God and follows it. Then (4) Sakhya, God as friend. There is here no fear. There is also the feeling of equality and familiarity. There are some Hindus who worship God as friend and playmate. Next comes (5) Madhura, sweetest love, the love of husband and wife. Of this St. Teresa and the ecstatic saints have been examples. Amongst the Persians, God has been looked upon as the wife, amongst the Hindus as the husband. We may recall the great queen Mira Bai, who preached that the Divine Spouse was all. Some carry this to such an extreme that to call

God 'mighty' or 'father' seems to them blasphemy. The language of this worship is erotic. Some even use that of illicit passion. To this cycle belongs the story of Krishna and the Gopi-girls. All this probably seems to you to entail great degeneration on the worshipper. And so it does. Yet many great saints have been developed by it. And no human institution is beyond abuse. Would you cook nothing because there are beggars? Would you possess nothing because there are thieves? 'O Beloved, one kiss of Thy lips, once tasted, hath made me mad!'

The fruit of this idea is that one can no longer belong to any sect, or endure ceremonial. Religion in India culminates in freedom. But even this comes out to be given up, and all is love for love's sake."[20]

Thus, freedom is love of and for religion that exceeds beyond the ordinary concept and comes out as the independent and supreme force of the identity of man as the love of All Love. To know that one is ever blessed is the highest goal of freedom which is true religion. It must be based on knowledge pure and perfect. And for purity and perfection freedom of the mind is of absolute importance. This will open the gateway of knowledge leading to omniscience. Freedom thus stands for religion of the highest and purest order leading us to understand, appreciate, respect and glorify the divinity inherent in every one of us.

How does knowledge come to us? How does it lead every one of us to realise the mind that shows the avenue of realising the Self that makes every one of us to be free from pleasure and pain, joy and sorrow to become ever blessed ? The seven grades of knowledge as Vivekananda chatacteristically describes actually expose the freedom of religion in all efflorescence of clarity of vision and truth:

While we are aware of thirsting after knowledge, we begin to seek here and there, wherever we think we can get some truth, and failing to find it we become dissatisfied and seek in a fresh direction. All search is vain, until we begin to perceive that knowledge is within ourselves, that no one can help us, that we must help ourselves. When we begin to practise the power of discrimination, the first sign that we are getting near truth will be that that dissatisfied state will vanish. We shall feel quite sure that we have found the truth, and that it cannot be anything else but the truth. Then we may know that the sun is rising, that the morning is breaking for us, and taking courage, we must persevere until the goal is reached. The second grade will be the absence of all pains. It will be impossible for anything in the universe, external or internal, to give us pain. The third will be the attainment of full knowledge. Omniscience will be ours. The fourth will be the attainment of the end of all duty through discrimination. Next will come what is called freedom of the Chitta. We shall realise that all difficulties and struggles, all vacillations of the mind, have fallen down, just as a stone rolls from the mountain top into the valley and never comes up again. The next will be that Chitta itself will realise that it melts away into its causes whenever we so desire. Lastly, we shall find that we are established in our Self, that we have been alone throughout the universe, neither body nor mind was ever related, much less joined, to us. They were working their own way, and we, through ignorance, joined ourselves to them. But we have been alone, omnipotent, omnipresent, ever blessed; our own Self was so pure and perfect that we required none else. We required none else to make us happy, for we are happiness itself. We shall find that this knowledge does not depend on anything else; throughout the universe there can be nothing that will not become effulgent before our knowledge. This will be the last state, and the Yogi will become peaceful and calm, never to feel any more pain, never to be again deluded, never to be touched by misery. He will know he is ever blessed, ever perfect, almighty.[21]

Real religion must be based on the spirit of freedom. It must endear freedom with all knowledge and wisdom, erudition and appreciation. It must be an exercise of one's own choice and experience crystallised by endless pursuit in truth and askance, purity and a generous and altruistic quest for fullness. It must break rigidity, ambiguity, force, compulsion and above all supremacy guided by ignorance and emotion.

Vivekananda banishes sentimentalism from religion outright and accords a warm and generous welcome to all religion in order to have 'a greater field for selection'. By exercising freedom and individuality, one can realise religion and the kingdom of God within him. In this connection he also refers to a splendid story on the study of the books on religion and freedom in quest of truth not by reading but by realisation of God through it:

> Love and charity for the whole human race, that is the test of true religiousness. I do not mean the sentimental statement that all men are brothers, but that one must feel the oneness of human life. So far as they are not exclusive, I see that the sects and creeds are all mine; they are all grand. They are all helping men towards the real religion. I will add, it is good to be born in a church, but it is bad to die there. It is good to be born a child, but bad to remain a child. Churches, ceremonies, and symbols are good for children, but when the child is grown, he must burst the church or himself. We must not remain children for ever. It is like trying to fit one coat to all sizes and growths. I do not deprecate the existence of sects in the world. Would to God there were twenty millions more, for the more there are, there will be greater field for selection. What I do object to it is trying to fit one religion to every case. Though all religions are essentially the same, they must have the varities of form produced by dissimilar circumstances among different nations. We must each have our own individual religion, individual so far as the externals of it go.
>
> Many years ago I visited a great sage of our own country, a very holy man. We talked of our revealed book, the Vedas, of your Bible, of the Koran, and of revealed books in general. At the close of our talk, this good man asked me to go to the table and take up a book; it was a book which, among other things, contained a forecast of the rainfall during the year. The sage

> said, 'Read that.' And I read out the quantity of rain that was to fall. He said, 'Now take the book and squeeze it,' I did so and he said, 'Why, my boy, not a drop of water comes out? Until the water comes out, it is all book, book. So until your religion makes you realise God, it is useless. He who only studies books for religion reminds one of the fable of the ass which carried a heavy load of sugar on its back, but did not know the sweetness of it.'[22]

Indeed, the sweetness of religion is that of freedom. When freedom is absent from the pursuit of religion and vice versa, it is neither freedom nor religion. It is simply an abstraction of both freedom and religion. True freedom is true religion in the sense that the feeling of being free prompts freedom into action. It goes beyond necessity and refines man through emancipation from the chain of causation.

Vivekananda unfolds the true nature of freedom in terms of feeling as the source of altruistic religion, the innate necessity of man as a free soul:

> Freedom of the will— it is as you feel you are free to act. But this freedom is a species of necessity. There is one infinite link before, after, and between the thought and the action but the latter takes the name of freedom— like a bird flitting through a bright room. We feel the freedom and feel it has no other cause. We cannot go beyond consciousness, therefore we feel we are free. We can trace it to no further than consciousness. Mahapurushas (saints) feel themselves identified with God; hence they also feel the real freedom.
>
> You may stop the water flowing out of the fountain by closing that part of the stream and gathering it all in the fountain; you have no liberty beyond it. But the source remains unchanged. Everything is predestination— and a part of that predestination is that you shall have such a feeling— the feeling of freedom. I am shaping my own action. Responsibility is the feeling of reaction. There is no absolute power. Power here is the conscious

> feeling of exercising any faculty which is created by necessity. Man has the feeling of 'I act'; what he means by power of freedom is the feeling. The power is attended with responsibility. Whatever may be done through us by predestination, we feel the reaction. A ball thrown by one, itself feels the reaction.[23]

Feeling is the heart of freedom and religion. It acts as an infinite cohesive power between religion and freedom. It takes one to a land of understanding and appreciation of the religion of the Self where freedom is never absent. It acts and reacts in tune with the progress of sense and sensibilities, visions and manifestations of the ever emerging force of consciousness. That consciousness is the greatest and most invaluable prize of harmony between freedom and religion. As Vivekananda vibrantly pronounces:

> Not two or many, 'tis but one,
> And thus in me all me's I have;
> I cannot hate, I cannot shun
> Myself from me, I can but love.
> From dreams awake, from bonds be free,
> Be not afraid.[24]

Do we listen and act accordingly?

References

1. Swami Vivekananda: *The Complete Works of Swami Vivekananda,* Advaita Ashrama, Kolkata, Mayavati Memorial Edition, 1989, Vol. I, pp. 324-325.
2. *Ibid.,* pp. 336-337.
3. *Ibid.,* Vol. IV, p. 394.
4. *Ibid.,* Vol. III, p. 100.
5. *Ibid.,* Vol. VI, pp. 83-84.
6. *Ibid.,* pp. 77-78.
7. *Ibid.,* pp. 44-45.
8. *Ibid.,* Vol. II, pp. 124-124.
9. *Ibid,* Vol. III, pp. 148-149.
10. *Ibid.,* Vol. VI, pp. 25-27.

11. *Ibid.*, p. 85.
12. *Ibid.*, pp. 35-36.
13. *Ibid.*, Vol. IV, pp. 255-256.
14. *Ibid.*, Vol. VII, p. 92.
15. *Ibid.*, p. 123.
16. *Ibid.*, Vol. III, pp. 285-286.
17. *Ibid.* pp. 286-287.
18. *Ibid.*, pp. 385-386.
19. *Ibid.*, Vol. VIII, pp. 153-154.
20. *Ibid.*, pp. 220-221.
21. *Ibid.*, Vol. I, pp. 258-259.
22. *Ibid.*, pp. 325-326.
23. *Ibid.*, Vol. VI, p. 117.
24. *Ibid.*, Vol. VIII, p. 164.

5

Freedom and Spirituality: Vivekananda's Quest

Freedom is the fundamental identity of man. It indicates the avenues of spirituality. It is the unending quest for which every one is striving for excellence and ascent. The mind of man is encapsulated with diverse and different thoughts on how to prove the real worth of inherent divinity. The ways and means are different. So are different the approaches and endeavour. In undertaking a serene journey for exploration and manifestation of spirituality, freedom genuinely acts as a passport to purity and poignance which are the two major components of quality and excellence.

As a pioneer in the fusion of freedom and spirituality par excellence, Swami Vivekananda considers both one and the same in terms of identity. If one is free, one cannot but be spiritual. Absence of freedom, therefore, means absence of spirituality because in the absence of the former, the latter becomes artificial, dull, drab and mechanical. In fact, freedom eliminated is spirituality abused in abstractions. The religion of freedom always incorporates the essence of spirituality as one of the most important characteristics from becoming to being and the beyond. Whenever freedom is exercised in understanding and appreciating spirituality, it calls forth the inner spirit of spirituality which breathes the aroma of excellence and ascent.

Apart from the fact that there is a very close relationship between freedom and spirituality, Vivekananda makes both a conjoint sojourn to what one ought to be from what one is at every moment. Indeed, time allows very little opportunity for any one to remain static, reserved and inactive. His vision of freedom and spirituality is a quest unending, thriving, spontaneous and living and beyond that. There is neither any room for artificiality, nor is there any scope for ambiguity because spirituality becomes real, meaningful, purposeful, simple and abiding only when it is safeguarded, nursed and enlightened in the true spirit of freedom and individuality.

The quest for freedom and spirituality for perfection and the beyond introduces one to the Holy Grail of superconsciousness which allows one to be hallowed with inherent divinity. When Vivekananda inspires us with the ever inspiring words of the Upanishads Thou art That— *Tat Tvamohsi,* the spiritual elegance of man in terms of freedom is brilliantly exposed. Moreover, freedom also stands for looking within for a crystallised vision and verification of spirituality. As it is a very practical and ever abiding exercise, Vivekananda always presents spirituality not merely in the theory but also in the practice of self-involvement, self-devotion and self-advancement besides extinction of personality. In following the invaluable words of the *Bhagavatgita*, one's duty is to be devoted to work without caring for the result, he places both freedom and spirituality as an indivisible and natural reality.

As spirituality leads one to cultivate freedom to be pure and perfect, one must learn how to be spiritual.This learning cannot be practised by means of books. It can only be possible by means of following a truly spiritual man who shows the way to self-involvement and self-exercise of spirituality where freedom paves the natural avenues of efflorescence. Vivekananda distinctly asserts:

> Every soul is destined to be perfect, and every being, in the end, will attain to that state. Whatever we are now is the result of whatever we have been or thought in the past; and whatever we shall be in the future will be the result of what we do or think now. But this does not preclude our receiving help from

> outside, so much so that in the vast majority of cases in the world, help from outside is almost absolutely necessary. Quickening influence comes from outside, and that works upon our own potentialities; and then the growth begins, spiritual life comes, and man becomes holy and perfect in the end. This quickening impulse which comes from outside cannot be received from books; the soul can receive impulse only from another soul, and from nothing else. We may study books all our lives, we may become very intellectual, but in the end we find we have not developed at all in spirituality. It does not follow that a high order of intellectual development always shows an equivalent development of the spiritual side of man; on the other hand, we find cases almost every day where the intellect has become very highly developed at the expense of the spirit.
>
> Now in intellectual development we can get much help from books, but in spiritual development, almost nothing. In studying books, sometimes we are deluded into thinking that we are being spiritually helped; but if we analyse ourselves, we shall find that only our intellect has been helped, and not the spirit. That is the reason why almost every one of us can *speak* most wonderfully on spiritual subjects, but when the time of action comes, we find ourselves so woefully deficient. It is because books cannot give us that impulse from outside. To quicken the spirit, that impulse must come from another soul.[1]

Transfer and transparency, the two very important attributes of freedom and spirituality, must be the guideline of any quest for ascent and excellence. This is very much alien to intellectual exercise for spiritual development. In fact, intellectual exercise fails to contribute to spiritual transmission and enrichment. This is why all teachers devoted to teaching for intellectual advancement must also be spiritually powerful. Vivekananda clearly unfolds this truth by explaining the role of the teacher in terms of spirituality:

> If a man wants to teach me something of dynamics or chemistry or any other physical science, he may be of any character;

he can still teach dynamics or any other science. For the knowledge that the physical sciences require is simply intellectual and depends on intellectual strength; a man can have in such a case a gigantic intellectual power without the least development of his soul. But in the spiritual sciences it is impossible from first to last that there can be any spiritual light in that soul which is impure. What can such a soul teach? It knows nothing. Spiritual truth is purity. "Blessed are the pure in heart, for they shall see God". In that one sentence is the gist of all religions. If you have learnt He was the only man who was ever ready to give up his life for animals to stop a sacrifice. He once said to a king, "If the sacrifice of a lamb helps you to go to heaven, sacrificing a man will help you better; so sacrifice me." The king was astonished. And yet this man was without any motive power. He stands as the perfection of the active type, and the very height to which he attained shows that through the power of work we can also attain to the highest spirituality.

To many the path becomes easier if they believe in God. But the life of Buddha shows that even a man who does not believe in God, has no metaphysics, belongs to no sect, and does not go to any church, or temple, and is a confessed materialist, even he can attain to the highest. We have no right to judge him. I wish I had one infinitesimal part of Buddha's heart. Buddha may or may not have believed in God; that does not matter to me. He reached the same state of perfection to which others come to Bhakti—love of God—Yoga, or Jnana. Perfection does not come from belief or faith. Talk does not count for anything. Parrots can do that. Perfection comes through the disinterested performance of action.[2]

The quest for freedom is the quest for absolute purity. It is a quest that leads to genuine spirituality. That spirituality enjoys the blessings of the All Pure in one who makes no distinction in the spiritual striving for the ascent of all. The vision of freedom exercised in honouring, embracing and worshipping purity in all women as the sacred passport to spirituality which Vivekananda has referred to by paying a glowing tribute to his Master, Shri Ramakrishna, remains a classic example for ever:

> This man [Shri Ramakrishna] meant by worshipping woman, that to him every woman's face was that of the Blissful Mother, and nothing but that. I myself have seen this man standing before those women whom society would not touch, and falling at their feet bathed in tears, saying, "Mother, in one form Thou art in the street, and in another form Thou art the universe. I salute Thee, Mother, I salute Thee." Think of the blessedness of that life from which all carnality has vanished, which can look upon every woman with that love and reverence when every woman's face becomes transfigured, and only the face of the Divine Mother, the Blissful One, the Protectress of the human race, shines upon it! That is what we want. Do you mean to say that the divinity back of a woman can ever be cheated? It never was and never will be. It always asserts itself. Unfailingly it detects fraud, it detects hypocrisy, unerringly it feels the warmth of truth, the light of spirituality, the holiness of purity. Such purity is absolutely necessary if real spirituality is to be attained.
>
> This rigorous, unsullied purity came into the life of this man. All the struggles which we have in our lives were past for him. His hard-earned jewels of spirituality, for which he had given three-quarters of his life, were now ready to be given to humanity, and then began his mission. His teaching and preaching were peculiar. In our country a teacher is a most venerated person, he is regarded as God Himself. We have not even the same respect for our father and mother. Father and mother give us our body, but the teacher shows us the way to salvation. We are his children, we are born in the spiritual line of the teacher. All Hindus come to pay respect to an extraordinary teacher, they crowd around him. And here was such a teacher, but the teacher had no thought whether he was to be respected or not, he had not the least idea that he was a great teacher, he thought that it was Mother who was doing

everything and not he. He always said, "If any good comes from my lips, it is the Mother who speaks; what have I to do with it?" That was his one idea about his world, and to the day of his death he never gave it up. This man sought no one. His principle was, first firm character, first earn spirituality and results will come of themselves. His favourite illustration was, 'When the lotus opens, the bees come of their own accord to seek the honey; so the lotus of your character be full-blown, and the results will follow.' "that, all that has been said in the past and all that it is possible to say in the future, you have known; you need not look into anything else, for you have all that is necessary in that one sentence; it could save the world, were all the other scriptures lost. A vision of God, a glimpse of the beyond never comes until the soul is pure. Therefore, in the teacher of spirituality, purity is the one thing indispensable; we must see *first* what he *is,* and *then* what he *says.* Not so much intellectual teachers; there we care more for what he says than what he is. With the teacher of religion we must first and foremost see what he is, and then alone comes the value of the words, because he is the transmitter. What will he transmit, if he has not that spiritual power in him? To give a simile: If a heater is hot, it can convey heat vibrations, but if not, it is impossible to do so. Even so is the case with the mental vibrations of the religious teacher which he conveys to the mind of the taught. It is a question of transference and not of stimulating only our intellectual faculties. Some power, real and tangible, goes out from the teacher and begins to grow in the mind of the taught.[3]

The growth of spirituality as above through the spiritual teacher is not enough. As the teacher is the means to an end in realising and appreciating spirituality in one's own mood and fashion and to the best of one's abilities and skilfulness, freedom must act as a real pathfinder to spiritual poignance and manifestation. It is one's own world continually reviewed and crystallised in harmony with freedom to advance and excel. Freedom thus serves as a definite pointer to look within and look beyond for efflorescence of the innermost one in every human being.

As an incomparable forerunner of freedom and spirituality, Vivekananda widens the horizon of human consciousness and dignifies the aspirations and possibilities of man as a free and spiritual visionary. He warns against externalities from which religion very often suffers and loses the radiance of spirituality in perfect tune with freedom. In his words:

> If there have been sages and Rishis in the past, be sure that there will be many now. If there have been Vyasas and Valmikis and Shankaracharyas in ancient times, why may not each one of you become a Sankaracharya? This is another point of our religion that you must always remember, that in all other scriptures inspiration is quoted as their authority, but this inspiration is limited to a very few persons, and through them the truth came to the masses, and we have all to obey them. Truth came to Jesus of Nazareth, and we must all obey him. But the truth came to the Rishis of India—the Mantra-drashtas, the seers of thought—and will come to all Rishis in the future, not to talkers, not to book-swallowers, not to scholars, not to philologists, but to seers of thought. The Self is not to be reached by too much talking, not even by the highest intellects, not even by the study of the scriptures. The scriptures themselves say so. Do you find in any other scripture such a bold assertion as that—not even by the study of the Vedas will you reach the Atman? You must open your heart. Religion is not going to church, or putting marks on the forehead, or dressing in a peculiar fashion; you may paint yourselves in all the colours of the rainbow, but if the heart has not been opened, if you have not realised God, it is all vain. If one has the colour of the heart, he [one] does not want any external colour. That is the true religious realisation. We must not forget that colours and all these things are good so far as they help; so far they are all welcome. But they are apt to degenerate and instead of helping they retard, and a man identifies religion with externalities.

> Going to the temple becomes tentamount to spiritual life. Giving something to a priest becomes tentamount to religious life. These are dangerous and pernicious, and should be at once checked.[4]

Be free from all motive power and you are on the right track of spirituality. This is what Vivekananda has radically and straightforwardly observed and followed in his principle and practice of freedom and spirituality. Extiction of all desires and motives is the way to spirituality of the highest order. This alone would lead one to understand and appreciate the way to perfection. While following the footprints of the Buddha as the ever emulating spiritual visionary in terms of freedom, he characteristically states:

> I want a good deal of metaphysics, for myself. I entirely differ in many respects, but, because I differ, is that any reason why I should not see the beauty of the man? He was the only man who was bereft of all motive power. There were other great men who all said they were the Incarnations of God Himself, and that those who would believe in them would go to heaven. But what did Buddha say in his dying breath? "None can help you; help yourself; work out your own salvation", he said about himself, "Buddha is the name of infinite knowledge, infinite as the sky; I, Goutama, have recorded that state; you will all reach that too if you struggle for it." Bereft of all motive power, he did not want to go to heaven, did not want money; he gave up his throne and everything else and went about begging his bread through the streets of India, preaching for the good of men and animals with a heart as wide as the ocean.[5]

The great lesson of spirituality quite independent and radical in all serenity and poignance, freshness and straightforwardness, simplicity and purity as we learn from Vivekananda through his Master, Shri Ramakrishna, represents the essence enriched in the practice of freedom in right earnest. It is freedom that represents spirituality in its true essence and ascent. It is a mockery to learn spirituality in a mechanical and passive way quite dissociated with life that is pure and steadfast, practical and full of the milk of human kindness as natural and spontaneous in manifestation and perfection.

To Vivekananda as to every one of us as it ought to be, spirituality is a challenge to eternity. As such, it cannot but be radical in order to be meaningful and purposeful, practical and useful for the ascent of man and the universe at large. Explaining the true essence of spirituality as freedom unending and evolving, he states:

> The word Mantra means 'thought out', cogitated by the mind; and the Rishi is the seer of these thoughts. They are neither the property of particular persons, nor the exclusive property of any man or woman, however great he or she may be; nor even the exclusive property of the greatest spirits— the Buddhas or Christs— whom the world has produced. They are as much the property of the lowest of the low, as they are the property of a Buddha, and as much the property of the smallest worm that crawls as of the Christ, because they are universal principles. They were never created. These principles have existed throughout time; and they will exist. They are non-create — uncreated by any laws which science teaches us today. They remain covered and become discovered, but are existing through all eternity in nature. If Newton had not been born, the law of gravitation would have remained all the same and would have worked all the same. It was Newton's genius which formulated it, discovered it, brought it into consciousness, made it a conscious thing to the human race. So are these religious laws, the grand truths of spirituality. They are working all the time. If all the Vedas and the Bibles and the Korans did not exist at all, if seers and prophets had never been born, yet these laws would exist. They are only held in abeyance, and slowly but surely would work to raise the human race, to raise human nature. But they are the prophets who see them, discover them, and such prophets are discoverers in the field of spirituality. As Newton and Galileo are prophets of physical science, so are they the prophets of spirituality.[6]

The beckoning of the infinite spiritual truth is due to the fact that man is an eternal lover of freedom. The Vedas teach us that religion is just born and it will discover and rediscover spirituality in terms of truth, man and none else is the lone architect. It is neither the work of a single prophet nor is it limited by time and space, but it rightly demands innumerable torchbearers of freedom and spirituality from time to time. As Vivekananda distinctly observes:

> Earth after earth, system after system will evolve, run for a certain time, and then dissolve back again into chaos; but the universe remains the same. Millions and millions of systems are being born, while millions are being destroyed. The universe remains the same. The beginning and the end of time can be told as regards a certain planet; but as regards the universe, time has no meaning at all. So are the laws of nature, the physical laws, the mental laws, the spiritual laws. Without beginning and without end are they; and it is within a few years, comparatively speaking, a few thousand years at best, that man has tried to reveal them. The infinite mass remains before us. Therefore, the one great lesson that we learn from the Vedas, at the start, is that religion has just begun. The infinite ocean of spiritual truth lies before us to be worked on, to be discovered, to be brought into our lives. The world has seen thousands of prophets, and the world has yet to see millions.[7]

A forerunner of freedom and spirituality in the true sense of the term, Vivekananda shows a positive approach to freedom in redefining and exploring newer avenues of leading a spiritual life for the progress of mankind in diverse directions. In explaining spirit and nature, he inspires us to exercise freedom so that we can be transparent in our thought and action, idea and devotion. It is a blunder to disbelieve the strength of freedom which never allows dependence and passivity in spirituality. It belittles realisation of the Self. In "Spirit and Nature", he strongly observes:

> Religion is a growth. Each one must experience it himself. The Christians believe that Jesus Christ died to save man. With you

> it is belief in a doctrine, and this belief constitutes your salvation. With us doctrine has nothing whatever to do with salvation. Each one may believe in whatever doctrine he likes, or in no doctrine. What difference does it make to you whether Jesus Christ lived in a certain time or not? What has it to do with you that Moses saw God in the burning bush? The fact that Moses saw God in the burning bush does not constitute your seeing Him, does it? If it does, then the fact that Moses ate is enough for you; you ought to stop eating. One is just sensible as the other. Records of great spiritual men of the past do us no good whatever except that they urge us onward to do the same, to experience religion ourselves. Whatever Christ or Moses or anybody else did does not help us in the least, except to urge us on.
>
> Each one has a special nature peculiar to himself, which he must follow and through which he will find his way to freedom.[8]

From the spiritual point of view, freedom takes a very important role to highlight the spirit in man. To understand this spirit, we will have to understand the fact that each of us is an Omnipresent Being. This proves that there is a great deal of difference between the Divine Being and the manifested being. As a manifested being, freedom ennobles the reflected spirit in man. How is spirituality reflected in man? As a spiritual being man must eliminate the baser elements of the reflections of the spirit.

In elucidating spirituality and freedom of the individual in terms of the above, Vivekananda characteristically points out:

> You have three things in you: (1) the body, (2) the mind, (3) the spirit. The spirit is intangible, the mind comes to birth and death, and so does the body. You are that spirit, but often you think that you are the body. When a man says, "I am here", he thinks of the body. Then comes another moment when you are on the highest plane; you do not say, "I am here". But if a man abuses you or curses you and you do not resent it, you are the spirit. "When I think I am the mind, I am one spark of that

eternal fire which Thou art; and when I feel I am the spirit, Thou and I are one"—so says a devotee to the Lord. Is the mind in advance of the spirit?

God does not reason; why should you reason if you knew? It is a sign of weakness that we have to go on crawling like worms to get a few facts and build generalisations, and the whole thing tumbles down again. The spirit is reflected in the mind and everything. It is the light of the spirit that makes the mind sensate. Everything is an expression of the spirit; the minds are so many mirrors. What you call love and fear, hatred, virtue, and vice are all reflections of the spirit; only when the reflector is base the reflection is bad.[9]

The spirit in man awaits freedom to be manifested and exercised in right earnest. If the exercise of spirituality is in perfect tune with freedom, divinity becomes an absolute reality. It allows understanding and appreciation in terms of causality where freedom paves the mind and stands for substance, time, space, and causation. The real "me", indestructible and, therefore, eternal is the spirit that enjoys the warmth of spirituality. As Vivekananda observes:

> The whole of nature is bound by the law of causation and is in time and space. We cannot see anything outside of space, yet we do not know space. We cannot perceive anything outside of time, yet we do not know time. We cannot understand anything except in terms of causality, yet we do not know what causation is. These three things—time, space, and causality—are in and through every phenomenon, but they are not phenomena. They are as it were the forms or moulds in which everything must be cast before it can be apprehended. Matter is substance plus time, space, and causation. Mind is substance plus time, space, and causation.
>
> This fact can be expressed in another way. Everything is substance plus name and form. Name and form come and go, but substance remains ever the same. Substance, form, and name make this pitcher. When it is broken, you do not call it pitcher

> any more, nor do you see its pitcher form. Its name and form vanish, but its substance remains. All the differentiation in substance is made by name and form. These are not real, because they vanish. What we call nature is not the substance, unchanging and indestructible. Nature is time, space, and causation. Nature is name and form. Nature is Maya. Maya means name and form, into which everything is cast. Maya is not real. We could not destroy it or change it if it were real. The substance is noumenon, Maya is phenomenon. There is the real "me" which nothing can destroy, and there is the phenomenal "me" which is continually changing and disappearing.[10]

The concept of freedom in terms of spirituality that embraces nature in relation to the indestructible and unchanging substance is the hallmark of Vivekananda's philosophy of "I am that I am". It welcomes the ever changing phenomenal "me" for ascent and excellence in spirituality. Freedom becomes really very meaningful in its delineation with spirituality where the real "I" represents worthwhile extinction of personality.

What type of modern India has Vivekananda envisioned ? How far has it been accepted right now in the mind-sets of marooned modernity? The distinct portrait of India in terms of spirituality in the perfect ambiance of freedom as he has presented has no parallel in the history of spiritual emancipation of man:

> On one side is modern Western science, dazzling the eyes with the brilliancy of myriad suns and driving in the chariot of hard and fast facts collected by the application of tangible powers direct in their incision; on the other are the hopeful and strengthening traditions of her ancient forefathers, in the days when she was at the zenith of her glory—traditions that have been brought out of the pages of her history by the great sages of her own land and outside, that run for numberless years and centuries through her every vein with the quickening of life drawn from universal love— traditions that reveal unsurpassed

valour, superhuman genius, and supreme spirituality, which are the envy of the gods—these inspire her with future hopes. On one side, rank materialism, plenitude of fortune, accumulation of gigantic power, and intense sense-pursuits have, through foreign literature, caused a tremendous stir; on the other, through the confounding din of all these discordant sounds, she hears, in low yet unmistakable accents, the heart-rending cries of her ancient gods, cutting her to the quick. There lie before her various strange luxuries introduced from the West – celestial drinks, costly well-served food, splendid apparel, magnificent palaces, new modes of conveyance, new manners, new fashions dressed in which moves about well-educated girl in shameless freedom—all these are arousing unfelt desires. Again, the scene changes, and in its place appear, with stern presence, Sita, Savitri, austere religious vows, fastings, the forest retreat, the matted locks and orange garb of the semi-naked Sannyasin, Samadhi and the search after the Self. On one side is the independence of Western societies based on self-interest; on the other is the extreme self-sacrifice of the Aryan society, in this violent conflict, is it strange that Indian society should be tossed up and down? Of the West, the goal is individual independence, the language money-making education, the means politics; of India, the goal is Mukti, the language the Veda, the means renunciation. For a time, modern India thinks, as it were, I am ruining this worldly life of mine in vain expectation of uncertain spiritual welfare hereafter which has spread its fascination over me; and again, lo! Spellbound she listens—*Eti samsare sfutataradoshah kathamihang manava tava santoshah*— 'Here, in this world of death and change, O man, where is thy happiness?'[11]

The pursuit of spirituality is an inner and eternal urge in the life of man. He becomes free only when he is spiritual in his thought and action, contemplation and realisation of the true worth of life. The spirit of man must remain free to expose truth from all points of view. All our thoughts and actions must be geared to the fact that religion upholds the spirit of man to be positive in the quest for the 'common heritage of man' to exercise and enjoy the real nature and purpose of freedom and spirituality.

Being unparalleled and incomparable in heralding the vision and glory of freedom and spirituality as 'the one central truth in our religion', Vivekananda positively suggests:

> Let us take our stand on the one central truth in our religion—the common heritage of the Hindus, the Buddhists, and Jains alike—the spirit of man, the Atman of man, the immortal, birthless, all-pervading, eternal soul of man whose glories the Vedas cannot themselves express, before whose majesty the universe with its galaxy of galaxy upon suns and stars and nebulae is a drop. Every man or woman, nay, from the highest Devas to the worm that crawls under our feet, is such a spirit evoluted or involuted. The difference is not in kind, but in degree.
>
> This infinite power of the spirit, brought to bear upon matter evolves material development, made to act upon thought evolves intellectually, and made to act upon itself makes of man a God.[12]

Freedom to manifest divinity in oneself is the best manifestation of spirituality. As such, to be divine is to be on the right track of being a God. Let each of us be Gods. That is the true manifestation of spirituality by means of an unending, sincere and endearing exercise of freedom. "Shivoham". I am God. This freedom to think, express, act upon and disseminate the inner force of spirituality is the march of man as a divine and spiritual being. As Vivekananda poignantly asserts:

> First, let us be Gods, and then help others to be Gods. "Be and make". Let this be our motto. Say not man is a sinner. Tell him that he is a God. Even if there were a devil, it would be our duty to remember God always, and not the devil.
>
> If the room is dark, the constant feeling and repeating of darkness will not take it away, but bring in the light. Let us know that all that is negative, all that is destructive, all that is mere criticism, is bound to pass away; it is the positive, the affirmative, the

> constructive that is immortal, that will remain for ever. Let us say, "We are" and "God is" and "We are God", "Shivoham, Shivoham", and march on. Not matter but spirit. All that has name and form is subject to all that has none. This is the eternal truth the Shrutis preach. Bring in the light; the darkness will vanish of itself. Let the lion of Vedanta roar; the foxes will fly to their holes. Throw the ideas broadcast, and let the result take care of itself. Let us put the chemicals together; the crystallisation will take its own course.[13]

A new wave of freedom in tune with spirituality is the only alternative to enshrine the inherent divinity in man. It is the solemn and serene identity of man who can freely declare, "Shivoham". The power of the spirit in him raises him from all constraints and keeps him alert and agile all the time. The innate spiritual instinct in him is always guarded by the power of freedom that cares for its upbringing and nourishment, dissemination and refinement. The spiritual foundation upon which the marvellous success of the ascent and advancement of man depends always looks forward to having a permanent atmosphere of freedom and spontaneity that serves as a sensitising sentinel of purity and integrity, goodness and serenity.

No bare sense of petty religion caring only for worthless personal satisfaction through sense-enjoyments is the goal of human life. It must prove its real worth by devoting itself to refinement of religion through spirituality. Freedom from narrowness of religion by leading a life of the religion of spirituality is the only avenue of the ascent of man. "If a man", as Vivekananda radically observes:

> uses all his mental energy in seeking to satisfy his body and its wants, show me the difference between him and an animal. Bhakti is a higher thing, higher than even desiring heaven. The idea of heaven is of a place of intensified enjoyment. How can that be God?
>
> Only the fools rush after sense-enjoyments. It is easy to live in the senses. It is easier to run in the old groove, eating and drinking; but what these modern philosophers want to tell you

> is to take these comfortable ideas and put the stamp of religion on them. Such a doctrine is dangerous. Death lies in the senses. Life on the plane of the Spirit is the only life, life on any other plane is mere death; the whole of this life can only be described as a gymnasium. We must go beyond it to enjoy real life.[14]

For a new religion of spirituality, what is of utmost importance is to provide ample and natural freedom of growth and development of every religion anywhere and everywhere. Every religion has its essence of freedom and spirituality. A consistent and sincere devotion to the culture of all religions is the essence of spiritual exercise. Such an endeavour not only allows freedom of the mind but also freedom of purity and steadfast devotion to spirituality. In this connection Vivekananda's invaluable words on religion serve as the most important guideline for the goal and methods of freedom and spirituality which broaden the vision of man:

> The greatest misfortune to befall would be if all mankind were to recognise and accept but one religion, one universal form of worship, one standard of morality. This would be the death-blow to all religious and spiritual progress. Instead of trying to hasten this disastrous event by inducing persons, through good or evil methods, to conform to our own highest ideal of truth, we ought rather to endeavour to remove all obstacles which prevent men from developing in accordance with their own highest ideals, and thus make their attempt vain to establish one universal religion.
>
> The ultimate goal of all mankind, the aim and end of all religions, is but one—re-union with God, or, what amounts to the same, with the divinity which is every man's true nature. But while the aim is one, the method of attaining may vary with the different temperaments of men.[15]

For the ideal of universal religion in terms of freedom and spirituality, it is an uphill task for man to eliminate whatever is crude and narrow and welcome whatever is crystallised and refined in tune with ascent and excellence. Our minds and the senses, actions and reactions must be directed towards this vision of spirituality by means of the best exercise and manifestation of freedom. For this, love and humanity, religion and identity, spiritual advancement and freedom become a marvellous fushion of transparency and transcendence.

As a pioneer in showing us how to make this fusion as above, Vivekananda poignantly reminds us:

> Wheresoever our senses reach, or wheresoever our minds imagine, we find therein the actions and reactions of two forces, the one counteracting the other and causing the constant play of the mixed phenomena that we see around us, and of those which we feel in our minds. In the external world, the action of these opposite forces is expressing itself as attraction and repulsion, or as centripetal and centrifugal forces; and in the internal, as love and hatred, good and evil. We repel some things, we attract others. We are attracted by one, we are repelled by another. Many times in our lives we find that without any reason whatsoever we are, as it were, attracted towards certain persons; at other times, similarly, we are repelled by others. This is patent to all, and the higher the field of action, the more potent, the more remarkable, are the influences of these opposite forces. Religion is the highest plane of human thought and life, and herein we find that the workings of these two forces have been most marked. The intensest love that humanity has ever known has come from religion, and the most diabolical hatred that humanity has known has also come from religion. The noblest words of peace that the world has ever heard have come from men on the religious plane, and the bitterest denunciation that the world has ever known has been uttered by religious men. The higher the object of any religion and the finer its organisation, the more remarkable are its activities. No other human motive has deluged the world with blood so much as religion; at the same time, nothing has brought into existence so many hospitals and asylums for the poor; no other human influence has taken such care, not only of humanity, but also of

> the lowest of animals, as religion has done. Nothing makes us so cruel as religion, and nothing makes us so tender as religion. This has been so in the past, and will also, in all probability, be so in the future. Yet out of the midst of this din and turmoil, this strife and struggle, this hatred and jealousy of religions and sects, there have arisen, from time to time, potent voices, drowning all this noise—making themselves heard from pole to pole, as it were—proclaiming peace and harmony. Will it ever come?[16]

A new wave of religion that embraces spirituality is the real outcome of freedom. Such a religion promises the glowing era of the spiritual man who is devoted to manifestation of spiritual thought in the light of freedom. The quest for having pleasure in a higher plane of spirituality which is the inherent and real nature of religion beckons us. As it is a beckoning of the Infinite in the spontaneous ambiance of freedom, it promises every one of us with the highest pleasure in life.

The motive power of religion in terms of freedom and spirituality from the points of view as above indicates the broader basis for which it actually stands. Otherwise, it turns into a narrow exercise of undesirable authority in life and society. A greater type of humanity always welcomes freedom to refine it by means of exercise of spirituality where the pursuit of the Infinite is absolutely necessary. "This pursuit of the Infinite", as Vivekananda characteristically points out:

> this struggle to grasp the Infinite, this effort to get beyond the limitations of the senses—out of matter, as it were—and to evolve the spiritual man—this striving day and night to make the Infinite one with our being—this struggle itself is the grandest and most glorious that man can make. Some persons find the greatest pleasure in eating. We have no right to say that they should not. Others find the greatest pleasure in possessing certain things. We have no right to say that they should not. But they have also no right to say "no" to the man who finds

his highest pleasure in spiritual thought. The lower the organisation, the greater the pleasure of the senses. Very few men can eat a meal with the same gusto as a dog or a wolf. But all the pleasures of the dog or the wolf have gone, as it were, into the senses. The lower types of humanity in all nations find pleasure in the senses, while the cultured and the educated find it in thought, in philosophy, in arts and sciences. Spirituality is a still higher plane. The subject being infinite, that plane is the highest, and the pleasure there is the highest for those who can appreciate it. So, even on the utilitarian ground that man is to seek for pleasure, he should cultivate religious thought, for it is the highest pleasure that exists. Thus, religion, as a study, seems to me to be absolutely necessary.

We can see it in its effects. It is the greatest motive power that moves the human mind. No other ideal can put into us the same mass of energy as the spiritual. So far as human history goes, it is obvious to all of us that this has been the case and that its powers are not dead. I do not deny that men, on simply utilitarian grounds, can be very good and moral. There have been many great men in this world perfectly sound, moral, and good, simply on utilitarian grounds. But the world-movers, men who bring, as it were, a mass of magnetism into the world, whose spirit works in hundreds and in thousands, whose life ignites others with a spiritual fire—such men, we always find, have that spiritual background. Their motive power came from religion. Religion is the greatest motive power for realising that infinite energy which is the birth-right and nature of every man. In building up character, in making for everything that is good and great, in bringing peace to others and peace to one's own self, religion is the highest motive power and, therefore, ought to be studied from that standpoint. Religion must be studied on a broader basis than formerly. All narrow, limited, fighting ideas of religion have to go. All sect ideas and tribal or national ideas of religion must be given up. That each tribe or nation should have its own particular God and think that every other

> is wrong is a superstition that should belong to the past. All such ideas must be abandoned.[17]

Freedom to be as one ought to be is the first lesson of spirituality. It is the lesson that baptises us with the real and positive religion of the identity of man. It eliminates all weakness, fear, superstitions and blindness to truth and self-respect. In a lecture on practical Vedanta delivered on 10th November 1896, Vivekananda strongly advises:

> Never tell yourselves or others that you are weak. Do good if you can, but do not injure the world. You know in your inmost heart that many of your limited ideas, this humbling of yourself and praying and weeping to imaginary beings are superstitious. Tell me one case where these prayers have been answered. All the answers that came were from your own hearts. You know there are no ghosts, but no sooner are you in the dark than you feel a little creepy sensation. This is so because in our childhood we have had all these fearful ideas put into our heads. But do not teach these things to others through fear of society and public opinion, through fear of incurring the hatred of friends, or for fear of losing cherished superstitions. Be masters of all these. What is there to be taught more in religion than the oneness of the universe and faith in one's self? All the works of mankind for thousands of years past have been towards this one goal, and mankind is yet working it out. It is your turn now and you already know the truth. For it has been taught on all sides. Not only philosophy and psychology, but materialistic sciences declared it. Where is the scientific man today who fears to acknowledge the truth of this oneness of the universe? Who is there who dares talk of many worlds ? All these are superstitions. There is only one life and one world, and this one life and one world is appearing to us as manifold. This manifoldness is like a dream. When you dream, one dream passes away and another comes. You do not live in your dreams. The dreams come one after another, scene after scene unfolds before you. So it is in this world of ninety per cent misery and

> ten per cent happiness. Perhaps after a while it will appear as ninety per cent happiness and we shall call it heaven, but a time comes to the sage when the whole thing vanishes, and this world appears as God Himself, and his own soul as God. It is not therefore that there are many worlds, it is not that there are many lives. All this manifoldness is the manifestation of that One. That One is manifesting Himself as many, as matter, spirit, mind, thought, and everything else. It is that One, manifesting Himself as many. Therefore, the first step for us to take is to teach the truth to ourselves and to others.
>
> Let this world resound with this ideal, and let superstitions vanish. Tell it to men who are weak and persist in telling it. You are the Pure One; awake and arise, O mighty one, this sleep does not become you. Awake and arise, this does not befit you. Think not that you are weak and miserable. Almighty, arise and awake, manifest your own nature. It is not fitting that you think yourself a sinner. It is not fit that you think yourself weak. Say that to the world, say it to yourselves, and see what a practical result comes, see how with an electric flash everything is manifested, how everything is changed. Tell that to mankind, and show them their power. Then we shall learn how to apply it in our daily lives.[18]

The inherent force of freedom and spirituality in symphony to ward off all narrowness and superstition and live a life of purity and boldness as Vivekananda asserts is the only way to make life really meaningful and worthy. It is the only way to honour onc's own self and enjoy the warmth of the Almighty as he really is. It is also the supreme force of transparency of truth in life and work.

Freedom is the condition of growth. It is the condition which is always a positive factor of spirituality. In religion and society as well, freedom, in sync with spirituality, makes positive and constructive inroads to inner growth in the light of the Vedanta. As Vivekananda distinctly observes in a lecture delivered in London:

> We, in India, allowed liberty in spiritual matters, and we have a tremendous spiritual power in religious thought even today.

> You grant the same liberty in social matters, and so have a splendid social organisation. We have not given any freedom to the expansion of social matters, and ours is a cramped society. We have never given any freedom in religious matters but with fire and sword have enforced your beliefs, and the result is that religion is a stunted, degenerated growth in the European mind. In India, we have to take off the shackles from society; in Europe, the chains must be taken from the feet of spiritual progress. Then will come a wonderful growth and development of man. If we discover that there is one unity running through all these developments, spiritual, moral, and social, we shall find that religion, in the fullest sense of the word, must come into society, and into our everyday life. In the light of Vedanta you will understand that all sciences are but manifestations of religion, and so in everything that exists in this world.
>
> We see, then, that through freedom the sciences were built; and in them we have two sets of opinions, the one the materialistic and denouncing, and the other the positive and constructive. It is a most curious fact that in every society you find them. Supposing there is an evil in society, you will find immediately one group rise up and denounce it in vindictive fashion, which sometimes degenerates into fanaticism. There are fanatics in every society, and women frequently join in these outcries, because of their impulsive nature. Every fanatic who gets up and denounces something can secure a following. It is very easy to break down; a maniac can break anything he likes, but it would be hard for him to build anything. These fanatics may do some good, according to their light, but much more harm.[19]

To eliminate fanaticism is the positive and constructive avenue of efflorescence of religion and spirituality. For that end-in-view, freedom takes recourse to the right approach to the infinite power of love. Actually, spirituality is realisation of the altruistic vision of infinite love. As soon as love takes the supreme goal of the role of freedom for manifestation of perfection already in every human being, no denunciation as we come across in a materialistic society will have its upper hand. The great spiritual saints look upon the world as it were a garden of love. They never agitate but affectionately hold high the spiritual power of man in every society. The freedom of love and spirituality they exercise shows how every human being is essentially spiritual. In fact, it is beyond the idea and knowledge of the fanatics how the great sages of the world love everyone with sympathy and forbearance under any circumstances by exercising freedom to embrace humanity as the emblem of spirituality. As Vivekananda characteristically points out:

> Fanatics little understand the infinite power of love in the hearts of these great sages who looked upon the inhabitants of this world as their children. They were the real fathers, the real gods, filled with infinite sympathy and patience for everyone; they were ready to bear and forbear. They knew how human society should grow, and patiently, slowly, surely, went on applying their remedies, not by denouncing and frightening people, but by gently and kindly leading them upwards step by step. Such were the writers of the Upanishads. They knew full well how the old ideas of God were not reconcilable with the advanced ethical ideas of the time; they knew full well that what the atheists were preaching contained a good deal of truth, nay, great nuggets of truth; but at the same time, they understood that those who sever the thread that bound the beads, who wanted to build a new society in the air, would entirely fail.[20]

To change the mind-set in order to find out the sameness in all—joy and sorrow, happiness and misery and so on— is to enjoy the warmth of equality. This sense of equality is the blessing of spirituality as the philosophy of the Vedanta upholds. It teaches us how to make the best use of freedom so that spirituality works wonders in the disturbed conditions of the mind.

In analysing the role of the Vedanta in terms of the above, Vivekananda significantly deliberates:

> We have seen that it is the subjective world that rules the objective. Change the subject, and the object is bound to change;

purify yourself, and the world is bound to be purified. This one thing requires to be taught now more than ever before. We are becoming more and more busy about our neighbours, and less and less about ourselves. The world will change if we change; if we are pure, the world will become pure. The question is why I should see evil in others. I cannot see evil unless I be evil. I cannot be miserable unless I am weak. Things that used to make me miserable when I was a child, do not do so now. The subject changed, so the object was bound to change; so says the Vedanta. All these things which we call causes of misery and evil, we shall laugh at when we arrive at that wonderful state of equality, that sameness. This is what is called in Vedanta attaining to freedom. The sign of approaching that freedom is more and more of this sameness and equality. In misery and happiness the same, in success and defeat the same—such a mind is nearing that state of freedom.

The mind cannot be easily conquered. Minds that rise into waves at the approach of every little thing at the slightest provocation or danger, in what a state that must be! What to talk of greatness or spirituality, when these changes come over the mind? This unstable condition of the mind must be changed. We must ask ourselves how far we can be acted upon by the external world, and how far we can stand on our own feet, in spite of all the forces outside us. When we have succeeded in preventing all the forces of the world from throwing us off our balance, then alone we have attained to freedom, and not before. That is salvation. It is here and nowhere else; it is this moment. Out of this idea, out of this fountain-head, all beautiful streams of thought have flowed upon the world, generally misunderstood in their expression, apparently contradicting each other. We find hosts of brave and wonderfully spiritual souls, in every nation, taking to caves or forests for meditation, severing their connection with the external world. This is the one idea. And, on the other hand, we find bright, illustrious beings coming into society, trying to raise their fellow men, the poor, the miserable.[21]

Freedom as a force of exercising spirituality has no parallel in the quest for excellence and ascent of man. This is best manifested in terms of duty. Normally we consider duty as an evaluation of man from the utilitarian points of view. This eliminates the true concept of duty as it should be looked upon and executed. The inner worth of duty as a free and spiritual exercise remains unknown or misunderstood.

Vivekananda significantly spells out the viewpoints on duty as above by referring to Karma-Yoga:

> Karma-Yoga teaches us that the ordinary idea of duty is on the lower plane; nevertheless, all of us have to do our duty. Yet, we may see that this the peculiar sense of duty is very often a great cause of misery. Duty becomes a disease with us; it drags us ever forward. It catches hold of us and makes our whole life miserable. It is the bane of human life. This duty, this idea of duty is the mid-day summer sun which scorches the innermost soul of mankind. Look at those poor slaves to duty! Duty leaves them no time to say prayers, no time to bathe. Duty is ever on them. They go out and work. Duty is on them! It is living a slave's life, at last dropping down in the street and dying in harness, like a horse. This is duty as it is understood. The only true duty is to be unattached and to work as free beings, to give up all work unto God. All our duties are His. Blessed are we that we are ordered out here. We serve our time; whether we do it ill or well, who knows? If we do it well, we do not get the fruits. If we do it ill, neither do we get the care. Be at rest, be free, and work. This kind of freedom is a very hard thing to attain. How easy it is to interpret slavery as duty—the morbid attachment of flesh for flesh as duty! Men go out into the world and struggle and fight for money or for any other thing to which they get attached. Ask them why they do it. They say, "It is a duty." It is the absurd greed for gold and gain, and they try to cover it with a few flowers.[22]

That freedom of man is not attachment but total dedication and detachment is at the core of spirituality. It transforms the mind and transcends it towards purity and poignancy. To seek for something infinite is the real nature of man. It denotes that we are by nature interested in the blessings of freedom that shows the avenues of spirituality.

In this connection, Vivekananda's viewpoints are very clear and explicit:

> In practical daily life we are hurt by small things; we are enslaved by little beings. Misery comes because we think we are finite—we are little beings. And yet, how difficult it is to believe that we are infinite beings! In the midst of all this misery and trouble, when a little thing may throw me off my balance, it must be my care to believe that I am infinite. And the fact is that we are, and that consciously or unconsciously we are all searching after that something which is infinite; we are always seeking for some thing that is free.
>
> There was never a human race which did not have a religion and worship some sort of God or gods. Whether the God or gods existed or not is no question; but what is the analysis of this psychological phenomenon? Why is all the world trying to find, or seeking for, a God? Why? Because in spite of all this bondage, in spite of nature and this tremendous energy of law grinding us down, never allowing us to turn to any side—wherever we go, whatever we want to do, we are thwarted by this law, which is everywhere—in spite of all this, the human soul never forgets its freedom and is ever seeking it. The search for freedom is the search of all religions; whether they know it or not, whether they can formulate it well or ill, the idea is there. Even the lowest man, the most ignorant, seeks for something which has power over nature's laws. He wants to see a demon, a ghost, a god—somebody who can subdue nature, for whom nature is not almighty, for whom there is no law. "Oh for somebody that can break the law!" that is the cry coming from the human heart. We are always seeking for someone who breaks the law. The rushing engine speeds along the railway track; the little worm crawls out of its way. We at once say,

> "The engine is dead matter, a machine; and the worm is alive," because the worm attempted to break the law. It is made to go in any direction man wants, and it cannot do otherwise; but the worm, small and little though it was, attempted to break the law and avoid the danger. It tried to assert itself against law, assert its freedom; and there was the sign of the future God in it.[23]

Radical and revolutionary as man is by nature, he cannot sacrifice freedom under any circumstances. This is why spirituality is also a natural entity of every human being as it embraces freedom first and freedom unendingly. A careful and cautious study of the self and the soul by him, however erroneous it might be at any stage of endeavour, is always directed towards the best ever fusion of freedom and spirituality. It is not merely an exercise but a matter of emancipation of the best worth of man as a divine, spiritual and free human being. In the invaluable and poignant words of Vivekananda:

> Everywhere we see this assertion of freedom, this freedom of the soul. It is reflected in every religion in the shape of God or gods; but it is all external yet—for those who only see the gods outside. Man decided that he was nothing. He was afraid that he could never be free; so he went to seek for someone outside of nature who was free. Then he thought that there were many and many such free beings, and gradually he merged them all into one God of gods and Lord of lords. Even that did not satisfy him. He came a little closer to truth, a little nearer; and then gradually found that whatever he was, he was in some way connected with the God of gods and Lord of lords; that he, though he thought himself bound and low and weak, was somehow connected with the God of gods. Then visions came to him; thought arose and knowledge advanced. And he began to come nearer and nearer to that God, and at last found out that God and all the gods, this whole psychological phenomenon connected with the search for an all-powerful free soul, was but a reflection of his own idea of himself. And then at last he

> discovered that it was not only true that "God made man after His own image", but that it was also true that man made God after his own image. That brought out the idea of divine freedom. The Divine Being was always within, the nearest of the near. Him we had ever been seeking outside, and at last found that He is in the heart of our hearts. You may know the story of the man who mistook his own heartbeat for somebody knocking at the door, and went to the door and opened it, but found nobody there, so he went back. Again he seemed to hear a knocking at the door, but nobody was there. Then he understood that it was his own heartbeat, and he had misinterpreted it as a knocking at the door. Similarly, man after his search finds out that this infinite freedom that he was placing in imagination all the time in the nature outside is the internal subject, the eternal Soul of souls; this Reality, he himself.[24]

The march for understanding, appreciating and enriching inner freedom never ends. It is a march that allows us to have an encounter with the Soul of souls. Again, it is an endearing search for the truth to encounter the All True. It is the quest for the All Free who is the permanent resident of the inner man within everyone everywhere. That I am existent is a natural phenomenon. That I am All Existent is the identity of spirituality born and bred up, nourished and strengthened with the spirit of the inner man always alert in honouring, enriching, and upholding the blessings of the Soul of souls.

The whirlpool of spirituality always looks forward to the awakening of freedom uninterrupted, everlasting, vibrant, pulsating and ever energising. The freshness of freedom is actually the freshness of the mind of man receptive to the call for celebration of inner freedom. This vastness like the ocean of wisdom and enlightenment, poignance of thought and feeling, being and beyonding is the hallmark of spirituality.

When would man be significantly justified to the synthesis of spirituality and freedom in the light of the invaluable viewpoints of Vivekananda?

References

1. Swami Vivekananda: *The Complete Works of Swami Vivekananda,* Advaita Ashrama, Kolkata, Mayavati Memorial Edition, 1989, Vol. IV, pp. 21-22.
2. *Ibid.,* Vol. IV, pp. 135-137.
3. *Ibid.,* pp. 26-27.
4. *Ibid.,* Vol. III, pp. 282-283.
5. *Ibid.,* pp. 176-177.
6. *Ibid.,* Vol. VI, pp. 8-9.
7. *Ibid.,* p. 9.
8. *Ibid.,* pp. 98-99.
9. *Ibid.,* Vol. VIII, pp. 179-180.
10. *Ibid.,* pp, 246-247.
11. *Ibid.,* Vol. IV, pp. 475-476.
12. *Ibid.,* pp. 350-351.
13. *Ibid.,* p. 351.
14. *Ibid.,* Vol. V, p. 267.
15. *Ibid.,* pp. 291-292.
16. *Ibid.,* Vol. II, pp. 375-376.
17. *Ibid.,* pp. 66-67.
18. *Ibid.,* pp. 302-304.
19. *Ibid.,* pp. 115-116.
20. *Ibid.,* p. 117.
21. *Ibid.,* Vol. I, pp. 426-427.
22. *Ibid.,* p. 103.
23. *Ibid.,* Vol. II, pp. 399-400.
24. *Ibid.,* 400-401.

6

Freedom and Aesthetics: Vivekananda's Uniqueness

Freedom as it generally welcomes from the conceptual point of view is independence. From a philosophical point of view, it denotes deliverance or liberation. But to Swami Vivekananda, it adorns and exercises Truth, Beauty and Goodness besides other finer visions and aspects of aesthetics. Freedom is a way of life diverse and different. To him, it is something more than that. It is the essence of quality and excellence, simplicity and cadence.

As an unparalleled synthesiser of freedom and aesthetics, Swami Vivekananda inspires us to exercise freedom of thought and expression in order to merge with the All Beautiful. This requires practice in extinction of personality in all poignance and objectivity. Although it is an endless striving, the only effective and desirable pointer to aesthetic efflorescence in terms of freedom is the 'emission of the divine Being' in every one of us. In his invaluable words:

> The soul that reigns within is independent and creates the desire for freedom. If we are not free, how can we hope to make the world better? We hold that human progress is the result of the action of the human spirit. What the world is, and what we ourselves are, are the fruits of the freedom of the spirit.
>
> We believe in one God, the Father of us all, who is omnipresent and omnipotent, and who guides and preserves His children

with infinite love. We believe in a Personal God as the Christians do, but we go further: we believe that we are He! That His personality is manifested in us, that God is in us, and that we are in God. We believe there is a germ of truth in all religions, and the Hindu bows down to them all; for in this world, truth is to be found not in subtraction but in addition. We would offer God a bouquet of the most beautiful flowers of all the diverse faiths. We must love God for love's sake, not for the hope of reward. We must do our duty for duty's sake, not for the hope of reward. Thus, in the purity of our hearts we shall see God. Sacrifices, genuflexions, mumblings, and mutterings are not religion. They are only good if they stimulate us to the brave performance of beautiful and heroic deeds and lifts our thoughts to the apprehension of the divine perfection.

What good is it, if we acknowledge in our prayers that God is the Father of us all, and in our daily lives do not treat every man as our brother? Books are only made so that they may point the way to a higher life; but no good results unless the path is trodden with unflinching steps! Every human personality may be compared to a glass of globe. There is the same pure white light— an emission of the divine Being— in the centre of each, but the glass being of different colours and thickness, the rays assume diverse aspects in the transmission. The equality and beauty of each central flame is the same, and the apparent inequality is only in the imperfection of the temporal instrument of its expression."[1]

Vivekananda's vision of freedom in the light of aesthetics is best reflected in the divinity nurtured in man. He considers every human being as the potential force of divinity. This allows freedom of individuality in the best possible efflorescence of aesthetics. When, as a Vedantist, he upholds the truth that every one is the endearing child of God, he cordially elucidates the spirit of aesthetics in terms of truth and the All True, God. In his thought provoking words:

We need reason to drive out all the superstitions; and what remains is Vedantism. There is a beautiful Sanskrit poem in which the sage says to himself: 'Why weepest thou, my friend? There is no fear, no death for thee. Why weepest thou? There is no misery for thee, for thou art like the infinite blue sky, unchangeable in thy nature. Clouds of all colour come before it, play for a moment, and pass away; it is the same sky. Thou hast only to drive away the clouds.'

We have to open the gates and clear the way. The water will rush in and fill in by its own nature, because it is there already.

Man is a good deal conscious, partly unconscious, and there is a possibility of getting beyond consciousness. It is only when we become *men* that we can go beyond all reason. The words *higher* or *lower* can be used only in the phenomenal world. To say them of the noumenal world is simply contradictory, because there is no differentiation there. Man-manifestation is the highest in the phenomenal world. The Vedantist says he is higher than the Devas. The gods will all have to die and will become men again, and in the man-body alone they will become perfect.

It is true that we create a system, but we have to admit that it is not perfect, because the reality must be beyond all systems. We are ready to compare it with other systems and are ready to show that this is the only rational system that can be; but it is not perfect, because reason is not perfect. It is, however, the only possible rational system that the human mind can conceive.

It is true to a certain extent that a system must disseminate itself to be strong. No system has disseminated itself so much as the Vedanta. It is the personal contact that teaches even now. A mass of reading does not make men; those who were real men were made so by personal contact. It is true that there are very few of these real men, but they will increase. Yet you cannot believe that there will come a day when we shall all be philosophers. We do not believe that there will come a time when there will be all happiness and no unhappiness.[2]

The sincere belief in man as the true architect of perfection in all directions upholds Vivekananda's philosophy of optimism.

He places man as the embodiment of a sum total of individuals who represent God. Such a vision of man idealises the aesthetic spirit of goodness as the exponent of divinity in man. An incomparable and unparalleled vision of aesthetic totality for which man alone can show and prove emerges from freedom of individuality. As Vivekananda highlights the spirit of freedom and individuality in terms of aesthetics and spirituality in perfect fusion:

> Neither need we trouble ourselves if a few fail. It is in the nature of things that many should fail, that troubles should come, that tremendous difficulties should arise, that selfishness and all the other devils in the human heart should struggle hard when they are about to be driven out by the fire of spirituality. The road to the Good is the roughest and steepest in the universe. It is a wonder that so many succeed, no wonder that so many fail. Character has to be established through a thousand stumbles.
>
> ** ** **
>
> A good world, a happy world, and social progress, are all terms equally intelligible with 'not ice' or 'dark light'. If we were good, it would not be the world. The soul foolishly thinks of manifesting the Infinite in finite matter, intelligence through gross particles; but at last it finds out its error and tries to escape. This going-back is the beginning of religion, and its method, destruction of self, that is, love. Not love for wife or child or anybody else, but love for everything else except this little self. Never be deluded by the tall talk, of which you will hear so much in America about 'human progress' and such stuff. There is *no progress* without corresponding digression. In one society there is one set of evils; in another, another.
>
> ** ** **
>
> The only knowledge that is of any value is to know that all this is humbug. But few, very few, will ever know this. 'Know the *Atman* alone, and give up all other vain words.' This is the only knowledge we gain from all this knowing about the universe.

> This is the only work, to call upon mankind to 'Awake, arise and stop not till the goal is reached'. It is renunciation, Tyaga, that is meant by religion, and nothing else.[3]

Knowledge as the sacred aesthetic component is God. We must be justified to knowledge which is endless and infinite. The more we are sincere and devoted to infinite knowledge, the more are we devoted to truth as an incomparable aesthetic component. This will prompt us to enjoy and experience freedom to think. This will also prepare us for understanding and experiencing the great aesthetic delight in the unity of all existence inherent in every one of us.

Referring to the Vedanta, Vivekananda exclusively points out the aesthetic delight in the unity we encounter in all existence:

> In our country we go down on our knees before the man who reads the Vedas, and we do not care for the man who is studying physics. That is superstition; it is not Vedanta at all. It is utter materialism. With God every knowledge is sacred. Knowledge is God. Infinite knowledge abides within every one in the fullest measure. You are not really ignorant, though you may appear to be so. You are incarnations of God, all of you. You are the incarnations of the Almighty, Omnipresent, Divine Principle. You may laugh at me now, but the time will come when you will understand. You must. Nobody will be left behind.
>
> What is the goal? This that I have spoken of— Vedanta— is not a new religion. So old—as old as God Himself. It is not confined to any time and place, it is everywhere. Everybody knows this truth. We are all working it out. The goal of the whole universe is that. This applies even to external nature—every atom is rushing towards that goal. And do you think any of the infinite pure souls are left without knowledge of the supreme truth? All have it, all are going to the same goal— the discovery of the innate Divinity. The maniac, the murderer, the superstitious man, the man who is lynched in this country—all are travelling to the same goal. Only that which we do ignorantly we ought to do knowingly, or better.

> The unity of all existence—you all have it already within yourselves. None was ever born without it. However, you may deny it, it continually asserts itself. What is human love? It is more or less an affirmation of that unity: 'I am one with thee, my wife, my child, my friend!' Only you are affirming the unity ignorantly. 'None ever loved the husband for the husband's sake, but for the sake of the Self that is in the husband.' The wife finds unity there.[4]

Freedom of the individual is freedom of the Self. The aesthetics of the idea of the Self is always independent and pays greatest importance to the ascent of the individual. When Vivekananda highlights the true nature of the Self in terms of knowledge, power and activity, the freedom of the individual becomes transparent:

> The presence of Sattva with knowledge does not prove that Sattva is the cause of knowledge; on the contrary, Sattva calls out what was already existing in man, as the fire hits an iron ball placed near it by arousing the heat latent in it, not by entering into the ball.
>
> Shankara says, knowledge is not a bondage, because it is the nature of God. The world ever is, whether manifested or unmanifested; so an eternal object exists.
>
> *Jnana-bala-kriya* (knowledge, power, activity) is God. Nor does He need form. Because the finite only needs form to interpose as an obstruction to catch and hold infinite knowledge; but God really needs no such help. There is no 'moving soul', there is only one Atman. Jiva (individual soul) is the conscious ruler of this body, in whom the five life principles come into unity, and yet that very Jiva is the Atman, because all is Atman. What you think about it is your delusion and not in the Jiva. You are God, and whatever else you may think is wrong. You must worship the Self in Krishna, not Krishna as Krishna. Only by worshipping the Self can freedom be won.[5]

That personal God is nothing but the Self objectified, stands for the uniqueness Vivekananda explains in terms of freedom and individuality. He adroitly elucidates the role of personal God as an embodiment of freedom and aesthetics for which the meaning of existence becomes true. In his words:

> So long as I say 'you', I have the right to speak of God protecting us. When I see another, I must take all the consequences and put in the third, the ideal, which stands between us; that is the apex of the triangle. The vapour becomes snow, then water, then Ganga; but when it is vapour, there is no Ganga, and when it is water, we think of no vapour in it. The idea of creation or change is inseparably connected with will. So long as we perceive this world in motion, we have to conceive will behind it. Physics proves the utter delusion of the senses; nothing really is as we see, hear, feel, smell, taste it. Certain vibrations producing certain results affect our senses; we know only relative truth.
>
> The Sanskrit word for truth is 'isness' (Sat). From our present standpoint, this world appears to us as will and consciousness. Personal God is as much an entity for Himself as we are for ourselves, and no more. God can also be seen as a form, just as we are seen. As men, we must have a God; as God, we need none. This is why Shri Ramakrishna constantly saw the Divine Mother ever present with him, more real than any other thing around him; but in Samadhi all went but the Self. Personal God comes nearer and nearer until He melts away, and there is no more Personal God and no more 'I', all is merged in Self.[6]

The merging of 'I' in the Self also upholds the aesthetic spirit of freedom in terms of morality. This is very much evident in the principle of freedom. The struggle to be free is actually guided by the desire and accomplishment of good action. Vivekananda distinctly explains this from the standpoint of the Vedanta:

> The fundamental principle is that there is eternal freedom for every one. Every one must come to it. We have to struggle, impelled by our desire to be free. Every other desire but that to

be free is illusive. Every good action, the Vedantist says, is a manifestation of that freedom.

I do not believe that there will come a time when all the evil in the world will vanish. How could that be? This stream goes on. Masses of water go out at one end, but masses are coming in at the other end.

The Vedanta says that you are pure and perfect, and that there is a state beyond good and evil, and that is your own nature. It is higher even than good. Good is only a lesser differentiation than evil.

We have no theory of evil. We call it ignorance.

** ** **

There is one thing to be remembered: that the assertion— I am God— cannot be made with regard to the sense-world. If you say in the sense-world that you are God, what is to prevent your doing wrong? So the affirmation of your divinity applies only to the noumenal. If I am God, I am beyond the tendencies of the senses and will not do evil. Morality of course is not the goal of man, but the means through which this freedom is attained. The Vedanta says that Yoga is one way that makes men realise this divinity. The Vedanta says this is done by the realisation of freedom within and that everything will give way to that. Morality and ethics will all range themselves in their proper places.[7]

The spirit of righteousness as an outcome of freedom always demands a strong backdrop of aesthetic sensibilities. This is why one must be free as a Yogi and devotedly strive for the aesthetics of austerity and calmness of mind in particular for realisation of the Self. As Vivekananda inspires us to live for an ideal that enjoys freedom and aesthetics in perfect harmony:

If you want to be a Yogi, you must be free and place yourself in circumstances where you are alone and free from all anxiety. He who desires for a comfortable and nice life and at the same

> time wants to realise the Self is like the fool who, wanting to cross the river, caught hold of a crocodile mistaking it for a log of wood. 'Seek ye first the Kingdom of God and His righteousness, and all these things shall be added unto you.' Unto him comes everything who does not care for anything. Fortune is like a flirt; she cares not for him who wants her, but she is at the feet of him who does not care for her. Money comes and showers itself upon one who does not care for it; so does fame come in abundance until it is a trouble and a burden. They always come to the Master. The slave never gets anything. The Master is he who can live in spite of them, whose life does not depend upon the little, foolish things of the world. Live for an ideal, and that one ideal alone. Let it be so great, so strong, that there may be nothing else left in the mind; no place for anything else, no time for anything else.[8]

The freedom to be true to oneself necessitates freedom to be true to knowledge. A man of truth never forsakes knowledge that promotes truth. Freedom to stick to truth all the time leads to knowledge pure and serene. The aesthetics of knowledge always safeguards truth because knowledge pure and serene never makes any compromise with ignorance.

While making a discourse on "The Evils of Adhikarivada", Vivekananda distinctly observes on the concept of knowledge and freedom in the light of truth:

> Knowledge means freedom from the errors which ignorance leads to. Knowledge paving the way to error! Enlightenment leading to confusion! Is it possible? Men are not bold enough to speak out broad truths, for fear of losing the respect of the people. They try to make a compromise between the real, eternal truths and the nonsensical prejudices of the people, and thus set up the doctrine that Lokacharas (customs of the people) and Deshacharas (customs of the country) must be adhered to. Throw away such texts as, '*tathapi lokacharah*—Yet the customs of the people will have to be followed.' Nonsense! The result of this sort of compromise is that the grand truths are soon buried

> under the heaps of rubbish, and the latter are eagerly held as real truths. Even the grand truths of the Gita, so boldly preached by Shri Krishna, received the gloss of compromise in the hands of future generations of disciples, and the result is that the grandest scripture of the world is now made to yield many things which lead men astray.
>
> This attempt at compromise proceeds from arrant downright cowardice. Be bold! My children should be brave, above all. Not the least compromise on any account. Preach the highest truths broadcast. Do not fear losing your respect or causing unhappy friction. Rest assured that if you serve truth in spite of temptations to forsake it, you will attain a heavenly strength in the face of which men will quail to speak before you things which you do not believe to be true. People will be convinced of what you will say to them if you can strictly serve truth for fourteen years continually, without swerving from it.[9]

How to stick to truth as a great aesthetic component of efflorescence of freedom? How to prepare oneself for practice and poignance of this great component of human ascent and excellence? The inevitable answer is to lead a life free from any form of desire and temptation.

In one of his inspired talks Vivekananda advises:

> Give up all desire for enjoyment in earth or heaven. Control the organs of the senses and control the mind. Bear every misery without even knowing that you are miserable. Think of nothing but liberation. Have faith in Guru, in his teachings, and in the surety that you can get free. Say "Soham, Soham" whatever comes. Tell yourself this even in eating, walking, suffering; tell the mind this incessantly—that what we see never existed, that there is only "I". Flash— the dream will break! Think day and night, this universe is zero, only God is. Have intense desire to get free.

** ** **

> The present only is existent. There is no past or future even in thought, because to think it, you have to make it the present. Give up everything, and let it float where it will. This world is all a delusion, do not let it fool you again. You have known it for what it is not, now know it for what it is. If the body is dragged anywhere, let it go; do not care where the body is. This tyrannical idea of duty is a terrible poison and is destroying the world.
>
> Do not wait to have a harp and rest by degrees; why not take a harp and begin here? Why wait for heaven? Make it here. In heaven there is no marrying or giving in marriage; why not begin at once and have none here? The yellow robe of the Sannyasin is the sign of the free. Give up this beggar's dress of the world; wear the flag of freedom, the ocre robe.[10]

Total abnegation or absolute refusal to prioritise what is material is the first step to ascent and excellence and only believing, striving and enriching the Self through renunciation are the means to develop aesthetic sensibilities of freedom. When we devote ourselves to the understanding and appreciation of freedom in terms of the aesthetic and spiritual concepts of superconsciousness and Brahmavit, the knower of God, as Vivekananda characteristically reveals, true liberation becomes a reality:

> Value nothing material and do not cling to it. If you cling to nothing, not even life, then there is no fear. "He goes from death to death who sees many in this world." There can be no physical death for us and no material death, when we see all is one. All bodies are mine; so even body is eternal, because the tree, the animal, the sun, the moon, the universe itself is my body; then how can it die? Every mind, every thought is mine, then how can death come? The Self is never born and never dies. When we realise this, all doubts vanish. "I am, I know, I love"—these can never be doubted. There is no hunger, for all that is eaten is eaten by me. If a hair falls out, we do not think, we die; so if one body dies, it is but a hair falling…

> The superconscious is God, is beyond speech, beyond thought, beyond consciousness... There are three states,—brutality (Tamas), humanity (Rajas), and divinity (Sattva). Those attaining the highest state simply *are.* Duty dies there; they only love and as a magnet draw others to them. This is freedom. No more you do moral acts, but whatever you do is moral. The Brahmavit (the knower of God) is higher than all gods. The angels came to worship Jesus when he had conquered delusion and had said, "Get thee behind me, Satan." *None* can help a Brahmavit, the universe itself bows down before him. His every desire is fulfilled, his spirit purifies others; therefore worship the Brahmavit if you wish to attain the highest. When we have the three great "gifts of God"— a human body, intense desire to be free, and the help of a great soul to show us the way— then liberation is certain for us. Mukti is ours.[11]

As an aesthetic concept, freedom stands for liberation from the bondage of both good and evil. This is one of the great challenges for man. How to liberate from such a bondage as good and evil tempt from time to time? Referring to the enviable and wonderful nature of a tortoise, Vivekananda observes:

> As the tortoise tucks its feet and head inside the shell, and you may kill it and break it in pieces, and yet it will not come out, even so the character of that man who has control over his motives and organs is unchangeably established. He controls his own inner forces, and nothing can draw them out against his will. By this continuous reflex of good thoughts, good impressions moving over the surface of the mind, the tendency for doing good becomes strong, and as the result we feel able to control the Indriyas (the sense-organs, the nerve-centres). Thus, alone will character be established, then alone a man gets to truth. Such a man is safe for ever; he cannot do any evil. You may place him in any company, there will be no danger for him. There is still a higher state than having this good tendency, and that is the desire for liberation. You must remember that freedom of the soul is the goal of all Yogas, and each one leads

> equally to the same result. By work alone men may get to where Buddha got largely by meditation or Christ by prayer. Buddha was a working Jnani, Christ was a Bhakta, but the same goal was reached by both of them. The difficulty is here. Liberation means entire freedom—freedom from the bondage of good, as well as from the bondage of evil. A golden chain is as much a chain as an iron one. There is a thorn in my finger, and I use another to take the first one out; and when I have taken it out, I throw both of them aside; I have no necessity for keeping the second thorn, because both are thorns after all. So the bad tendencies are to be counteracted by the good ones, and the bad impressions of the mind are to be removed by the fresh waves of good ones, until all that is evil almost disappears, or is subdued or held in control in a corner of the mind; but after that, the good tendencies have also to be conquered. Thus, the "attached" becomes the "unattached".[12]

To be unattached is to be dependent on one's unique strength, and to be dependent on the latter is to enjoy freedom to effloresce. How should one be free as such? Vivekananda provides us with the serene and aesthetic answer of living in perfect freedom through personal effort. In analysing his point, he interestingly refers to an instance on the aesthetic religion of freedom:

> A huge locomotive has rushed on over the line and a small worm that was creeping upon one of the rails saved its life by crawling upon out of the path of the locomotive. Yet this little worm, so insignificant that it can be crushed in a moment, is a living something, while this locomotive, so huge, so immense, is only an engine, a machine. You say the one has life and the other is only dead matter and all its power and strength and speed are only those of a dead machine, a mechanical contrivance. Yet the poor little worm which moved upon the rail and which the least touch of the engine would have deprived of its life is a magestic being compared to that huge locomotive. It is a small part of the Infinite and, therefore, it is greater than this powerful engine. Why should that be so? How do we know

> the living from the dead? The machine mechanically performs all the movements its maker made it to perform, its movements are not those of life. How can we make the distinction between the living and the dead, then? In the living there is freedom, there is intelligence; in the dead all is bound and freedom is not possible, because there is no intelligence. This freedom that distinguishes us from mere machines is what we are all striving for. To be more free is the goal of all our efforts, for only in perfect freedom can there be perfection. This effort to attain freedom underlies all forms of worship, whether we know it or not.[13]

To deny the bond of nature and establish one's identity is the aesthetic goal of freedom. It is to break all bondage and proclaim the victory of man, 'the Master of nature' as a Being who always strives for higher and higher ends-in-view of life and the beyond. The cry of the soul in tune with the cry of the individual must be attuned because they are striving for reaching the same destination through exercise of the aesthetics of freedom. At the same time, born rebels as we are, we continually strive for breaking the bonds of nature and enjoy freedom as aesthetically as we can.

In support of the viewpoints as stated above, we might recall Vivekananda's poignant observations:

> Even hells stand out with this miraculous fact that we are born rebels; and the first fact of life—the inrushing of life itself—against this we rebel and cry out, "No law for us." As long as we obey the laws we are like machines, and on goes the universe, and we cannot break it. Laws as laws become man's nature. The first inkling of life on its higher level is in seeing this struggle within us to break the bond of nature and to be free. "Freedom, O Freedom! Freedom, O Freedom!" is the song of the soul. Bondage, alas, to be bound in nature, seems its fate.
>
> Why should there be serpent, or ghost, or demon worship and all these various creeds and forms for having miracles? Why do we say that there is life, there is being in anything? There must

> be a meaning in all this search, this endeavour to understand life, to explain being. It is not meaningless and vain. It is man's ceaseless endeavour to become free. The knowledge which we now call science has been struggling for thousands of years in its attempt to gain freedom, and people ask for freedom. Yet there is no freedom in nature. It is all law. Still the struggle goes on. Nay, the whole of nature from the very sun to the atoms is under law, and even for man there is no freedom. But we cannot believe it. We have been studying laws from the beginning and yet cannot—nay, will not—believe that man is under law. The soul cries ever, "Freedom, O Freedom!" With the conception of God as a perfectly free Being, man cannot rest eternally in this bondage. Higher he must go, and unless the struggle were for himself, he would think it too severe.[14]

A timeless thinker of freedom and the role of man as an aesthetic being, Vivekananda extends the horizon of freedom in terms of the science of oneness of the universe as 'the essential unity of things'. That we are all mentally, spiritually, physically, and, above all, one in all is the grand aesthetic vision of man.

Emphasising on the ever abiding aesthetic vision of man and freedom, Vivekananda clarifies the role of knowledge in terms of the above:

> Knowledge does not mean the knowledge we have, but the essence of that, that which is expressing itself in the course of evolution in human beings or in other animals as knowledge. The essence of that knowledge is meant, the ultimate fact beyond, if I may be allowed to say so, even consciousness. That is what is meant by knowledge and what we see in the universe as the essential unity of things. To my mind, if modern science is proving anything again and again, it is this, that we are one—mentally, spiritually, and physically. It is wrong to say we are even physically different. Supposing we are materialists, for argument's sake, we shall have to come to this, that the whole universe is simply an ocean of matter, of which you and I are like the whirlpools. Masses of matter are coming into each

whirlpool, taking the whirlpool form, and coming out as matter again. The matter that is in my body may have been yours a few years ago, or in the sun, or may have been the matter in a planet, and so on, in a continuous state of flux. What is meant by your body and my body? It is the oneness of the body. So with thought. It is an ocean of thought, one infinite mass, in which your mind and my mind are like whirlpools. Are you not seeing the effect now, how my thoughts are entering into yours, and yours into mine? The whole of our lives is one; we are one, even in thought. Coming to a still further generalisation, the essence of matter and thought is their potentiality of spirit; this is the unity from which all have come, and that must essentially be one. We are absolutely one; we are physically one, we are mentally one, and as spirit, it goes without saying, that we are one, if we believe in spirit at all. This oneness is the one fact that is being proved every day by modern science. To a proud man it is told: You are the same as that little worm there; think not that you are something enormously different from it; you are the same. You have been that in a previous incarnation, and the worm has crawled up to this man state, of which you are so proud. This grand preaching, the oneness of things, making us one with everything that exists, is the great lesson to learn, for most of us are very glad to be made one with higher beings, but nobody wants to be made one with lower beings. Such is human ignorance, that if anyone's ancestors were men whom society honoured, even they were brutish, if they were robbers, even robber barons, everyone of us would try to trace our ancestry to them; but if among our ancestors we had poor, honest gentleman, none of us wants to trace our ancestry to them. But the scales are falling from our eyes, truth is beginning to manifest itself more and more, and that is a great gain to religion.[15]

The new religion thus christened in freedom and aesthetics shows the avenues of advancement of man in diverse directions. It teaches us the great and invaluable truth that God, the All Good, is in every one of us irrespective of the apparent distinction between the virtuous and the sinner, the wise and the ignorant, the rich and the poor, the happy and the miserable. It is a fact that at a certain point of time all these differences will disappear and everyone would manifest the inherent divinity.

Referring to a classic anecdote, Vivekananda positively elucidates:

> Two birds of a beautiful plumage, inseparable companions, sat upon the same tree, one on the top and one below. The beautiful bird below was eating the fruits of the tree, sweet and bitter, one moment a sweet one and another a bitter. The moment he ate a bitter fruit, he was sorry, but after a while he ate another and when it was too bitter, he looked up and saw the other bird who ate neither the sweet nor the bitter, but was calm and majestic, immersed in his own glory. And then the poor lower bird forgot and went on eating the sweet and bitter fruits again, until at last he ate one that was extremely bitter; and then he stopped again and once more looked up at the glorious bird above. Then he came nearer and nearer to the other bird; and when he had come near enough, rays of light shone upon him and enveloped him, and saw he was transformed into the higher bird. He became calm, majestic, free, and found that there had been but one bird all the time on the tree. The lower bird was but the reflection of the one above. So we are in reality one with the Lord, but the reflection makes us seem many, as the one sun reflects in a million dew-drops and seems a million tiny suns. The reflection must vanish if we are to identify ourselves with our real nature which is divine. The universe itself can never be the limit of our satisfaction. That is why the miser gathers more and more money, that is why the robber robs, the sinner sins, that is why you are learning philosophy. All have one purpose. There is no other purpose on life, save to reach this freedom. Consciously or unconsciously, we are all striving for perfection. Every being must attain to it.

> The man who is groping through sin, through misery, the man who is choosing the path through hells, will reach it, but it will take time. We cannot save him. Some hard knocks on his head will help him to turn to the Lord. The path of virtue, purity, unselfishness, spirituality, becomes known at last and what all are doing unconsciously, we are trying to do consciously. The idea is expressed by St. Paul, "The God that ye ignorantly worship, Him declare I unto you." This is the lesson for the whole world to learn. What have these philosophies and theories of nature to do, if not to help us to attain to this one goal in life? Let us come to that consciousness of the identity of everything and let man see himself in everything. Let us be no more the worshippers of creeds or sects with small limited notions of God, but see Him in everything in the universe. If you are knowers of God, you will everywhere find the same worship as in your heart.[16]

The omnipresence of God in everyone despite apparent differences is an unparalleled aesthetic concept with which religion as Vivekananda prominently highlights stands for exposition in the illumined vision of freedom. He places religion on a citadel where everyone is divine in the earnest and ceaseless endeavour for fulness and perfection. Freedom, then, adorns the true reality of the existence of man.

The true identity of man is the Self which has Its existence in him. He is the Self. He should always strive for real knowing and bliss through exercise of freedom. Then he can prove that he is a refined being with aesthetic sensibilities. As Vivekananda serenely observes:

> The Self is the condition of all in the universe, but It can never be conditioned. As soon as we know that we are It, we are free. As mortals we are not and never can be free. Free mortality is a contradiction in terms, for mortality implies change, and only the changeless can be free. The Atman alone is free, and that is one real essence. We feel this inner freedom; in spite of all theories, all beliefs, we know it, and every action proves that we

> know it. The will is not free, its apparent freedom is but a reflection from the Real. If the world were only an endless chain of cause and effect, where could one stand to help it? There must needs be a piece of dry land for the rescuer to stand on, else how can he drag anyone out of the rushing stream and save him from drowning? Even the fanatic who cries "I am a worm", thinks that he is on the way to become a saint. He sees the saint even in the worm.
>
> There are two ends or aims of human life, real knowing (Vijnana) and bliss. Without freedom, these two are impossible. They are the touchstone of all life. We should feel the Eternal Unity so much, that we should weep for all sinners, knowing that it is *we* who are sinning. The eternal law is self-sacrifice, not self-assertion.[17]

To eliminate self-assertion is to enjoy freedom of the mind. Unless the mind is free, no good can come out as an essence of life. When we speak of goodness, we consider freedom as its torchbearer and vice versa. Thus, freedom and goodness eliminate all points of differences. The inherent power of freedom to be as one ought to be must be exercised. Otherwise, goodness will never come out through its natural efflorescence. That will reveal the true history of man, civilisation, advancement and religion by totally eliminating all forms of superstition.

As a radical thinker of freedom in terms of aesthetics, Vivekananda advises us:

> If you can get an explanation of a phenomenon from within its nature, it is nonsense to look for an explanation from outside. If the world explains itself, it is nonsense to go outside for an explanation. Have you found any phenomena in the life of a man that you have ever seen which cannot be explained by the power of the man himself? So what is the use of going to the stars or anything else in the world? My own Karma is sufficient explanation of my present state. So in the case of Jesus himself. We know that his father was only a carpenter. We need not go

> to anybody else to find an explanation of his power. He was the outcome of his own past, all of which was a preparation for that Jesus. Buddha goes back and back to animal bodies and tells how he ultimately became Buddha. So what is the use of going to the stars for explanation? They may have a little influence; but it is our duty to ignore them rather than hearken to them and make ourselves nervous. This I lay down as the first essential in all I teach: anything that brings spiritual, mental, or physical weakness, touch it not with the toes of your feet. Religion is the manifestation of the natural strength that is in man. A spring of infinite power is coiled up and is inside this little body, and that spring is spreading itself. And as it goes on spreading, body after body is found insufficient; it throws them off and takes higher bodies. This is the history of man, of religion, civilisation, or progress. That giant Prometheus, who is bound, is getting himself unbound. It is always a manifestation of strength, and all these ideas such as astrology, although there may be a grain of truth in them, should be avoided.[18]

The indomitable power of freedom is revealed in self-sacrifice and renunciation which are the great aesthetic components of fullness. Life is transitory but it becomes really meaningful, purposeful, and permanent in the pursuit and fullness of self-sacrifice and renunciation for the cause of altruism. From freedom to greater freedom is the endless aesthetic quest for man.

In the lecture delivered in Oakland on salvation, Vivekananda points out the significance of the above:

> The two great watchwords of every great religion are renunciation and self-sacrifice. We all want the truth, and we know that it must come, whether we want it or not. In a way we are all striving for that good. And what prevents our reaching it? It is ourselves. Your ancestors used to call it the devil; but it is our own false self.
>
> We live in slavery, and we would die if we were out of it. We are like the man who lived in total darkness for ninety years and

when taken out into the warm sunshine of nature, prayed to be taken back to his dungeon. You would not leave this old life to go into a newer and greater freedom which opens out.[19]

To enjoy and disseminate the innate spirit of freedom in terms of goodness for one and all is a great aesthetic exercise for man. It is the surest way to regain the true self. By means of continuous and sincere crystallisation of the self, the spirit of goodness becomes a part and parcel of life. Realisation of the Atman is the genesis of freedom. It ignores all forms of causation and directs our attention towards the realisation of Atman only as true followers of aesthetic vision of purity and perfection. Referring to the invaluable words of the Upanishad, Vivekananda characteristically deliberates: Jnana says, 'Kill desire and so get rid of it.' That is the only way. Cast out all causation and realise the Atman. Only freedom can produce true morality. If there were only an endless chain of cause and effect, Nirvana could not be. It is extinction of the seeming self, bound by this chain. That is what constitutes freedom, to get beyond causality.

Our true nature is good, it is free, the pure being that can never be or do wrong. When we read God with our eyes and minds, we call Him this or that; but in reality there is but One, all variations are our interpretations of that One. We *become* nothing; we *regain* our true Self. Buddha's summary of misery as the outcome of 'ignorance and caste' (inequality) has been adopted by the Vedantists because it is the best ever made. It manifests the wonderful insight of this greatest among men. Let us then be brave and sincere: whatever path we follow with devotion, must take us to freedom. Once lay hold on one link of the chain and the whole must come after it by degrees. Water the root of the tree and the whole tree is watered. It is of little advantage to waste time to water each leaf. In other words, seek the Lord and getting Him we get all. Churches, doctrines, forms — these are merely the hedges to protect the tender plant of religion; but later on they must all be broken down, that the little plant may become a tree. So the various religious sects, Bible, Vedas, and scriptures are just 'tubs' for the little plant; but it has to get out of the tub and fill the world.[20]

Freedom and religion are so aesthetically intertwined that if we consider one as separable from the other, man stands as extinct from both. The soul of freedom is the soul of religion and vice versa. It is the soul that shows the serene avenues of aesthetic enrichment. It points out the positive points of advance towards higher and more poignant visions of both religion and freedom in terms of aesthetic endeavour. When we speak of the quest for religion, the assertion of freedom stands out mandatory and supreme. Otherwise, the ascent of man becomes impossible.

Unless the idea of religion as the realisation of the Self in oneself is manifested, the aesthetic vision of freedom becomes turbulent. This turbulence shows how to be truly involved in the religion of living, loving and having the idea of man, the God of all gods. It is an endless search to be perfect in the idea of self-realisation bereft of which freedom remains absent or becomes meaningless and dormant. Freedom to understand anything is actually a way towards better and finer transparency. Unless the endeavour of transparency finds the true substance of thinking and reasoning in perfect tune with feeling, freedom loses much of its connotation as an infinite force of advancement.

As an aesthetic thinker, Vivekananda significantly asserts on the true concept of knowledge and clarifies it through an example as follows:

> Whichever way we turn in trying to understand things in their reality, if we analyse far enough, we find that at last we come to a peculiar state of things, seemingly a contradiction: something which our reason cannot grasp and yet is a fact. We take up something—we know it is finite; but as soon as we begin to analyse it, it leads us beyond our reason, and we never find an end to all its qualities, its possibilities, its powers, its relations. It has become infinite. Take even a common flower, that is finite enough; but who is there that can say he knows all about the flower? There is no possibility of anyone's getting to the end of knowledge about that one flower. The flower has become infinite—the flower which was finite to begin with. Take a grain

> of sand. Analyse it. We start with the assumption that it is finite, and at last we find that it is not, it is infinite; all the same, we have looked upon it as finite. The flower is similarly treated as a finite something.
>
> So with all our thoughts and experiences, physical and mental. We begin, we may think, on a small scale, and grasp them as little things; but very soon they elude our knowledge and plunge into the abyss of the infinite. And the greatest and the first thing perceived is ourselves. We are also in the same dilemma about existence. We exist. We see we are finite beings. We live and die. Our horizon is narrow. We are here, limited, confronted by the universe all around. Nature can crush us out of existence in a moment. Our little bodies are just held together, ready to go to pieces at a moment's notice. We know that. In a region of action how powerless we are! Our will is being thwarted at every turn. So many things we want to do, and how few we can do! There is no limit to our willing. We can will everything, want everything, we can desire to go to the dogstar. But how few of our desires can be accomplished! The body will not allow it. Well, nature is against the accomplishment of our will. We are weak. What is true of the flower, of the grain of sand, of the physical world, and of every thought, is a hundredfold true of ourselves. We are also in the same dilemma of existence, being finite and infinite at the same time. We are like waves in the ocean; the wave is the ocean and yet not the ocean. There is not any part of the wave of which you cannot say, 'It is the ocean.' the name 'ocean' applies to the wave and equally to every other part of the ocean, and yet it is separate from the ocean. So in this infinite ocean of existence we are like wavelets. At the same time, when we want really to grasp ourselves, we cannot—we have become the infinite.[21]

To love the good is to love God, and to love God as such is to be free from all narrowness of vision. It is the freedom of the mind of a person to take recourse to the spirit of the aesthetics of love in the form of All Love without self-interest that affects serenity and magnanimity. True freedom always opens the mind with the aesthetic spirit of altruism. That spirit enables us to be devoted to service without any personal interest or attachment.

In analysing the role of freedom and goodness as the ideal of a universal religion through the teachings of Karma-Yoga, 'the attainment of God through work', Vivekananda radically observes:

> It is evident that in society there are many persons who seem to be born for some sort of activity or other, whose minds cannot be concentrated on the plane of thought alone, and who have but one idea, concretised in work, visible and tangible. There must be a science for this kind of life too. Each one of us is engaged in some work, but the majority of us fritter away the greater portion of our energies, because we do not know the secret of work. Karma-Yoga explains this secret and teaches where and how to work, how to employ to the greatest advantage the largest part of our energies in the work that is before us. But with this secret we must take into consideration the great objection against work, namely that it causes pain. All misery and pain come from attachment. I want to do work, I want to do good to a human being; and it is ninety to one that that human being whom I have helped will prove ungrateful and go against me; and the result to me is pain. Such things deter mankind from working; and it spoils a good portion of the work and energy of mankind, this fear of pain and misery. Karma-Yoga teaches us how to work for work's sake, unattached, without caring who is helped, and what for. The Karma-Yogi works because it is his nature, because he *feels* that it is good for him to do so, and he has no object beyond that. His position in this world is that of a giver, and he never cares to receive anything. He knows that he is giving, and does not ask for anything in return, and, therefore, he eludes the grasp of misery. The grasp of pain, whenever it comes, is the result of the reaction of 'attachment'.[22]

Indeed, to be attached is to be under yoke, and to be under yoke is to be deprived of freedom. The human mind frantically seeks freedom primarily because it dignifies individuality. There is no room for commonality because it totally eats up all simplicity, vitality, straightforwardness and manliness which are the essential fruits of freedom. Unless goodness, beauty and truth— the three most elemental components of aesthetics— adorn freedom, there is every possibility of being swayed down by vainglory and pride. The pride of freedom, if any, is always altruism and humility.

To be in quest of God is actually to be in quest of nature and to be in quest of nature must be a quest for freedom. Such freedom allows us to be true to the aesthetics of attaining perfect knowledge. It leads us towards freedom of existence. It also makes us aware of the great spirit of the existence of God in all nature and man.

From the Vedantic spirit of the true nature of God in terms of freedom and aesthetics, Vivekananda radically observes:

> The whole of nature is worship of God. Wherever there is life, there is this search for freedom and that freedom is the same as God. Necessarily this freedom gives us mastery over all nature and is impossible without knowledge. The more we are knowing, the more we are becoming masters of nature. Mastery alone is making us strong and if there be some being entirely free and masters of nature, that being must have a perfect knowledge of nature, must be omnipresent and omniscient. Freedom must go hand in hand with these, and that being alone who has acquired these will be beyond nature.
>
> Blessedness, eternal peace, arising from perfect freedom, is the highest concept of religion underlying all the ideas of God in Vedanta—absolutely free Existence, not bound by anything, no change, no nature, nothing that can produce a change in Him. The same freedom is in you and in me and is the only real freedom.[23]

Again, freedom as Vivekananda points out is everywhere in the universe. This expands the aesthetic spirit of freedom. This also opens a fresh thinking of freedom in terms of stern realities of life that defies death. Vivekananda elucidates this point from his own personal experience of courageously 'facing the terrible':

> Freedom breathes in the throb of the universe. Unless there is unity at the universal heart, we cannot understand variety. Such is the conception of the Lord in the Upanishads. Sometimes it rises even higher, presenting to us an ideal before which we stand aghast—that we are in essence one with God. He who is the colouring in the wings of the butterfly, and the blossoming of the rose-bud, is the power that is in the plant and in the butterfly. He who gives us life is the power within us. Out of His fire comes life, and the direst death is also His power. He whose shadow is death, His shadow is immortality also. Take a still higher conception. See how we are flying like hunted hares from all that is terrible, and like them, hiding our heads and thinking we are safe. See how the whole world is flying from everything terrible. Once when I was in Varanasi, I was passing through a place where there was a large tank of water on one side and a high wall on the other. It was in the grounds where there were many monkeys. The monkeys of Varanasi are huge brutes and are sometimes surly. They now took it into their heads not to allow me to pass through their street, so they howled and shrieked and clutched at my feet as I passed. As they pressed closer, I began to run, but the faster I ran, the faster came the monkeys and they began to bite at me. It seemed impossible to escape, but just then I met a stranger who called out to me, 'Face the brutes.' I turned and faced the monkeys, and they fell back and finally fled. That is a lesson for all life—face the terrible, face it boldly. Like the monkeys, the hardships of life fall back when we cease to flee before them. If we are ever to gain freedom, it must be by conquering nature, never by running away.[24]

To eliminate fear is to enjoy the freedom of boldness, and to be bold is to aesthetically march for advancement and ascent. The spirit of self-refinement finds the best possible efflorescence of freedom to progress. Worries and woes are no longer there because freedom to think and act becomes an inseparable and aesthetic way of life.

Towards the end of his reply to the address of welcome accorded to him after his arrival in Kolkata, Vivekananda poignantly reminds us:

> Be not afraid, for all great power, throughout the history of humanity, has been with the people. From out of their ranks have come all the greatest geniuses of the world, and history can only repeat itself. Be not afraid of anything. You will do marvellous work. The moment you fear, you are nobody. It is fear that is the great cause of misery in the world. It is fear that is the greatest of all superstitions. It is fear that is the cause of our woes, and it is fearlessness that brings heaven even in a moment.[25]

As an ardent follower of freedom, fearlessness is the only key to open the gateway, as it were, of aesthetic fullness of life. It is a promise to poignance of freedom. It is a fulfilment yet to be made. It can never be averted because it is the essence of freedom. Let us listen to Vivekananda's vibrant voice of freedom in "The Song of the Sannyasin":

> Strike off thy fetters! Bonds that bind thee down,
> Of shining gold, or darker, baser ore;
> Love, hate—good, bad—and all the dual throng,
> Know, slave is slave, caressed or whipped, not free;
> For fetters, though of gold, are not less strong to bind;
> Then off with them,...[26]

When would we be the true followers of freedom and aesthetics as above?

References

1. Swami Vivekananda: *The Complete Works of Swami Vivekananda,* Advaita Ashrama, Kolkata, Mayavati Memorial Edition, 1989, Vol. IV, pp. 190-191.
2. *Ibid.*, Vol. V, pp. 283-284.
3. *Ibid.*, Vol. VIII, pp. 383-385.
4. *Ibid.*, pp. 137-138.

5. *Ibid.,* Vol. VII, pp. 56-57.
6. *Ibid.,* pp. 57-58.
7. *Ibid.,* Vol. V, p. 282.
8. *Ibid.,* pp. 251-252.
9. *Ibid.,* pp. 264-265.
10. *Ibid.,* Vol. VII, pp. 92-93.
11. *Ibid.,* pp. 93-94.
12. *Ibid.,* Vol. I, pp. 55-56.
13. *Ibid.,* p. 333.
14. *Ibid.,* p. 335.
15. *Ibid.,* pp. 372-374.
16. *Ibid.,* pp. 339-341.
17. *Ibid.,* Vol. VIII, p. 23.
18. *Ibid.,* pp. 184-185.
19. *Ibid.,* p. 239.
20. *Ibid.,* p. 27.
21. *Ibid.,* Vol. II, pp. 397-398.
22. *Ibid.,* pp. 391-392.
23. *Ibid.,* Vol. I, p. 337.
24. *Ibid.,* pp. 338-339.
25. *Ibid.,* Vol. III, pp. 320-321.
26. *Ibid.,* Vol. IV, p. 393.

7

Freedom and Humanism: Vivekananda's Radical Thoughts

The focal point of humanism is freedom. To be free is to honour humanism, and to honour humanism is to admit and enrich the inner essence of man. Freedom is a very crucial component of self-identity. Unless the identity of the self is not clear and transparent, man becomes a meaningless living being. Again, this identity of man by means of the exercise of the self is the only avenue of the efflorescence of the Divine Self inherent in man.

When we speak or think of divine humanism it is evident that freedom plays one of the most significant role in the whole process and exposure of the divinity already in man. It is not an easy task to uphold freedom under all eventualities. Only the sane and serene man knows how to honour the inner call of freedom that cares for acceleration of humanism.

A dynamic exponent of humanism, Swami Vivekananda inspires us how to rise up as one man freely and fairly to serve the downtrodden humanity. In a letter written from Chicago in 1894 to Alasinga, one of his followers, he writes:

> What India wants is a new electric fire to stir up a fresh vigour in the national veins. This was ever, and always will be, slow work. Be content to work, and, above all, be true to yourself. Be pure, staunch, and sincere to the very backbone, and

> everything will be all right. If you have marked anything in the disciples of Shri Ramakrishna, it is this—they are sincere to the backbone. My task will be done, and I shall be quite content to die, if I can bring up and launch one hundred such men over India. He, the Lord, knows best. Let ignorant men talk nonsense. We neither seek aid nor avoid it—we are the servants of the Most High. The petty attempts of small men should be beneath our notice. Onward! Upon ages of struggle a character is built. Be not discouraged. One word of truth can never be lost; for ages it may be hidden under rubbish, but it will show itself sooner or later. Truth is indestructible, virtue is indestructible, purity is indestructible. Give me a genuine man; I do not want masses of converts.[1]

Coming down straight to the downtrodden humanity, Vivekananda reminds us that unless man is free from the constraints of caste, creed, community and so on, unless man is free from ignorance and weakness, selfishness and humiliation, the efflorescence of humanism is a myth and total abstraction. Addressing Alasinga in the same letter in its concluding part, he welcomes us to think and act upon humanism and freedom anew and afresh:

> Let us pray, "Lead, Kindly Light"—a beam will come through the dark, and a hand will be stretched forth to lead us. I always pray for you: you must pray for me. Let each one of us pray day and night for the down-trodden millions in India who are held fast by poverty, priestcraft, and tyranny—pray day and night for them. I care more to preach religion to them than to the high and the rich. I am no metaphysician, no philosopher, nay, no saint. But I am poor, I love the poor. I see what they call the poor of this country, and how many there are who feel for them! What an immense difference in India! Who feels there for the two hundred millions of men and women sunken forever in poverty and ignorance? Where is the way out? Who feels for them? They cannot find light or education. Who will bring the light to them—who will travel from door to door bringing

> education to them? Let these people be your God—think of them, work for them, pray for them incessantly—the Lord will show you the way. Him I call a Mahatman (great soul) whose heart bleeds for the poor, otherwise he is a Duratman (wicked soul). Let us unite our wills in continued prayer for their good. We may die unknown, unpitied, unbewailed, without accomplishing anything—but not one thought will be lost. It will take effect, sooner or later. My heart is too full to express my feeling; you know it, you can imagine it. So long as the millions live in hunger and ignorance, I hold every man a traitor who, having been educated at their expense, pays not the least heed to them![2]

That every man is Divine is the kernel of the spirit of humanism. Unless we admit it from the inmost core of our hearts, all philosophy of man becomes narrow and worthless. It also affects the future of humanism as a mere symbol and never a positive force for the march of man as a real humanist. The central truth about man as Vivekananda asserts is:

> The Divine within; every being, however degraded, is the expression of the Divine. The Divinity becomes covered, hidden from view. I call to mind an incident of the Indian Mutiny. A Swami, who for years had fulfilled a vow of eternal silence, was stabbed by a Mohammedan. They dragged the murderer before his victim and cried out, 'Speak the word, Swami, and he shall die.' After many years of silence, he broke it to say with his last breath: 'My children, you are all mistaken. That man is God Himself.' The great lesson is, that unity is behind all. Call it God, Love, Spirit, Allah, Jehovah—it is the same that animates all life from the lowest animal to the noblest man. Picture to yourself an ocean ice-bound, pierced with many different holes. Each of these is a soul, a man, emancipated according to his degree of intelligence, essaying to break through the ice.[3]

Freedom to exercise self-evaluation rather than blaming and finding fault with others and even misunderstanding or misinterpreting the All Good is the sign of positive humanism.

As one with such a foundation of freedom and humanism, the glory of man is never duped or affected by any form of desolation or failure, futility and frustration. Man must be strong in contemplation and action, positive in performances and strategies, and adventurous in knowing the unknown and solving the unsolved not with the help of others expected or likely to be expected but alone, all alone.

To find fault with others is to dehumanise man. Every man must make his own destiny. None is there to share any responsibility for him. Not even the All Merciful whose love and affection is always impartial and all pervading. Everyone must reap what he sows. This is positive humanism. Such humanism never fades and becomes an everlasting promise and poignance of the march of man.

As a pioneer in positive humanism and advancement of man, Vivekananda elegantly introspects:

> We human beings are very slow to recognise our own weakness, our own faults, so long we can lay the blame upon somebody else. Men in general lay all the blame of life on their fellow-men, or, failing that, on God, or they conjure up a ghost, and say it is fate. Where is fate, and who is fate? We reap what we sow. We are the makers of our own fate. None else has the blame, none has the praise. The wind is blowing; those vessels whose sails are unfurled catch it, and go forward on their way, but those which have their sails furled do not catch the wind. Is that the fault of the wind? Is it the fault of the merciful Father, whose wind of mercy is blowing without ceasing, day and night, whose mercy knows no decay, is it His fault that some of us are happy and some unhappy? We make our own destiny. His sun shines for the weak as well as for the strong. His wind blows for saint and sinner alike. He is the Lord of all, the Father of all, merciful, and impartial. Do you mean to say that He, the Lord of creation, looks upon the petty things of our life in the same light as we do? What a degenerate idea of God that would be! We are like little puppies, making life-and-death struggles here, and foolishly thinking that even God Himself will take it as

> seriously as we do. He knows what the puppies' play means. Our attempts to lay the blame on Him, making Him the punisher, and the rewarder, are only foolish. He neither punishes, nor rewards any. His infinite mercy is open to every one, at all times, in all places, under all conditions, unfailing, unswerving. Upon *us* depends how we use it. Upon *us* depends how we utilise it. Blame neither man, nor God, nor anyone in the world. When you find yourselves suffering, blame yourselves, and try to do better.
>
> This is the only solution of the problem. Those that blame others–and alas! the number of them is increasing every day—are generally miserable with helpless brains; they have brought themselves to that pass through their own mistakes and blame others, but this does not alter their position. It does not serve them in any way. This attempt to throw the blame upon others only weakens them the more. Therefore, blame none for your own faults, stand upon your feet, and take the whole responsibility upon yourselves. Say, "This misery that I am suffering is of my own doing, and that very thing proves that it will have to be done by me alone." That which I created, I can demolish; that which is created by some one else I shall never be able to destroy. Therefore, stand up, be bold, be strong. Take the whole responsibility on your own shoulders, and know that you are the creator of your own destiny. All the strength and succour you want is within yourselves.[4]

To honour oneself is to honour the Divine Spirit inherent in oneself, which is the true philosophy of humanism. It is spontaneous and dynamic, practical and enthusiastic. It accelerates man towards the right direction of living for continuous striving characteristic of serene humanism. As one believing and acting upon the goodness of one and all, one finds the meaning of man from the altruistic vision of the Divine Man. As Vivekananda elucidates:

> Why is it that all great men have preached the brotherhood of mankind, and greater men the brotherhood of all lives? Because

> whether they were conscious of it or not, behind all that, through all their irrational and personal superstitions, was peering forth the eternal light of Self denying all manifoldness, and asserting that the whole universe is but one.
>
> Again, the last word gave us one universe, which through the senses we see as matter, through the intellect as souls, and through the spirit as God. To the man who throws upon himself veils, which the world calls wickedness and evil, this very universe will change and become a hideous place; to another man, who wants enjoyments, this very universe will change its appearance and become a heaven, and to the perfect man the whole thing will vanish and become his own Self.
>
> Now, as society exists at the present time, all these three stages are necessary, the one does not deny the other, one is simply the fulfilment of the other. The Advaitist or the qualified Advaitist does not say that dualism is wrong; it is a right view, but a lower one. It is on the way to truth; therefore let everybody work out of his own vision of this universe, according to his own ideas. Injure none, deny the position of none; take man where he stands and, if you can, lend him a helping hand and put him on a higher platform, but do not injure and do not destroy. All will come to truth in the long run.[5]

Freedom to think and act for humanism is the ultimate goal of man as a Divine Being. He should always hope for a renewed humanity that cares for spiritual excellence and ascent. In all his efforts in bringing about a radical and revolutionary change of consciousness, he must always be above all forms of narrowness and selfishness. Only then he would be blessed with the blessings of humanism.

The blessings of humanism in terms of freedom that we seek in joy can be best explained by means of realisation of truth. The joy derived from senses simply builds the moratorium of progress and humanism. Unless we overpower our little joys and sorrows, happiness and miseries, the progress of humanity will never be attained. Vivekananda significantly explains the philosophy of our sense-enjoyments in terms of freedom and humanism:

> Our pleasures are always changing. If a young man dreams of heaven, he dreams of a heaven where he will have a beautiful wife. When that same man becomes old he does not want a wife. It is our necessities which make our heaven, and the heaven changes with the change of our necessities. If we had a heaven like that desired by those to whom sense-enjoyment is the very end of existence, then we would not progress. That would be the most terrible curse we could pronounce on the soul. Is this all we can come to? A little weeping and dancing, and then to die like a dog! What a curse you pronounce on the head of humanity when you long for these things! That is what you do when you cry after the joys of this world, for you do not know what true joy is. What philosophy insists on is not to give up joys, but to know what joy really is. The Norwegian heaven is a tremendous fighting place where they all sit before Odin; they have a wild boar hunt, and then they go to war and slash each other to pieces. But in some way or other, after a few hours of such fighting, the wounds are all healed up, and they go into a hall where the boar has been roasted, and have a carousal. And then the wild boar takes form again, ready to be hunted the next day. That is much the same thing as our heaven, not a whit worse, only our ideas may be a little more refined. We want to hunt wild boars, and get to a place where all enjoyments will continue, just as the Norwegian imagines that the wild boar is hunted and eaten every day, and recovers the next day.
>
> Now, philosophy insists that there is a joy which is absolute, which never changes. That joy cannot be the joys and pleasures we have in this life, and yet Vedanta shows that everything that is joyful in this life is but a particle of that real joy, because that is the only joy there is. Every moment really we are enjoying the absolute bliss, though covered up, misunderstood, and caricatured. Wherever there is any blessing, blissfulness, or joy, even the joy of the thief in stealing, it is that absolute bliss

> coming out, only it has become obscured, muddled up, as it were, with all sorts of extraneous conditions, and misunderstood. But to understand that, we have to go through the negation, and then the positive side will begin. We have to give up ignorance and all that is false, and then truth will begin to reveal itself to us. When we have grasped the truth, things which we gave up at first will take new shape and form, will appear to us in a new light, and become deified. They will have become sublimated, and then we shall understand them in their true light. But to understand them, we have first to get a glimpse of truth; we must give them up at first, and then we get them back again, deified. We have to give up all our miseries and sorrows, all our little joys.[6]

The great lesson of humanism in perfect tune with freedom can only be learnt when man becomes an optimist and looks upon everything as the fountain of advancement. How to be justified to this essential point of humanism? How to be prepared for acting upon the essence of freedom? It is to realise one's own real nature and goal of life. It is one's own life with all varieties of visions and experiences that gets the free spurt of positive humanism. Let us recall the inspiring words of Vivekananda holding high the flag of freedom and positive humanism:

> The struggle is the great lesson. Mind you, the great benefit in this life is struggle. It is through that we pass. If there is any road to Heaven, it is through Hell. Through Hell to Heaven is always the way. When the soul has wrestled with circumstance and has met death, a thousand times death on the way, but nothing daunted has struggled forward again and again and yet again—then the soul comes out as a giant and laughs at the ideal he has been struggling for, because he finds how much greater is he than the ideal. I am the end, my own Self, and nothing else, for what is there to compare to my own Self? Can a bag of gold be the ideal of my Soul? Certainly not! My Soul is the highest ideal that I can have. Realising my own real nature is the one goal of my life.

> There is nothing that is absolutely evil. The devil has a place here as well as God, else he would not be here. Just as I told you, it is through Hell that we pass to Heaven. Our mistakes have places here. Go on! Do not look back if you think you have done something that is not right. Now, do you believe you could be what you are today, had you not made those mistakes before? Bless your mistakes, then. They have been angels unawares. Blessed be torture! Blessed be happiness! Do not care what be your lot. Hold on to the ideal. March on! Do not look back upon little mistakes and things. In this battlefield of ours, the dust of mistakes must be raised. Those who are so thin-skinned that they cannot bear the dust, let them get out of the ranks.[7]

A down-to-earth visionary of freedom and humanism, Vivekananda inspires man to be free from all matter. That is the surest way of devotion to spirituality, the way that shows how to lead our day-to-day life in meditation. That is the way to honour and welcome the 'marvellous touch of the Soul'. Reminding us of the body which is only a painting and drawing our attention to the endless flames of the Great Painter, Vivekananda accelerates freedom and humanism in terms of exercise of spirituality free from all expectations and purposes, interests and passions like a child:

> The body is our enemy, and yet is our friend. Which of you can bear the sight of misery? And which of you cannot do so when you see it only as a painting? Because it is unreal, we do not identify ourselves with it; we know it is only a painting; it cannot bless us, it cannot hurt us. The most terrible misery painted upon a piece of canvas, we may even enjoy; we praise the technique of the artist, we wonder at his marvellous genius, even though the scene he paints is most horrible. That is the secret; that non-attachment. Be the Witness!
>
> No breathing, no physical training of Yoga, nothing is of any use until you reach to the idea, "I am the Witness." Say, when the tyrant hand is on your neck, "I am the Witness! I am the Witness!" Say, "I am the Spirit! Nothing external can touch

> me." When evil thoughts arise, repeat that, give that sledge-hammer blow on their heads, "I am the Spirit! I am the Witness, the Ever-Blessed! I have no reason to do, no reason to suffer, I have finished with everything. I am rhe Witness. I am in my picture gallery—this universe is my museum, I am looking at these successive paintings. They are all beautiful. Whether good or evil. I see the marvellous skill, but it is all one. Infinite flames of the Great Painter!" Really speaking, there is naught—neither volition, nor desire. He is all. He—She—the Mother, is playing, and we are like dolls, Her helpers in this play. Here, she pits one now in the garb of a beggar, another moment in the garb of a king, the next moment in the garb of a saint, and again in the garb of a devil. We are putting on different garbs to help the Mother Spirit in Her play.
>
> When the baby is at play, she will not come even if called by her mother. But when she finishes her play, she will rush to her mother, and will have no play. So there come moments in our life, when we feel our play is finished, and we want to rush to the Mother. Then all our toil here will be of no value; men, women, and children—weälth, name, and fame, joys and glories of life—punishments and successes—will be no more, and the whole life will seem like a show. We shall see only the infinite rhythm going on, endless and purposeless, going we do not know where. Only this much shall we say: our play is done.[8]

To exercise freedom in spirituality as a radical humanist is a great challenge in the ascent and excellence of man. It necessitates sincerity and earnestness, empathy and whole-hearted involvement for all round progress of humanity. As such, it calls for dedication and devotion to service to the masses irrespective of caste, creed, religion and so on. It also demands service without caring for the self in any form and under any circumstances. In replying to a question made by one of his followers on how India will rise again, Vivekananda shows the path of practical humanism:

> The dawn has already appeared in the eastern sky, and there is little delay in the sun's rising. You all set your shoulders to the

> wheel! What is there in making the world all in all, and thinking of "My Samsara (family and property), my Samsara"? Your duty at present is to go from one part of the country to another, from village to village, and make the people understand that mere sitting idly won't do any more. Make them understand their real condition and say, "O ye brothers, arise! Awake! How much longer would you remain asleep!" Go and advise them how to improve their own condition, and make them comprehend the sublime truths of the Shastras (scriptures), by presenting them in a lucid and popular way. So long the Brahmins have monopolised religion; but since they cannot hold their ground against the strong tide of time, go and take steps so that one and all in the land may get that religion. Impress upon their minds that they have the same right to religion as the Brahmins. Initiate all, even down to the Chandalas (people of the lowest castes), in these fiery Mantras. Also instruct them, in simple words, about the necessities of life, and in trade, commerce, agriculture, etc. If you cannot do this, then fie upon your education and culture, and fie upon your studying the Vedas and the Vedanta![9]

A radical thinker par excellence in freedom and humanism, Vivekananda, upholds the dignity, glory, individuality and freedom. He advises us never to compromise with any form of constraints, and strive for the efflorescence of goodness and truth which are the hallmarks of freedom. His religion is liberty. His realisation is the ascent of man.

In his letter written on 1st February, 1895 from New York to Miss Mary Hale, Vivekananda distinctly exposes:

> In one word, I have a message to give, I have no time to be sweet to the world, and every attempt at sweetness makes me a hypocrite. I will die a thousand deaths rather than lead a jelly-fish existence and yield to every requirement of this foolish world, no matter whether it be my own country or a foreign country. You are mistaken, utterly mistaken, if you think I have

a *work,* as Mrs. Bull thinks; I have no *work* under and beyond the sun. I have a message, and I will give it after my own fashion. I will neither Hinduise my message, nor Christianise it, nor make it any "ise" in the world. I will only my-ise it and that is all. *Liberty,* Mukti, is all my religion, and everything that tries to curb it, I will avoid by fight or flight. Pooh! I try to pacify the priests!! Sister, do not take this amiss. You babies and babies must submit to be taught. You have not yet drunk of that fountain which makes "reason unreason, mortal immortal, this world a zero, and of man a god". Come out if you can of this network of foolishness they call this world. Then I will call you indeed brave and free. If you cannot, cheer those that dare dash this false God, society, to the ground and trample on its unmitigated hypocrisy; if you cannot cheer them, pray, be silent, but do not try to drag them down again into the mire with such false nonsense as compromise and becoming nice and sweet.

I hate this world, this dream, this horrible nightmare, with its churches and chicaneries, its books and blackguardisms, its fair faces and false hearts, its howling righteousness on the surface and utter hollowness beneath, and, above all, its sanctified shopkeeping. What! Measure my soul according to what the bond-slaves of the world say?— Pooh! Sister, you do not know the Sannyasin. "He stands on the heads of the Vedas!" say the Vedas, because he is free from churches and sects and religions and prophets and books and all of that ilk![10]

Apart from the fact that Vivekananda never admits narrowness and absence of sense and sensibilities which are fine components of freedom and humanism, he also strongly upholds the radical and transparent vision of religion that has its roots in strengthening the feeling of infinity so much so that man looks upon this world as a promoter of the spirit of infinity. Therefore, this universe is never the be all and end all for man but it simply denotes a fraction of his quest for the unknown and the infinite. Even the body and the mind stand for a part of his identity of his infinite thirst after the meaning and significance of life beyond life. Therein lies the true meaning of man and humanism.

In the light of the above, Vivekananda poignantly observes:

> The question has been raised as to from whom this universe comes, in whom it rests, and to whom it goes; and the answer has been given that from freedom it comes, in bondage it rests, and goes back into that freedom again. So, when we speak of man as no other than that infinite being which is manifesting itself, we mean that only one very small part thereof is man; this body and this mind which we see are only one part of the whole, only one spot of the infinite being. This whole universe is only one speck of the infinite being; and all our laws, our bondages, our joys and our sorrows, our happinesses and our expectations, are only within this small universel all our progression and digression are within its small compass. So you see how childish it is to expect a continuation of this universe—the creation of our minds—and to expect to go to heaven, which after all must mean only a repetition of this world that we know. You see at once that it is an impossible and childish desire to make the whole of infinite existence conform to the limited and conditioned existence which we know. When a man says that he will have again and again this same thing which he is having now, or, as I sometimes put it, when he asks for a *comfortable* religion, you may know that he has become so degenerate that he cannot think of anything higher than what he is now; he is just his little present surroundings and nothing more. He has forgotten his infinite nature, and his whole idea is confined to these little joys, and sorrows, and heart-jealousies of the moment. He thinks that his finite thing is the infinite; and not only so, he will not let his foolishness go. He clings on desperately unto Trishna, and the thirst after life, what the Buddhists call Tanha and Tissa. There may be millions of kinds of happiness, and beings, and laws, and progress, and causation,

> all acting outside the little universe that we know; and, after all, the whole of this comprises but one section of our infinite nature.[11]

The quest from the finite to the infinite is the genesis of freedom. It is this freedom of which man is ever proud. It is also a blessing for his own identity because it haunts him at every moment 'to strive to seek to find and not to yield'. It promises him with welcome moments of entering into the cathedral of infinity where he finds how insignificant his contributions are as the exponent of the progress of humanism. His strivings never accept victory or defeat, success or failure, because he knows that all such moments are simply transitory and call forth more involvements and more enlightenments for ascent and excellence of humanism.

Freedom beyond, therefore, is the ultimate end-in-view of humanism. It is freedom that prompts man to be ever adventurous in the march for humanism. Unless the spirit of the infinite beckons, the meaning and significance of man exercising or representing freedom and humanism becomes meaningless. In the invaluable words of Vivekananda:

> Perfect equilibrium, or what the Christians call the peace that passeth all understanding, cannot be had in this universe, nor in heaven, nor in any place where our mind and thoughts can go, where the senses can feel, or which the imagination can conceive. No such place can give us that freedom, because all such places would be within our universe, and it is limited by space, time and causation.There may be places that are more ethereal than this earth of ours, where enjoyments may be keener, but even those places must be in the universe and, therefore, in bondage to law; so we have to go beyond, and real religion begins where this little universe ends. These little joys, and sorrows, and knowledge of things end there, and the reality begins. Until we give up the thirst after life, the strong attachment to this our transient conditioned existence, we have no hope of catching even a glimpse of that infinite freedom

> beyond. It stands to reason then that there is only one way to attain that freedom which is the goal of all the noblest aspirations of mankind, and that is by giving up this little life, giving up this little universe, giving up this earth, giving up heaven, giving up the body, giving up the mind, giving up everything that is limited and conditioned. If we give up our attachment to this little universe of the senses or of the mind, we shall be free immediately.[12]

To be free from desire is to be on the right track of humanism. Unless we are free, we cannot be free from all sorts of narrowness of vision. The advancement of selflessness which is one of the most essential components of perfection of the spirit of humanism can never be possible in the presence of desire that simply welcomes more worldly desire affecting all our efforts in quest of truth. As Vivekananda characteristically explains:

> We are like moths plunging into the flaming fire, knowing that it will burn us, knowing that the senses only burn us, that they only enhance desire. 'Desire is never satiated by enjoyment; enjoyment only increases desire as butter fed into fire only increases the fire.' Desire is increased by desire. Knowing all this, people still plunge into it all the time. Life after life they have been going after the objects of desire, suffering extremely in consequence, yet they cannot give up desire. Even religion, which should rescue them from this terrible bondage of desire, they have made a means of satisfying desire. Rarely do they ask God to free them from bondage to the body and senses, from slavery to desires. Instead, they pray to Him for health and prosperity, for long life: 'O God, cure my headache, give me some money or something!'
>
> The circle of vision has become so narrow, so degraded, so beastly, so animal! None is desiring anything beyond this body. Oh, the terrible degradation, the terrible misery of it! What little flesh, the five senses, the stomach! What is the world but a combination of stomach and sex? Look at millions of men

> and women—that is what they are living for. Take these away from them and they will find their life empty, meaningless, and intolerable. Such are we. And such is our mind; it is continually hankering for ways and means to satisfy the hunger of the stomach and sex. All the time this is going on. There is also endless suffering; these desires of the body bring only momentary satisfaction and endless suffering. It is like drinking a cup of which the surface layer is nectar, while underneath all is poison. But we still hanker for all these things.[13]

Renunciation of the senses and desires in order to be spiritual is the true meaning of man. It is this truth which is inseparably related to freedom and humanism. Unless man is free from degraded visions and missions of life writ large in the day-to-day beastly life of narrow pleasures, humanism becomes an abstraction.

As a positive humanist fired with the spirit of freedom, Vivekananda suggests:

> What can be done? Renunciation of the senses and desires is the only way out of this misery. If you want to be spiritual, you must renounce. This is the real test. Give up the world—this nonsense of the senses. There is only one real desire: to know what is true, to be spiritual. No more materialism, no more this egoism, I must become spiritual. Strong, intense must be the desire. If a man's hands and feet were so tied that he could not move and then if a burning piece of charcoal were placed on this body, he would struggle with all his power to throw it off. When I shall have that sort of extreme desire, that restless struggle, to throw off this burning world, then the time will have come for me to glimpse the Divine Truth.[14]

To have a 'glimpse of the Divine Truth' through spiritual excellence and ascent is the nectar of freedom and humanism for which man should endlessly strive. Degradation has become the identity of man. With desires for momentary things encapsulating aggravating senses and material desires and happiness, the quest for the Divine Truth as a pointer to spiritual humanism in an ambiance of freedom remains absent. As Vivekananda unfolds the real nature of man in the light of the Gita:

> Degradation—that is what religion has turned out to be. The whole thing is becoming sham. And the years are rolling on and nothing spiritual is being attained. But man should hunger for one thing alone, the spirit, because spirit alone exists. That is the ideal. If you cannot attain it now, say, "I cannot do it, that is the ideal, I know, but I cannot follow it yet." But that is not what you do. You degrade religion to your low level and seek matter in the name of spirit. You are all atheists. You do not believe in anything except the senses. "So-and-so said such-and-such—there may be something in it. Let us try and have the fun. Possibly some benefit will comel possibly my broken leg will get straight."
>
> Miserable are the diseased people; they are great worshippers of the Lord, for they hope that if they pray to Him He will heal them. Not that that is altogether bad—if such prayers are honest and if they remember that that is not religion. Shri Krishna says in the Gita (VII. 16), "Four classes of people worship Me: the distressed, the seeker of material things, the inquirer, and the knower of truth." People who are in distress approach God for relief. If they are ill, they worship Him to be healed; if they lose their health, they pray to Him to get it back. There are other people who ask Him for all kinds of things, because they are full of desires—name, fame, wealth, position and so on. They will say, "O Virgin Mary, I will make an offering to you if I get what I want. If you are successful in granting my prayer, I will worship God and give you a part of everything." Men not so material as that, but still with no faith in God, feel inclined to know about Him. They study philosophies, read scriptures, listen to lectures, and so on. They are the inquirers. The last class are those who worship God and know Him. All these four classes of people are good, not bad. All of them worship Him.[15]

Freedom from the external world is the true freedom of man. Our sense of humanism is yet to be liberated from external wants.

External wants are constraints to the true religion of man. Devotion to religion as such necessitates freedom from petty necessities and unending striving for something beyond the temptations of diverse materialistic wants of the world. As a practical thinker of devotion in terms of freedom and religion, Vivekananda strongly points out:

> Religion is not for the many, that is impossible. A sort of knee-drill, standing up and sitting down, may be suited for the many, but religion is for the few. There are in every country only a few hundreds who can be, and will be religious. The others cannot be religious, because they will not be awakened, and they do not want to be. The chief thing is to *want* God. We want everything except God, because our ordinary wants are supplied by the external world; it is only when our necessities have gone beyond the external world that we want a supply from the internal, from God. So long as our needs are confined within the narrow limits of this physical universe, we cannot have any need for God; it is only when we become satiated with everything here that we look beyond for a supply. It is only when the need is there that the demand will come. Have done with this child's play of the world as soon as you can, and then you feel the necessity of something beyond the world, and the first step of religion will come.
>
> There is a form of religion which is fashionable. My friend has much furniture in her parlour; it is the fashion to have a Japanese vase, so she must have one even if it costs a thousand dollars. In the same way she will have a little religion and join a church. Bhakti is not for such. That is not *want.* Want is that without which we cannot live. We want breath, we want food, we want clothes, without them we cannot live. When a man loves a woman in this world, there are times when he feels that without her he cannot live, although that is a mistake. When a husband dies, the wife thinks she cannot live without him, but she lives all the same. This is the secret of necessity; it is that without which we cannot live, either it must come to us or we die.

> When the time comes that we feel the same about God, or in other words, we want something beyond this world, something above all material forces, then we may become Bhaktas. What our little lives when for a moment the cloud passes away, and we get one glimpse from beyond, and for that moment all these lower desires seem like a drop in the ocean? Then the soul grows, and feels the want of God, and must have Him.[16]

The yearning of the Bhakta for God beyond all material wants is the freedom of man to be a true religious humanist. Only then he understands the role of freedom in the religion of man. There must be the poignant desire for freedom, otherwise, humanism will be detached from reality. It is that humanism which leads us from the unreal to the real, from the matter-of-factness to the beyond. To worship the spirit as spirit, and everything else will be transformed and manifested in the light of the spirit. Our intense desire to be free-will then be blessed with the spirit of enlightened humanism.

What, then, is our goal of freedom for humanism? It is persistent effort in bringing about a radical mind-set for the welfare of others in order to be blessed with the ascent of man. No materialistic hunger, no so-called freedom from misery, disease and death, but ever glowing freedom to be devoted to extinction of personality.

Tracing the history of freedom and blissful humanism from the Gita and the Upanishad, Vivekananda expresses in a letter written to Mr. J. J. Goodwin from Switzerland on 8th August, 1896:

> Great work requires great and persistent effort for a long time. Neither need we trouble ourselves if a few fail. It is in the nature of things that many should fall, that troubles should come, that tremendous difficulties should arise, that selfishness and all the other devils in the human heart should struggle hard when they are about to be driven out by the fire of spirituality. The road to the Good is the roughest and steepest in the universe. It is a wonder that so many succeed, no wonder that so many fall. Character has to be established through a thousand stumbles.

> I am much refreshed now. I look out of the window and see the huge glaciers just before me and feel that I am in the Himalayas. I am quite calm. My nerves have regained their accustomed strength; and little vaxations, like those you write of, do not touch me at all. How shall I be disturbed by this child's play? The whole world is a mere child's play—preaching, teaching, and all included. "Know him to be the Sannyasin who neither hates nor desires" (Gita, V. 3). And what is there to be desired in this little mud-puddle of a world, with its ever-recurring misery, disease, and death? "He who has given up all desires, he alone is happy."
>
> This rest, eternal, peaceful rest, I am catching a glimpse of now in this beautiful spot. "Having once known that the Atman alone, and nothing else, exists, desiring what, or for whose desire, shall you suffer misery about the body?" (Brihadaranyaka, IV. iv. 12.)
>
> I feel as if I had my share of experience on what they call "work". I am finished, I am longing now to get out. "Out of thousands, but one strives to attain the Goal. And even of those who struggle hard, but few attain." (Gita, VII. 3); for the senses are powerful, they drag men down.[17]

The role of freedom to win over the senses is legion. This is the primary lesson of humanism. Even when we speak about the role of intellectual exercise in religion, the point of humanism is missed in the mist of meaningless arguments where the role of freedom to think is lost in doctrines and documents. The existence of God in every individual cannot gain ground in denying freedom to exercise one's own identity which is the first lesson of humanism.

The concept of religion as realisation is an outcome of freedom that stands for true humanism. This striving for realisation is a long term, strenuous, sincere and patient endeavour. As a practical thinker of humanism in terms of religion, Vivekananda adroitly spells out:

> Man makes a great mistake when he thinks that he can at once jump to the highest state. If a baby thinks that he is going to be

> an old man in a day, he is mistaken; and I hope you will always bear in mind this one ideal, that religion is neither in books, nor in intellectual consent, nor in reasoning. Reasons, theories, documents, doctrines, books, religious ceremonies, are all *helps* to religion: religion itself consists in *realisation.* We all say: "There is a God." Have you seen God? That is the question. You hear a man say, "There is God in heaven." You ask him if he has seen Him, and if he says he has, you would laugh at him and say he is a maniac. With most people religion is a sort of intellectual assent and goes no further than a document. I would not call it religion. It is better to be an atheist than to have that sort of religion. Religion does not depend on our intellectual assent or dissent. You say there is a soul. Have you seen the soul? How is it we all have souls and do not see them? You have to answer the question and find out the way to see the soul. If not, it is useless to talk of religion. If any religion is true, it must be able to show us the soul and show us God and the truth in ourselves. If you and I fight for all eternity about one of these doctrines or documents, we shall never come to any conclusion. People have been fighting for ages, and what is the outcome? Intellect cannot reach there at all. We have to go beyond the intellect; the proof of religion is in direct perception. The proof of the existence of this wall is that we see it; if you sit down and argue about its existence or non-existence for ages, you could never come to any conclusion; but directly you see it, it is enough. If all the men in the world told you it did not exist, you would not believe them, because you know that the evidence of your own eyes is superior to that of all the doctrines and documents in the world.[18]

The strong religious note baked and blessed in the positive and radical humanistic spirit in 'Om Tat Sat, Om'—Thou art That— is a bold efflorescence of freedom. With such a force of freedom that never yields to conservatism or orthodoxy, the meaning of man becomes transparent. Death or life, pain or pleasure, love or hate— all are subject to the positive force of freedom. One becomes really calm and patient in an ambience of discipline in the teeth of all constraints. In "The Song of the Sannyasin" composed at the Thousand Island Park, New York, in July, 1895, Vivekananda serenely muses:

> Wake up the note! The song that had its birth
> Far off, where worldly taint could never reach,
> In mountain caves and glades of forest deep,
> Whose calm no sigh for lust or wealth or fame
> Could ever dare to break; where rolled the stream
> Of knowledge, truth, and bliss that follows both.
> Sing high that note, Sannyasin bold! Say—
> "Om Tat Sat, Om!"
> Strike off thy fetters! Bonds that bind thee down,
> Of shining gold, or darker, baser ore;
> Love, hate—good, bad—and all the dual throng,
> Know, slave is slave, caressed or whipped, not free;
> For fetters, though of gold, are not less strong to bind;
> Then off with them, Sannyasin bold! Say—
> "Om Tat Sat, Om![19]

The longing for freedom is the essence of humanism. It is a longing which is interesting and everlasting, adventurous and enchanting. It always allows man to know the unknown, feel the unfelt, and see the unseen. It always discards absolute sameness of thought and feeling, imagination and emotion. In the social life of man, this turns out to be one of the major contributions to the differentiating components derived from freedom and humanism.

Vivekananda characteristically elucidates the above in terms of sameness:

> On the physical plane, we always find the two forces most distinctly at work, separating the individuals, making them more

> and more distinct from other individuals, and again making them into species and classes, and bringing out similarities of expressions, and form. The same holds good as regards the social life of man. Since the time when society began, these two forces have been at work, differentiating and unifying. Their action appears in various forms, and is called by various names, in different places, and at different times. But the essence is present in all, one making for differentiation, and the other for sameness; the one making for caste, and the other breaking it down; the one making for classes and privileges, and the other destroying them. The whole universe seems to be the battle-ground of these two forces. On the one hand, it is urged, that though this unifying process exists, we ought to resist it with all our might, because it leads towards death, that perfect unity is perfect annihilation, and that when the differentiating process that is at work in this universe ceases, the universe comes to an end. It is differentiation that causes the phenomena that are before us; unification would reduce them all to a homogeneous and lifeless matter. Such a thing, of course, mankind wants to avoid. The same argument is applied to all the things and facts that we see around us. It is urged that even in physical body and social classification, absolute sameness would produce natural death and social death. Absolute sameness of thought and feeling would produce mental decay and degeneration. Sameness, therefore, is to be avoided. This has been the argument on the one side, and it has been urged in every country and in various times, with only a change of language.[20]

As a radical thinker of freedom and humanism, Vivekananda insists on accepting the knowledge of man. He strongly asserts that the highest knowledge is the knowledge of man. He does not impose upon the role of man as the only exponent of knowledge. He promotes the existence of man in stressing on the divinity inherent in him. Thus, humanism takes a new habitation and a new name with the progress of freedom exercised in the process of defining and explaining unity in diversity, the finite and the Infinite, and vice versa. Referring to a story told by Max Muller, Vivekananda elucidates:

> I remember a story told by Prof. Max Muller in one of his books, an old Greek story, of how a Brahmin visited Socrates in Athens. The Brahmin asked, "What is the highest knowledge?" And Socrates answered, "To know man is the end and aim of all knowledge." "But how can you know man without knowing God?" replied the Brahmin. The one side, the Greek side, which is represented by modern Europe, insisted upon the knowledge of man; the Indian side, mostly represented by the old religions of the world, insisted upon the knowledge of God. The one sees God in nature, and the other sees nature in God. To us, at the present time, perhaps, has been given the privilege of standing aside from both these aspects, and taking an impartial view of the whole. This is a fact that variation exists, and so it must, if life is to be. This is also a fact that in and through these variations unity must be perceived. This is a fact that God is perceived in nature. But it is also a fact that nature is perceived in God. The knowledge of man is the highest knowledge, and only by knowing man, can we know God. This is also a fact that the knowledge of God is the highest knowledge, and knowing God alone we can know man. Apparently contradictory though these statements may appear, they are the necessity of human nature. The whole universe is a play of unity in variety, and of variety in unity. The whole universe is a play of differentiation and oneness; the whole universe is a play of the finite in the Infinite. We cannot take one without granting the other. But we cannot take them both as facts of the same perception, as facts of the same experience; yet in this way it will always go on.[21]

The spirit of humanism in consonance with freedom makes man more adaptive to the changing circumstances in life and work. The more are we concerned about humanism, the more we are on the right track of the destiny of man entirely framed and acted upon by means of the exercise of freedom. Here freedom stands for naturalness and spontaneity, frankness and clarity of vision and actualisation. In the vast context of humanism and religion, freedom shows a wider avenue of welcome to The Impersonal God to understand and assimilate the fact that God is the sum total of the whole universe, and man exercises freedom as best as possible. As Vivekananda poignantly introspects:

> The sum total of this whole universe is God Himself. Is God then matter? No, certainly not, for matter is that God perceived by the five senses; that God as perceived through the intellect is mind; and when the spirit sees, He is seen as He. Whatever is real in this chair is He, for the chair requires two things to make it. Something was outside which my senses brought to me, and to which my mind contributed something else, and the combination of these two is the chair. That which existed eternally, independent of the senses and of the intellect, was the Lord Himself. Upon Him the senses are painting chairs, and tables, and rooms, houses, and worlds, and moons, and suns, and stars, and everything else. How is it, then, that we all see this same chair, that we are all alike painting these various things on the Lord, on this Existence, Knowledge, and Bliss? It need not be that all paint the same way, but those who paint the same way are on the same plane of existence and therefore they see one another's paintings as well as one another. There may be millions of beings between you and me who do not paint the Lord in the same way, and them and their paintings we do not see.
>
> On the other hand, as you all know, the modern physical researches are tending more and more to demonstrate that what is real is but the finer; the gross is simply appearance. However that may be, we have seen that if any theory of religion can stand the test of modern reasoning, it is the Advaita, because it fulfils its two requirements. It is the highest generalisation, beyond even personality, generalisation which is common to every being. A generalisation ending in the Personal God can never be universal, for, first of all, to conceive of a

> Personal God we must say, He is all-merciful, all-good. But this world is a mixed thing, some good and some bad. We cut off what we like, and generalise that into a Personal God! Just as you say a Personal God is this and that, so you have also to say that He is not this and not that. And you will always find that the idea of a Personal God has to carry with it a personal devil. That is how we clearly see that the idea of a Personal God is not a true generalisation, we have to go beyond, to the Impersonal.[22]

The role of freedom in religious humanism is more often than not dwarfed and arrested in leaving off the radical march in thinking for Impersonal God. There is no denying the fact that freedom to think and make a harmonious bond between the Personal God and the Impersonal God enhances the true spirit of humanism. In fact, self-realisation in terms of the Impersonal God makes inroads to the inherent freedom that shows the avenue of how to be conscious of the beyond. With innumerable and varied changes in man lead to the fact that man understands all the transformations he undergoes. As a consequence, he identifies his constant quality—the Impersonal being with all manifestations.

Vivekananda explicitly presents the nature and role of religion in terms of freedom and humanism, where the idea of the Personal God necessitates a clear concept of the Impersonal God:

> Will religion stand as a factor in human life, our consoler, our helper? What becomes of the desire of the human heart to pray for help to some being? That will all remain. The Personal God will remain, but on a better basis. He has been strengthened by the Impersonal. We have seen that without the Impersonal, the Personal cannot remain. If you mean to say there is a Being entirely separate from this universe, who has created this universe just by His will, out of nothing, that cannot be proved. Such a state of things cannot be. But if we understand the idea of the Impersonal, then the idea of the Personal can remain there also. This universe, in its various forms, is but the various readings of the same Impersonal. When we read it with the five senses, we call it the material world. If there be a being with more

senses than five, he will read it as something else. If one of us gets the electrical sense, he will see the universe as something else again. There are various forms of that same Oneness, of which all these various ideas of worlds are but various readings, and the Personal God is the highest reading that can be attained to, of that Impersonal, by the human intellect. So that the Personal God is true as much as this chair is true, as much as this world is true, but no more. It is not absolute truth. That is to say, the Personal God is that very Impersonal God and, therefore, it is true, just as I, as a human being, am true and not true at the same time. It is not true that I am what you see I am; you can satisfy yourself on that point. I am not the being that you take me to be. You can satisfy yourself on that point. I am not the being that you take me to be. You can satisfy your reason as to that, because light, and various vibrations, or conditions of the atmosphere, and all sorts of motions inside me have contributed to my being looked upon as what I am, by you. If any one of these conditions change, I am different again. You may satisfy yourself by taking a photograph of the same man under different conditions of light. So I am what I appear in relation to your senses, and yet, in spite of all these facts, there is an unchangeable something of which all these are different states of existence, the impersonal me, of which thousands of me's are different persons. I was a child, I was young, I am getting older. Every day of my life, my body and thoughts are changing, but in spite of all these changes, the sum-total of them constitutes a mass which is a constant quantity. That is the impersonal me, of which all these manifestations form, as it were, parts.

Similarly, the sum-total of this universe is immovable, we know, but everything pertaining to this universe consists of motion, everything is in a constant state of flux, everything changing and moving. At the same time, we see that the universe as a whole is immovable, because motion is a relative term. I move with regard to the chair, which does not move. There must be

> at least two to make motion. If this whole universe is taken as a unit there is no motion; with regard to what should it move? Thus, the Absolute is unchangeable and immovable, and all the movements and changes are only in the phenomenal world, the limited. The whole is Impersonal, and within this Impersonal are all these various persons beginning with the lowest atom, up to God, the Personal God, the Creator, the Ruler of the Universe, to whom we pray, before whom we kneel, and so on. Such a Personal God can be established with a great deal of reason. Such a Personal God is explicable as the highest manifestation of the Impersonal.[23]

The freedom of man to switch over from the finite to the infinite, from the personal to the impersonal is at the core of spiritual humanism. Such an exercise of humanism becomes crystal clear with the unending striving for the beyond in the endeavour of perfection for excellence and ascent. As there is no specific means for such an endeavour as freedom is opposed to stigmatised inroads to inner consciousness, man finds delight in knowing the unknown and seeing the unseen. The wings of freedom are, as it were, symbols of the different patterns of the human psyche. These steer man to find out, select and introduce the operational strategies as best as possible. Thus, freedom serves as a genuine guideline for efflorescence of humanism.

What, then, should be the significant end-in-view of freedom and humanism? Here are Vivekananda's suggestions:

> To whom shall I tell the truth?—Who will see?
> Free thyself from the mighty attraction—
> The maddening wine of love, the charm of sex.
> Break the harp! Forward with the ocean's cry!
> Drink tears, pledge even life— let the body fall.
> Awake, O hero! Shake off thy vain dreams,
> Death stands at thy head—does fear become thee?
> A load of misery, true though it is—

This Becoming—know this to be thy God!
His temple—the Shmashan among corpses
And funeral pyres; unending battle—
That verily is His sacred worship;
Constant defeat—let that not unnerve thee;
Shattered be little self, hope, name, and fame;
Set up a pyre of them and make thy heart
A burning ground.[24]

To make the heart 'a burning ground' to find out the truth and be victorious is the essence of humanism that should always be in the warmth of freedom. Freedom is actually like an enzyme of freshness for the human mind which must be controlled so much so that the mind can most satisfactorily act like a search-light for transparency and transcendence. As a radical and introspective exponent of freedom and humanism in terms of the 'perfect man' – the Permanent Being— Vivekananda serenely observes:

> When we are not passing through changes, we will not have bodies (so-called). "Matter" beyond the limit of time, space, and causality will not be matter at all. Time and space exist only in us, we are the one Permanent Being. All forms are transitory, that is why all religions say, "God has no form". Menander was a Greco-Bactrian king. He was converted to Buddhism about 150 B.C. by one of the Buddhist missionary monks and was called by them "Milinda". He asked a young monk, his teacher, "Can a perfect man (such as Buddha) be in error or make mistakes?" The young monk's answer was: The perfect man can remain in ignorance in minor matters not in his experience, but he can *never* be in error as to what his insight has actually realised. He is perfect here and now. He knows the whole mystery, the Essence of the universe, but he may not know the mere external variation through which that Essence is manifested in time and space. He knows the *clay* itself, but has not had experience of every shape it may be wrought into. The perfect man knows the Soul itself, but not every form and

> combination of its manifestation. He would have to attain more relative knowledge just as we do, though on account of his immense power, he would learn it more quickly.
>
> The tremendous "search-light" of a controlled mind, when thrown on any subject, would rapidly reduce it to possession. It is very important to understand this, because it saves so much foolish explanation as to how a Buddha or a Jesus could be mistaken in ordinary relative knowledge, as we well know they were. The disciples should not be blamed as having put down the sayings erroneously. It is humbug to say that one thing is true and another untrue in their statements. Accept the whole account, or reject it. How can *we* pick out the true from the false?[25]

Freedom invites a generous mind and welcomes all irrespective of caste, creed, religion and so on as a characteristic component of humanism. It never dwarfs exposure of individuality because the arrest of freedom and frankness affects efflorescence of humanism. As Vivekananda radically reminds us through his invaluable words of advice:

> Get rid, in the first place, of all these limited ideas and see God in every person—working through all hands, walking through all feet, and eating through every mouth. In every being He lives, through all minds He thinks. He is self-evident, nearer unto us than ourselves. To know this is religion, is faith, and may it please the Lord to give us this faith! When we shall feel that oneness, we shall be immortal.[26]

When comes such an incomparable apostle of freedom and humanism?

References

1. Swami Vivekananda: *The Complete Works of Swami Vivekananda*, Advaita Ashrama, Kolkata, Mayavati Memorial Edition, 1989, Vol. V, p. 57.
2. *Ibid.*, pp. 57-58.
3. *Ibid.*, pp. 191-192.

4. *Ibid.*, Vol. II, 224-225.
5. *Ibid.*, pp. 252-253.
6. *Ibid.*, pp. 166-167.
7. *Ibid.*, Vol. V, pp. 252-253.
8. *Ibid.*, pp. 253-254.
9. *Ibid.*, p. 381.
10. *Ibid.*, pp. 72-73.
11. *Ibid.*, Vol. I, pp. 96-97.
12. *Ibid.*, pp. 97-98.
13. *Ibid.*, Vol. VIII, pp. 117-118.
14. *Ibid.*, p. 118.
15. *Ibid.*, pp. 119-120.
16. *Ibid.*, pp. 122-123.
17. *Ibid.*, pp. 383-384.
18. *Ibid.*, Vol. IV, pp. 33-34.
19. *Ibid.*, pp. 392-393.
20. *Ibid.*, Vol. I, pp. 430-431.
21. *Ibid.*, pp. 432-433.
22. *Ibid.*, pp. 375-376.
23. *Ibid.*, pp. 378-379.
24. *Ibid.*, Vol. IV, p. 510.
25. *Ibid.*, Vol. VIII, pp. 16-17.
26. *Ibid.*, Vol. I, p. 341.

8

Freedom and Mysticism: Vivekananda's Poignance

Mysticism is the voice of the innermost man. It is the voice that proclaims the poignance of the beyond. It caters to the greatest thoughts and emotions of man in terms of the consciousness of the beyond where advancement is the beginning with no end because it believes and nurses the spirit beyond, the spirit unending.

As an inseparable partner to mysticism, freedom is not only essential but also obligatory. Otherwise, it is diluted in matter-of-factness and loses much of its serenity and depth of vision and action. Indeed, freedom strengthens the foundation of mysticism. It serves as a potent force to the latter, and makes inner avenues of thoughts refined and conscious for the sojourn beyond. It does not allow stray thoughts and emotions overpowering and supreme, for the mystic mind with sovereignty and gravity of the beyond always makes the mind voidless. All passions spent is thus the nature of mysticism that is always in perfect unison with freedom that guarantees 'calmness of mind, all passions spent'.

Indeed, freedom is, as it were, the unending muse of mysticism. It caresses and vitalises the mystic mind with a crystallising end-in-view of consciousness. The more are we refined, the more we are the partners to the spirit of a mystic mind that cares for the selfless Self. When we are in the right spirit of freedom, we begin to exercise the spirit of "I" that welcomes the void "I" to be merged in the voidless. As a result, the call of the beyond becomes more significant than anything else for which the mind erroneously pines, and becomes ready for a visit to the Holy Grail. This is a characteristic point of freedom that provides us with an opportunity for self-realisation in terms of mystic consciousness of the beyond.

With freedom, whatever is finite is eliminated because it arrests higher thoughts and nobler visions with commonality and drabness, mechanised rules and regulations. Over and above, with a mind caged, cornered and camouflaged, there is no room for exercise of introspection. Therefore, it welcomes the Infinite because it is the true identity of man, the Divine Being, who cannot but love and respect the call of the beyond. This is a wonderful experience of man, perhaps the most wonderful of all to be a sailing partner to the All True who continually beckons him to join the feast of unending joy in the Holy Grail.

The mystic mind is eternally free. Freedom is a natural passort to man who evolves for superiority of awareneness that promises march for unison with the All True. The passions that disturb the inner mind are no longer as powerful as in the past. The present becomes a challenge for the past to make a pilgrimage for the future of man. The muse of mysticism is an inborn affair with which the birth of man is blessed. It is now or never to be reborn in the womb of mysticism well fortified in freedom.

As a practical and radical visionary of freedom and mysticism, Swami Vivekananda explains mysticism in terms of the Sankhya Yoga upon which the basis of Raja-Yoga depends:

> According to the Sankhya philosophy, the genesis of perception is as follows: the effections of the external objects are carried by the other instruments to their respective brain centres or organs, the organs carry the affections to the mind, the mind to the determinative faculty, from this the Purusha (the soul) receives them, when perception results. Next he gives the order back, as it were, to the motor centres to do the needful. With the exception of the Purusha all of these are material, but the mind

> is much finer matter than the external instruments. That material of which the mind is composed goes also to form the subtle matter called the Tanmatras. These become gross and make the external matter. That is the psychology of the Sankhya. So that between the intellect and the grosser matter outside there is only a difference in degree. The Purusha is the only thing which is immaterial. The mind is an instrument, as it were, in the hands of the soul, through which the soul catches external objects. The mind is constantly changing and vacillating, and can, when perfected, either attach itself to several organs, to one, or to none. For instance, if I hear the clock with great attention, I will not, perhaps, see anything although my eyes may be open, showing that the mind was not attached to the seeing organ, while it was to the hearing organ. But the perfected mind can be attached to all the organs simultaneously. It has the reflexive power of looking back into its own depths. This reflexive power is what the Yogi wants to attain; by concentrating the powers of the mind, and turning them inward, he seeks to know what is happening inside. There is in this no question of mere belief; it is the analysis arrived at by certain philosophers. Modern psychologists tell us that the eyes are not the organ of vision, but that the organ is in one of the nerve centres of the brain, and so with all the senses; they also tell us that these centres are formed of the same material as the brain itself. The Sankhyas also tell us the same thing. The former is a statement on the physical side, and the latter on the psychological side; yet both are the same.[1]

With inwardness as a stepping stone for a journey to the beyond where freedom makes the absolute framework of mysticism, Vivekananda highlights on non-uniformity which is the identity of freedom that leads to the spirit of the beyond. Analysing the role of freedom in terms of the Vedanta, he refers to the soul which is free to lead man to the path of ascent and the beyond. In his words:

> I work through freedom. I walk for five minutes; but before those five minutes of walking, which are uniform, there was

> the action of the will, which gave the impulse to walk. Therefore, man says he is free, because all his actions can be cut up into small periods; and although there is smallness in the same periods, beyond the period there is not the same sameness. In this perception of non-uniformity is the idea of freedom. In nature we see only very large periods of uniformity; but the beginning and end must be free impulses. The impulse of freedom was given just at the beginning, and that has rolled on; but this, compared with other periods, is much longer. We find by analysis on philosophic grounds that we are not free. But there will remain this factor, this consciousness that I am free. What we have to explain is, how that comes. We will find that we have these two impulsions in us. Our reason tells us that all our actions are caused, and at the same time, with every impulse we are asserting our freedom. The solution of the Vedanta is that there is freedom inside—that the soul is really free—but that that soul's actions are percolating through body and mind, which are not free.[2]

With mind as the initial step for the freedom to exercise as a means for mystic ascent, all our devotion and dedication are directed towards the beckoning of the beyond. It is endless but interesting, difficult but fascinating. A sense of serenity in and through discipline becomes the guiding force without which poignancy of the mind becomes a myth.

Analysing freedom in terms of the above, Vivekananda distinctly observes:

> In this world we are bound by laws, and we are always striving to break through these laws, we are always trying to disobey, to trample on nature. For instance, nature gives us no houses, we build them. Nature made us naked, we clothe ourselves. Man's goal is to be free, and just in so far as we are incompetent to break nature's laws shall we suffer. We only obey nature's law in order to be *outlawed*—beyond law. The whole struggle of life is *not* to obey. (That is why I sympathise with Christian Scientists, for they teach the liberty of man and the divinity of soul.)

> The soul is superior to all environment. "The universe is my father's kingdom; I am the heir-apparent"—that is the attitude for man to take.[3]

To assert oneself capable of going beyond is the positive outcome of freedom. This assures one of one's striving for superior values and convictions in life beyond life. This also ignites one to go ahead for greeting the ever new and unknown. The cup of life to taste the 'dark drink' is the infinite mystic passion for which one must be prepared. The journey yet to be undertaken for encountering the hardships of life must be accorded a warm welcome. Despite the fact that this an ever going process for beauty of the beyond as a characteristic prize of mystic poignance, the task never ends but attracts life more with renewed consciousness.

In tune with the above, Vivekananda serenely states in his mystic poem "The Cup":

> This is your cup—the cup assigned
> to you from the beginning.
> Nay, My child, I know how much
> of that dark drink is your own brew
> Of fault and passion, ages long ago,
> In the deep years of yesterday, I know.
>
> This is your road—a painful road and drear.
> I made the stones that never give you rest.
> I set your friend in pleasant ways and clear,
> And he shall come like you, unto My breast.
> But you, My child, must travel here.
>
> This is your task. It has no joy nor grace,
> But it is not meant for any other hand,
> And in My universe hath measured place,
> Take it. I do not bid you understand.[4]

To fulfil the task of realisation of God, one requires the understanding of the Personal God, the self must be revealed to identify and express our own nature. The Self cannot be objectified in terms of the Personal God which is the same when it is free. As freedom enjoys subjectivity, the self gets the fillip for the Self to be in unison with the Personal God for the beyond. In the words of Vivekananda, this freedom of the Self for the beyond becomes explicit:

> The Personal God is the same Absolute looked at through the haze of Maya. When we approach Him with the five senses, we can see Him only as the Personal God. The idea is that the Self cannot be objectified. How can the Knower know Itself? But it can cast a shadow, as it were, if that can be called objectification. So the highest form of that shadow, that attempt at objectifying Itself, is the Personal God. The Self is the eternal subject, and we are struggling all the time to objectify that Self. And out of that struggle has come this phenomenal universe and what we call matter, and so on. But these are very weak attempts, and the highest objectification of the Self possible to us is the Personal God. This objectification is an attempt to reveal our own nature. According to the Sankhya, nature is showing all these experiences to the soul, and when it has got real experience it will know its own nature. According to the Advaita Vedantist, the soul is struggling to reveal itself. After long struggle, it finds that the subject must always remain the subject; and then begins non-attachment, and it becomes free.[5]

The religion of freedom as a mystic spirit is the eternal call for the inner man who loves the call of the beyond. His religion of realisation has an endless avenue of making a journey to the ever beckoning beyond. This necessitates an ever enticing quest for truth with the aroma of mystic suspense and wonder, serenity and grandeur. From the standpoint of Raja-Yoga, Vivekananda characteristically elucidates:

> It is not much to talk about religion, until one has felt it. Why is there so much disturbance, so much fighting and quarrelling in the name of God? There has been more bloodshed in the

name of God than for any other cause, because people never went to the fountain-head; they were content only to give a mental assent to the customs of their forefathers, and wanted others to do the same. What right has a man to say he has a soul if he does not feel it, or that there is a God if he does not see Him? If there is a God we must see Him, if there is a soul we must perceive it; otherwise it is better not to believe. It is better to be an outspoken atheist than a hypocrite. The modern idea, on the other hand, with the "learned" is that religion and metaphysics and all search after a Supreme Being are futile; on the other hand, with the semi-educated, the idea seems to be that these things really have no basis; their only value consists in the fact that they furnish strong motive powers for doing good to the world. If men believe in a God, they may become good, and moral, and so make good citizens. We cannot blame them for holding such ideas, seeing that all the teaching these men get is simply to believe in an eternal rigmarole of words, without any substance behind them. They are asked to live upon words; can they do it? If they could, I should not have the least regard for human nature. Man wants truth, wants to experience truth for himself; when he has grasped it, realised it, felt it within his heart of hearts, then alone, declared the Vedas, would all doubts vanish, all darkness be scattered, and all crookedness be made straight.[6]

Mysticism in an ambience of freedom opens the world of truth in askance, serenity in cadence, and catholicity in poignance. The journey to the beyond becomes an exciting and moving adventure of the mind and the heart, the body and the soul. From the philosophical points of view of the Absolute and manifestation, Vivekananda traces the philosophy of Oneness of the soul and exposes the fact that freedom always paves path to morality as an expression of positive humanity. He refers to sublime poetry, points out the essence of mysticism by referring to the old Upanishads, Plato, Buddha, Shankaracharya and the Advaita system and consolidates the point that the religion of the beyond is a sure signal for a higher platform of humanity. In his elegant words:

> In the old Upanishads we find sublime poetry; their authors were poets. Plato says, inspiration comes to people through poetry, and it seems as if these ancient Rishis, seers of Truth, were raised above humanity to show these truths through poetry. They never preached, nor philosophised, nor wrote. Music came out of their hearts. In Buddha, we had the great, universal heart and infinite patience, making religion practical and bringing it to everyone's door. In Shankaracharya, we saw tremendous intellectual power, throwing the scorching light of reason upon everything. We want today that bright sun of intellectuality joined with the heart of Buddha, the wonderful infinite heart of love and mercy. This union will give us the highest philosophy. Science and religion will meet and shake hands. Poetry and philosophy will become friends. This will be the religion of the future, and if we can work it out, we may be sure that it will be for all times and peoples. This is the one way that will prove acceptable to modern science, for it has almost come to it. When the scientific teacher asserts that all things are the manifestation of one force, does it not remind you of the God of whom you hear in the Upanishads: "As the one fire entering into the universe expresses itself in various forms, even so that One Soul is expressing Itself in every soul and yet is infinitely more besides?" Do you not see whither science is tending? The Hindu nation proceeded through the study of the mind, through metaphysics and logic. The European nations start from external nature, and now they too are coming to the same results. We find that searching through the mind we at last come to that Oneness, the Universal One, the Internal Soul of everything, the Essence and Reality of everything, the Ever-Free, the Ever-Blissful, the Ever-Existing. Through material science we come to the same Oneness. Science today is telling us that all things are but the manifestation of one energy which is the sum-total of everything which exists, and the trend of humanity is towards

> freedom and not towards bondage. Why should men be moral? Because through morality is the path towards freedom, and immorality leads to bondage.[7]

Freedom in religion is freedom in realisation. If it is not so, it loses the mystic aroma of truth and independent thinking and reasoning to march ahead with consciousness and the beyond. Even morality, goodness and virtue apart from social and intellectual depths of vision which become excellent in mystic introspection are really based on how freedom is exercised in perfect tune with the spirit of mystic inwardness of contemplation and action. In fact, religion in the warmth of mystic realisation of any one who aspires after Truth becomes absolute and effulgent.

In the light of the above, Vivekananda exposes the true nature and identity of religion and morality that supersedes mere intellectual exercise and paves free avenues of the mystic response from the soul. As a radical and mystic thinker, he strongly observes:

> This turmoil and fight and difference in religions will cease only when we understand that religion is not in books and temples. It is an actual perception. Only the man who has actually perceived God and soul has religion. There is no real difference between the highest ecclesiastical giant who can talk by the volume, and the lowest, most ignorant materialist. We are all atheists; let us confess it. Mere intellectual assent does not make us religious. Take a Christian, or a Mohammedan, or a follower of any other religion in the world. Any man who truly realised the truth of the Sermon on the Mount would be perfect, and become a god immediately. Yet it is said that there are many millions of Christians in the world. What is meant is that mankind may at some time try to realise that Sermon. Not one in twenty millions is a real Christian.
>
> So, in India, there are said to be three hundred millions of Vedantins. But if there were one in a thousand who has actually realised religion, this world would soon be greatly changed. We are all atheists, and yet we try to fight the man who admits it.

> We are all in the dark; religion is to us a mere intellectual assent, a mere talk, a mere nothing. We often consider a man religious who can talk well. But this is not religion. "Wonderful methods of joining words, rhetorical powers, and explaining texts of the books in various ways—these are only for the enjoyment of the learned, and not religion." Religion comes when that actual realisation in our souls begins. That will be the dawn of religion; and then alone we shall be moral. Now we are not much more moral than the animals. We are only held down by the whips of society. If society said today, "I will not punish you if you steal", we should just make a rush for each other's property. It is the policeman that makes us moral. It is social opinion that makes us moral, and really we are little better than animals. We understand how much this is so in the secret of our own hearts. So let us not be hypocrites. Let us confess that we are not religious and have no right to look down on others. We are all brothers, and we shall be truly moral when we have realised religion.[8]

To realise religion is to be free, and to be free is to be mystic so that we can realise religion as a means of exercising the spirit of the beyonding of consciousness. With the spirit of religion exercised as such, we find a new language of religion that welcomes everyone to know that truth is an identity of anyone who himself is truth. This also expands the horizon of religion to the beyond because it does not believe in morality as we generally accept and encounter but embraces both good and evil in order to exceed beyond that in the freshness of freedom.

As an incomparable introspective visionary who knows well how to realise the Atman as a mystic force of freedom, Vivekananda elucidates the role of the Self in every individual and unfolds the truth of work or thought in terms of 'character':

> The Atman is the only exercise in the human body which is immaterial. Because it is immaterial, it cannot be a compound, and because it is not a compound, it does not obey the law of

cause and effect, and so it is immortal. That which is immortal can have no beginning because everything with a beginning must have an end. It also follows that it must be formless; there cannot be any form without matter. Everything that has a form must have a beginning and an end. We have none of us seen a form which had not a beginning and will not have an end. A form comes out of a combination of force and matter. This chair has a peculiar form, that is to say a certain quantity of matter is acted upon by a certain amount of force and made to assume a particular shape. The shape is the result of a combination of matter and force. The combination cannot be eternal; there must come to every combination a time when it will dissolve. So all forms have a beginning and an end. We know our body will perish; it had a beginning and it will have an end. But the Self having no form, cannot be bound by the law of beginning and end. It is existing from infinite time; just as time is eternal, so is the Self of man eternal. Secondly, it must be all-pervading. It is only form that is conditioned and limited by space; that which is formless cannot be confined in space. So, according to Advaita Vedanta, the Self, the Atman, in you, in me, in every one, is omnipresent. You are as much in the sun now as in this earth, as much in England as in America. But the Self acts through the mind and the body, and where they are, its action is visible.

Each work we do, each thought we think, produces an impression, called in Sanskrit Samskara, upon the mind and the sum total of these impressions becomes the tremendous force which is called "character". The character of a man is what he has created for himself; it is the result of the mental and physical actions that he has done in his life. The sum total of the Samskaras is the force which gives a man the next direction after death. A man dies; the body falls away and goes back to the elements; but the Samskaras remain, adhering to the mind which, being made of fine material, does not dissolve, because the finer the material, the more persistent it is. But the mind also dissolves in the long run, and that is what we are struggling for. In this connection, the best illustration that comes to my mind is that of the whirlwind. Different currents of air coming from different directions meet and at the meeting-point become united and go on rotating; as they rotate, they form a body of dust, drawing in bits of paper, straw, etc., at one place, only to drop them and go on to another, and so go on rotating, rising, and forming bodies out of the materials which are before them. Even so the forces, called Prana in Sanskrit, come together and form the body and the mind out of matter, and move on until the body falls down, when they raise other materials to make another body, and when this falls, another rises, and thus the process goes on. Force cannot travel without matter. So when the body falls down, the mind-stuff remains, Prana in the form of Samskaras acting on it; and then it goes on to another point, raises up another whirl from fresh materials, and begins another motion; and so it travels from place to place until the force is all spent; and then it falls down, ended. So when the mind will end, be broken to pieces entirely, without leaving any Samskara, we shall be entirely free, and until that time we are in bondage; until then the Atman is covered by the whirl of the mind, and imagines it is being taken from place to place. When the whirl falls down, the Atman finds that It is all-pervading. It can go where It likes, is entirely free, and is able to manufacture any number of minds or bodies It likes; but until then It can go only with the whirl. This freedom is the goal towards which we are moving.[9]

The realisation of freedom in terms of the Self as a never-ending mystical force for ascent and the beyond is the real identity of man. It is this identity for which humanity is cherished with the bliss of the All-Being and All-Beyonding which works like a whirlwind in all thoughts and actions. To believe in the real man free from all desires and passions is to believe in the spirit of freedom which leads to the beyonding of awareness and an earnest adherence and devotion to the divine being already in man.

To concentrate on the spirit of freedom in terms of mystic poignance is to understand and appreciate the role of the soul as a guiding mystic force of the mind. This leads us to realise the Self as 'a practical God' as Vivekananda analyses in terms of the mystic poignance of freedom:

> Where is there a more practical God than He whom I see before me—a God omnipresent, in every being, more real than our senses? For you are He, the Omnipresent God Almighty, the Soul of your souls, and if I say you are not, I tell an untruth. I know it, whether at all times I realise it or not. He is the Oneness, the Unity of all, the Reality of all life and all existence.[10]

That mere intellectual endeavour will not enable anyone to understand the spirit of Oneness or Divinity in man and cannot go beyond the realm of reality is the idea well nurtured in the spirit of freedom and mysticism as an outcome of altruism. Vivekananda clearly explains the concept and function of the intellect and clarifies Oneness as a potent force of All Love:

> The world cannot find time to work it up from the lowest steps. But what is the use of our standing on higher steps if we cannot give the truth to others coming afterwards? Therefore, it is better to study it in all its workings; and first, it is absolutely necessary to clear the intellectual portion, although we know that intellectuality is almost nothing; for it is the heart that is of most importance. It is through the heart that the Lord is seen, and not through the intellect. The intellect is only the street-cleaner, cleansing the path for us, a secondary worker, the policeman; but the policeman is not a positive necessity for the workings of society. He is only to stop disturbances, to check wrong-doing, and that is all the work required of the intellect. When you read intellectual books, you think when you have mastered them, "Bless the Lord that I am out of them", because the intellect is blind and cannot move of itself, it has neither hands nor feet. It is feeling that works, that moves with speed infinitely superior to that of electricity or anything else. Do you feel?—that is the question. If you do, you will see the

> Lord. It is the feeling that you have today that will be intensified, deified, raised to the highest platform, until it feels everything, the oneness in everything, till it feels God in itself and in others. The intellect can never do that.[11]

That feeling is more important than intellect as a means of understanding oneness and love has been further spelt out by Vivekananda:

> Intellect is necessary, for without it we fall into crude errors and make all sorts of mistakes. Intellect checks these; but beyond that, do not try to build anything upon it. It is an inactive, secondary help; the real help is feeling, love. Do you feel for others? If you do, you are growing in oneness. If you do not feel for others, you may be the most intellectual giant ever born, but you will be nothing; you are but dry intellect, and you will remain so. And if you feel, even if you cannot read any book and do not know any language, you are in the right way. The Lord is yours.[12]

The role of feeling as an inevitable component of freedom is undeniable for catholicity of mystic vision. Mere cultivation of knowledge is an exercise of information and reason. That does not satisfy the human mind which always pines for something beyond knowledge. The cosmic world beckons him. He becomes resless. He wants to come out of himself and develops an earnestness for making an intense and serene entry into the world of freedom and mysticism. To go beyond reason and consciousness then becomes his steadfast quest for freedom beyond cognition.

From the standpoint of knowledge in the light of freedom and mysticism, Vivekananda significantly points out:

> Knowledge is pigeon-holing a new impression with old ones, recognising a new impression. What is meant by recognition? Finding association with similar impressions that one already has. Nothing further is meant by knowledge. If that is the case, if knowledge means finding the associations, then it must be that to know anything we have to see the whole series of its

similars. Is it not so? Suppose you take a pebble; to find the association, you have to see the whole series of pebbles similar to it. But with our perception of the universe as a whole we cannot do that, because in the pigeon-hole of our mind there is only one single record of the perception, we have no other perception of the same nature or class, we cannot compare it with any other. We cannot refer it to its associations. This bit of the universe, cut off by our consciousness, is a startling new thing, because we have not been able to find its associations. Therefore, we are struggling with it, and thinking it horrible, wicked, and bad; we may sometimes think it is good, but we always think it is imperfect. It is only when we find its associations that the universe can be known. We shall recognise it when we go beyond the universe and consciousness, and then the universe will stand explained. Until we can do that, all the knocking of our heads against the wall will never explain the universe, because knowledge is the finding of similars, and this conscious plane only gives us one single perception of it. So with our idea of God. All that we see of God is only a part, just as we see only one portion of the universe, and all the rest is beyond human recognition. "I, the universal; so great am I that even this universe is but a part of Me." That is why we see God as imperfect, and do not understand Him. The only way to understand Him and the universe is to go beyond reason, beyond consciousness. "When thou goest beyond the heard and the hearing, the thought and the thinking, then alone wilt thou come to Truth." "Go thou beyond the scriptures, because they teach only up to nature, up to the three qualities." When we go beyond them, we find the harmony, and not before.[13]

The knowledge of religion in terms of images necessitates freedom of the mind which ensures mysticism in the exercise of the beyond. Here consciousness welcomes freshness of thought in terms of images irresistibly and ceaselessly. The alert mind is never satisfied with the stereotyped process of thinking. It looks forward to becoming entirely free from all dictates and dogmas in order to make ample room for finding out the right image through radical thinking. As a mystic visionary of freedom, Vivekananda characteristically explains this point:

> All over the world you will find images in some form or other. With some, it is in the form of a man, which is the best form. If I wanted to worship an image I would rather have it in the form of a man than of an animal, or building, or any other form. One sect thinks a certain form is the right sort of image, and another thinks it is bad. The Christian thinks that when God came in the form of a dove it was all right, but if He comes in the form of a fish, as the Hindus say, it is very wrong and superstitious. The Jews think if an idol be made in the form of a chest with two angels sitting on it, and a book on it, it is all right, but if it is in the form of a man or a woman, it is awful. The Mohammedans think that when they pray, if they try to form an image of the temple with the Caaba, the black stone in it, and turn towards the west, it is all right, but if you form the image in the shape of a church it is idolatry. This is the defect of image-worship. Yet, all these seem to be necessary stages.
>
> In this matter it is of supreme importance to think what we ourselves believe. What we have realised, is the question. What Jesus, or Buddha, or Moses did is nothing to us, unless we too do it for ourselves. It would not satisfy our hunger to shut ourselves up in a room and think of what Moses ate, nor what Moses thought save *us*. My ideas are very radical on these points. Sometimes I think that I am right when I agree with all the ancient teachers, at other times I think they are right when they agree with me. I believe in thinking independently. I believe in becoming entirely free from the holy teachers; pay all reverence to them, but look at religion as an independent research. I have to find my light, just as they found theirs. Their finding the light will not satisfy us at all. You have to *become* the Bible, and not to follow it, excepting as paying reverence to

> it as a light on the way, as a guide-post, a mark: that is all the value it has.[14]

With radical thoughts of freedom and a quest for the mystic grandeur of ascent and excellence, Vivekananda takes recourse to a mystic identity of sense perception which must rise above 'the totality of material and mental phenomena' and prove the real worth of being and beyonding of consciousness. What, then, is reality? How to identify it? Here is an invaluable analysis:

> It may be argued that there is no necessity whatsoever of postulating any such substance or being beyond the mass of mental and material phenomena. The totality of phenomena is all that we know or can know, and it requires nothing beyond itself to explain itself. An analysis beyond the senses is impossible, and the feeling of a substance in which everything inheres is simply an illusion.
>
> We see, that from the most ancient times, there has been these two schools among thinkers. One party claims that the unavoidable necessity of the human mind to form concepts and abstractions is the natural guide to knowledge, and that it can stop nowhere until we have transcended all phenomena and formed a concept which is absolute in all directions, transcending time and space and causality. Now if this ultimate concept is arrived at by analysing the whole phenomena of thought and matter, step by step, taking the cruder first and resolving it into a finer, and still finer, until we arrive at something which stands as the solution of everything else, it is obvious that everything else beyond this final result is a momentary modification of itself, and as such, this final result alone is real and everything else is but its shadow. The reality, therefore, is not in the senses but beyond them.
>
> On the other hand, the other party holds that the only reality in the universe is what our senses bring to us, and although a sense of something beyond hangs on to all our sense-perceptions, that is only a trick of the mind, and therefore unreal.[15]

Analysing freedom in terms of illusion, Vivekananda further highlights on an altogether new concept of mysticism that upholds the fact that neither the body nor the will is free but beyond that:

> From the highest thinker to the most ignorant man everyone knows that he is free. Now every man at the same time finds out with a little thinking that every action of his had motives and conditions, and given those motives and conditions his particular action can be as rigorously deduced as any other fact in causation.
>
> Here, again, the same difficulty occurs. Man's will is as rigorously bound by the law of causation as the growth of any little plant or the falling of a stone, and, yet, through all this bondage runs the indestructible idea of freedom. Here also the totality side will declare that the idea of freedom is an illusion and man is wholly a creature of necessity.
>
> Now, on one hand, this denial of freedom as an illusion is no explanation; on the other hand, why not say that the idea of necessity or bondage or causation is an illusion of the ignorant? Any theory which can fit itself to facts which it wants to explain, by first cutting as many of them as prevents its fitting itself into them, is on the face of it wrong. Therefore, the only way left to us is to admit at first that the body is not free, neither is the will, but that there must be something beyond both the mind and the body which is free.[16]

The quest for freedom in tune with mysticism is never-ending. Man must strive for freedom of the right kind which ensures freedom of the right mind. This is the starting point of mysticism, a call for consciousness of the beyond. Once the selection is made for appropriate efflorescence of freedom, the rest goes on continually. The mind is now in quest of the beyond. The depth of vision for introspection makes many more inroads to consciousness to encounter the All Poignant.

To encounter the All Poignant is to be convinced of the fact that life is a continuous chain of slavery like any thing. Emancipation from plurality and adoration of the One show inroads to inner consciousness—an assured sojourn for spiritual and mystic marvels of life. How to be blessed with a free mind of this sort? How to make life really free as a mystic? In his discourse on meditation, Vivekananda significantly points out:

> You are all running after life, and we find that is foolishness. There is something much higher than life even. This life is inferior, material. Why should I live at all? I am something higher than life. Living is always slavery. We always get mixed up.
>
> * *　　　* *　　　* *
>
> The whole of the universe has been demonstrated into one. That science is called the science of Vedanta. The whole universe is one. The one runs through all this seeming variety.
>
> We have all these variations now and we see them—what we call the five elements: solid, liquid, gaseous, luminous, ethereal. After that the state of existence is mental and beyond that spiritual. Not that spirit is one and mind is another, and so on. It is the one existence appearing in all these variations. To go back, the solid must become liquid. The way [the elements evolved] they must go back. The solids will become liquid, etherised. This is the idea of the macrocosm—and universal. There is the external universe and universal spirit, mind, ether, gas, luminosity, liquid, solid.
>
> The same with the mind. I am just exactly the same in the microcosm. I am the spirit; I am mind; I am the ether, solid, liquid, gas. What I want to do is to go back to my spiritual state. It is for the individual to live the life of the universe in one short life. Thus, man can be free in this life.[17]

To be worthy of freedom as an efflorescence of mysticism is to consider man as an infinite being. To understand the universe as a small part of an individual is to accept the role of freedom introspectively. The greater part lies in the mystic beyonding of man. Looking at man from this point introspectively, Vivekananda makes a very distinct and poignant introspection:

> The question has been raised as to from whom this universe comes, in whom it rests, and to whom it goes; and the answer has been given that from freedom it comes, in bondage it rests, and goes back into that freedom again. So, when we speak of man as no other than that infinite being which is manifesting itself, we mean that only one very small part thereof is man; this body and this mind which we see are only one part of the whole, only one spot of the infinite being. This whole universe is only one spec of the infinite being; and all our laws, our bondages, our joys and our sorrows, our happiness and our expectations, are only within this small universe; all our progression and digression are within its small compass. So you see how childish it is to expect a continuation of this universe—the creation of our minds—and to expect to go to heaven, which after all must mean only a repetition of this world that we know. You see at once that it is an impossible and childish desire to make the whole of infinite existence conform to the limited and conditioned existence which we know. When a man says that he will have again and again this same thing which he is having now, or, as I sometimes put it, when he asks for a *comfortable* religion, you may know that he has become so degenerate that he cannot think of anything higher than what he is now; he is just his little present surroundings and nothing more. He has forgotten his infinite nature, and his whole idea is confined to these little joys, and sorrows, and heart-jealousies of the moment, he thinks that this finite thing is the infinite; and not only so, he will not let this foolishness go. He clings on desperately unto Trishna, and the thirst after life, what the Buddhists call Tanha and Tissa. There may be millions of kinds of happiness, and beings, and laws, and progress, and causation, all acting outside the little universe that we know; and, after all, the whole of this comprises but one section of our infinite nature.[18]

To a mystic, the whole universe is Maya, an illusion. To get out of this illusion is to respond to the call of the infinite. It is the call of freedom. It is the call of infinity. It is the call of the wonder and grandeur of mysticism. It is the call that endears us to happily embrace and translate into reality the great saying of the Upanishad—*Tena Tyektena Bhunjitha.* It is the call that prompts us to welcome the universe unknown, reject this earth or heaven, body, mind, everything and prepare ourselves to be worthy of the lotus land of purity and poignance, freedom and excellence. It is the call for a renewal of renewals, a renaissance, as it were, of renaissance in and through refinement of freedom and catholicity of mystic vision as an infinite saga of life and work. As Vivekananda reflects:

> Until we give up the thirst after life, the strong attachment to this our transcient conditioned existence, we have no hope of catching even a glimpse of that infinite freedom beyond. It stands to reason then that there is only one way to attain to that freedom which is the goal of all the noblest aspirations of mankind, and that is by giving up this little life, giving up this little universe, giving up this earth, giving up heaven, giving up the body, giving up the mind, giving up everything that is limited and conditioned. If we give up our attachment to this little universe of the senses or of the mind, we shall be free immediately. The only way to come out of bondage is to go beyond the limitations of law, to go beyond causation.
>
> But it is a most difficult thing to give up the clinging to this universe; few ever attain to that. There are two ways to do that mentioned in our books. One is called "Neti, Neti" (not this, not this), the other is called "Iti" (this); the former is the negative, and the latter is the positive way. The negative way is the most difficult. It is only possible to the men of the very highest, exceptional minds and gigantic wills who simply stand up and say, "No, I will not have this," and the mind and body obey their will, and they come out successful. But such people are very rare. The vast majority of mankind choose the positive way, the way through the world, making use of all the bondages

themselves to break those very bondages. This is also a kind of giving up; only it is done slowly and gradually, by knowing things, enjoying things and thus obtaining experience, and knowing the nature of things until the mind lets them all go at last and becomes unattached.[19]

To be unattached is to be on the right road to freedom and mysticism. The mind becomes serene and the heart pulsates with a new beckoning. It is the beckoning for undertaking an adventure for whatever is beyond our reach. Meanwhile, consciousness takes a new challenge. It is the challenge to be free from every aspect of littleness in thought and action. It is a quest within as a pointer to the quest of the beyond which is the essence of mysticism.

In the poem "No one to blame" written on 16th May, 1895, Vivekananda introduces us with the core of mysticism cradled in the essence of freedom:

The sun goes down, its crimson rays
Light up the dying day;
A startled glance I throw behind
And count my triumph shame;
No one but me to blame.

Each day my life I make or mar,
Each deed begets its kind,
Good good, bad bad, the tide once set
No one can stop or stem;
No one but me to blame.

I am my own embodied past;
Therein the plan was made;
The will, the thought, to that conform,
To that the outer frame;
No one but me to blame.

Love comes reflected back as love,
Hate breeds more fierce hate,

They mete their measures, lay on me
Through life and death their claim;
No one but me to blame.

I cast off fear and vain remorse,
I feel my Karma's sway
I face the ghosts my deeds have raised—
Joy, sorrow, censure, fame;
No one but me to blame.[20]

To be prepared for realisation of the beyond is primarily to be free from all constraints, and to be free from all constraints is to welcome oneself in reverence as an omnipotent being. Thus, freedom in sync with mysticism raises us to the status of a being both personal and impersonal. The All Being in every one of us blesses us as personalised impersonal beings. Vivekananda explains his own idea on this point in the light of freedom and mysticism:

> My idea is that what you call a Personal God is the same as the Impersonal Being, a Personal and Impersonal God at the same time. We are personalised impersonal beings. If you use the word in the absolute sense, we are impersonal; but if you use it in a relative meaning, we are personal. Each one of you is a universal being, each one is omnipresent. It may seem staggering at first, but I am as sure of this as that I stand before you. How can the spirit help being omnipresent? It has neither length, nor breadth, nor thickness, nor any material attribute whatsoever; but if we are all spirits we cannot be limited by space. Space only limits space, matter matter. If we were limited to this body, we would be a material something. Body and soul and everything would be material, and such words as "living in the body", "embodying the soul" would be only words used for convenience; beyond that they would have no meaning.[21]

How to be prepared for the freedom of the soul? How to be truly omnipresent as a personal and impersonal being? Where would we find the mystic bliss, and how? How would we address the Soul? Here is Vivekananda's poignant poetic muse:

> Speed forth, O Soul! upon thy star-strewn path;
> Speed, blissful one! where thought is ever free,
> Where time and space no longer mist the view,
> Eternal peace and blessings be with thee!
>
> Thy service true, complete thy sacrifice,
> Thy home the heart of love transcendent find;
> Remembrance sweet, that kills all space and time,
> Like altar roses fill thy place behind!
>
> Thy bonds are broke, thy quest in bliss is found,
> And one with That which comes as Death and Life;
> Thou helpful one! unselfish e'er on earth,
> Ahead! still help with love this world of strife![22]

When would we be truly mystic in the serenity of freedom?

References

1. Swami Vivekananda: *The Complete Works of Swami Vivekananda,* Advaita Ashrama, Kolkata, Mayavati Memorial Edition, 1989, Vol. I, pp. 134-135.
2. *Ibid.,* Vol. V, p. 290.
3. *Ibid.,* Vol. VI, p. 140.
4. *Ibid.,* p.177.
5. *Ibid.,* Vol. V, p. 266.
6. *Ibid.,* Vol. I, pp. 127-128.
7. *Ibid.,* Vol. II, pp. 140-141.
8. *Ibid.,* pp. 163-164.
9. *Ibid.,* pp. 254-256.
10. *Ibid.,* pp. 305-306.
11. *Ibid.,* p. 306.
12. *Ibid.,* p. 307.
13. *Ibid.,* pp. 448-449.
14. *Ibid.,* Vol. IV, pp. 44-45.

15. *Ibid.*, pp. 381-382.
16. *Ibid.*, pp. 382-383.
17. *Ibid.*, pp. 232-233.
18. *Ibid.*, Vol. I, pp. 96-97.
19. *Ibid.*, pp. 97-98.
20. *Ibid.*, Vol. VIII, pp. 175-176.
21. *Ibid.*, p. 188.
22. *Ibid.*, Vol. IV, p. 389.

9

Freedom and Values: Vivekananda's Suggestions

Freedom is the real identity of a man who cares for values. It promotes him to think and re-think of his very existence as a man. It also boosts him towards radicalism and asserts the values that are at the very core of his march for advancement and excellence. Complex and crucial as diverse problems and possibilities are, spread all over life and beyond that, values always need a forewarning in all thoughts and contemplations, rubrics and suggestions. Needless to say, freedom shows the right way of negotiating these aspects from the assimilative, subjective and distinctive points of values.

As a radical and revolutionary thinker of values, Swami Vivekananda has unparalleled and incomparable suggestions on how values can be an unfailing and useful partner of freedom for ascent and excellence. In his address at the Parliament of Religions, he upholds the dignity of man and religion as one of the most precious values for all times which ennobles the soul of man. As he poignantly suggests:

> The present is determined by our past actions, and the future by the present. The soul will go on evolving up or reverting back from birth to birth and death to death. But here is another question: Is man a tiny boat in a tempest, raised one moment on the foamy crest of a billow and dashed down into a yawning chasm the next, rolling to and fro at the mercy of good and bad

> actions—a powerless, helpless wreck in an ever-raging, ever-rushing, uncompromising current of cause and effect; a little moth placed under the wheel of causation, which rolls on crushing everything in its way and waits not for the widow's tears or the orphan's cry? The heart sinks at the idea, yet this is the law of Nature. Is there no hope? Is there no escape?—was the cry that went up from the bottom of the heart of despair. It reached the throne of mercy, and words of hope and consolation came down and inspired a Vedic sage, and he stood up before the world and in trumpet voice proclaimed the glad tidings: "Hear, ye children of immortal bliss! Even ye that reside in higher spheres! I have found the Ancient One who is beyond all darkness, all delusion: knowing Him alone you shall be saved from death over again." "Children of immortal bliss"—what a sweet, what a hopeful name! Allow me to call you, brethren, by that sweet name—heirs of immortal bliss—yea, the Hindu refuses to call you sinners. Ye are the children of God, the sharers of immortal bliss, holy and perfect beings. Ye divinities on earth—sinners! It is a sin to call a man so; it is a standing libel on human nature. Come up, O lions, and shake off the delusion that you are sheep; you are souls immortal, spirits free, blest and eternal; ye are not matter, ye are not bodies; matter is your servant, not you the servant of matter.[1]

The valuation of man in terms of divinity as an inherent and incomparable force of freedom as Vivekananda highlights is yet to be translated in right earnest. There is no point of defeat in work and life. Work is to be genuinely known and performed by appropriately unfolding and manipulating its secret. Life also is to be led in terms of poignance and perfection. There is no short cut to life and work. Despite the fact that there is an absence of equality almost in every sphere of life, both demand freedom as an invaluable component of success in theory and practice. Vivekananda splendidly submits:

> Just as inequality is necesary for creation itself, so the struggle to limit it is also necessary. If there were no struggle to become

> free and get back to God, there would be no creation either. It is the difference between these two forces that determines the nature of the motives of men. There will always be these motives to work, some tending towards bondage and others towards freedom.
>
> This world's wheel within wheel is a terrible mechanism; if we put our hands in it, as soon as we are caught we are gone. We all think that when we have done a certain duty, we shall be at rest; but before we have done a part of that duty, another is already in waiting. We are all being dragged along by this mighty, complex world-machine. There are only two ways out of it; one is to give up all concerns with the machine, to let it go and stand aside, to give up our desires. That is very easy to say, but is almost impossible to do. I do not know whether in twenty millions of men one can do that. The other way is to plunge into the world and learn the secret of work, and that is the way of Karma-Yoga. Do not fly away from the wheels of the world-machine, but stand inside it and learn the secret of work. Through proper work done inside, it is also possible to come out. Through this machinery itself is the way out.[2]

Freedom to think is freedom to manifest individuality. Unless individuality is exercised in a sincere and catholic way, the value of a man becomes meaningless. He simply becomes lifeless and dull, purposeless and artificial. The thirst for life must be exposed in all spontaneity and serenity. In his reply to the address of the Maharaja of Khetri, Vivekananda upholds the grandeur and value of the 'domineering spirit' of every individual who cares not for himself but remains steadfast in dedicating himself for the well-being of others:

> To the worldly-minded, everything that can be converted into money is real, that which cannot be so converted is unreal. To the man of domineering spirit, anything that will conduce to his ambition of ruling over his fellow-men is real—the rest is naught; and man finds nothing in that which does not echo back the heart-beats of his special love in life.

> Those whose only aim is to barter the energies of life for gold, or name, or any other enjoyment; those to whom the tramp of embattled cohorts is the only manifestation of power; those to whom the enjoyments of the senses are the only bliss that life can give—to these, India will ever appear as an immense desert whose every blast is deadly to the development of life, as it is known by them.
>
> But to those whose thirst for life has been quenched for ever by drinking from the stream of immortality that flows from far away beyond the world of the senses, whose souls have cast away—as a serpent its slough—the three-fold bondages of lust, gold, and fame, who, from their height of calmness, look with love and compassion upon the petty quarrels and jealousies and fights for little gilded puff-balls, filled with dust, called "enjoyment" by those under a sense-bondage; to those whose accumulated force of past good deeds has caused the scales of ignorance to fall-off from their eyes, making them see through the vanity of name and form— to such wheresoever they be, India, the motherland and eternal mine of spirituality, stands transfigured, a beacon of hope to everyone in search of Him who is the only real Existence in a universe of vanishing shadows.[3]

Freedom to exercise the finer values in life is the birth-right of man. Even though occasional failures bring forth desolation and disappointments, it is evident that in the long run freedom pays earnest dividends in the form of unalloyed glory. Therefore, all values are charged by challenges which a man with a brave heart never fails to accept and march on accordingly.

In a poem titled "Hold on yet a while, Brave Heart" Vivekananda suggests as an ever inspiring optimist:

> If the sun by the cloud is hidden a bit,
> If the welkin shows but gloom,
> Still hold on yet a while, brave heart,
> The victory is sure to come.

No winter was but summer came behind,
Each hollow crests the wave,
They push each other in light and shade;
Be steady then and brave.

The duties of life are sore indeed,
And its pleasures fleeting, vain,
The goal so shadowy seems and dim,
Yet plod on through the dark, brave heart,
With all thy might and main.

Not a work will be lost, no struggle vain,
Though hopes be blighted, powers gone;
Of thy loins shall come the heirs to all,
Then hold on yet a while, brave soul,
No good is e'er undone.

Though the good and the wise in life are few,
Yet theirs are the reins to lead,
The masses know but late the worth;
Heed none and gently guide.

With thee are those who see afar,
With thee is the Lord of might,
All blessings pour on thee, great soul,
To thee may all come right![4]

The values of misery are immense but it eludes us because we are more often than not without being free from the sufferings and pains brought forth from it. If we exercise freedom to embrace misery with courage and steadfastness, tolerance and calmness, sooner or later we will win over it. As an ever-abiding optimist, Vivekananda advises us:

> Superhuman power is not strong enough. Superdivine strength is the only way, the one way out. By it we can pass through all these intricacies, through these showers of miseries, unscathed.

> We may be cut to pieces, torn asunder, yet our hearts must grow nobler and nobler all the time.
>
> It is very difficult, but we can overcome the difficulty by constant practice. We must learn that nothing can happen to us, unless we make ourselves susceptible to it. I have just said, no disease can come to me until the body is ready; it does not depend alone on the germs, but upon a certain predisposition which is already in the body. We get only that for which we are fitted. Let us give up our pride and understand this, that never is misery undeserved. There never has been a blow undeserved; there never has been an evil for which I did not pave the way with my own hands. We ought to know that. Analyse yourselves and you will find that every blow you have received, came to you because you have prepared yourselves for it. You did half, and the external world did the other half: that is how the blow came. That will sober us down. At the same time, from this very analysis will come a note of hope, and the note of hope is: "I have no control of the external world, but that which is in me and nearer unto me, my own world, is in my control. If the two together are required to make a failure, if the two together are necessary to give me a blow, I will not contribute the one which is in my keeping; and how then can the blow come? If I get real control of myself, the blow will never come.[5]

To keep onself prepared to any eventuality is the fundamental force of values and freedom. It is the person and not any other man or thing on which depends the values of life and work handled independently and with all sincerity. It is our duty to work sincerely and the rest follows automaticaly. The power of freedom also finds its convenient avenues for efflorescence of apposite values as we derive from different sources.

From the Vedantic standpoint, Vivekananda suggests how work in this complex world of ours should be done so that it welcomes both values and freedom in a symphony of thought and action:

> Work incessantly, holding life as something deified, as God Himself, and knowing that this is all we have to do, this is all

> we should ask for. God is in everything, where else shall we go to find Him? He is already in every work, in every thought, in every feeling. Thus, knowing, we must work—this is the only way, there is no other. Thus, the effects of work will not bind us. We have seen how false desires are the cause of all the misery and evil we suffer, but when they are thus deified, purified, through God, they bring no evil, they bring no misery. Those who have not learnt this secret will have to live in a demoniacal world until they discover it. Many do not know what an infinite mine of bliss is in them, around them, everywhere; they have not yet discovered it. What is a demoniac world? The Vedanta says, ignorance.[6]

The value of perseverance can only be understood and experienced in terms of freedom personally exercised and not from anywhere and anyhow passively. It is a sustained and relentless devotion to inwardness of vision which finally brings the joy of value-cultivation. Vivekananda explains this point from his personal experience:

> From my childhood I have heard of seeing God everywhere and in everything, and then I can really enjoy the world, but as soon as I mix with the world, and get a few blows from it, the idea vanishes. I am walking in the street thinking that God is in every man, and a strong man comes along and gives me a push and I fall flat on the footpath. Then I rise up quickly with clenched fist, the blood has rushed to my head, and the reflection goes. Immediately I have become mad. Everything is forgotten; instead of encountering God I see the devil. Ever since we were born we have been told to see God in all. Every religion teaches that—see God in everything and everywhere. Do you not remember in the New Testament how Christ says so? We have all been taught that; but it is when we come to the practical side, that the difficulty begins. You all remember how in *Aesop's Fables* a fine stag is looking at his form reflected in a lake and is saying to his young one, "How powerful I am, look at my splendid head, look at my limbs, how strong and muscular they

> are; and how swiftly I can run." In the meantime he hears the barking of dogs in the distance, and immediately takes to his heels, and after he has run several miles, he comes back panting. The young one says, "You just told me how strong you were, how was it that when the dog barked, you ran away?" "Yes, my son; but when the dogs bark all my confidence vanishes." Such is the case with us. We think highly of humanity, we feel ourselves strong and valiant, we make grand resolves; but when the "dogs" of trial and temptation bark, we are all like the stag in the fable. Then, if such is the case, what is the use of teaching all these things? There is the greatest use. The use is this, that perseverance will finally conquer. Nothing can be done in a day.[7]

As a radical thinker of freedom and values, Vivekananda introduces creation and imagination not in a stereotyped and common manner but with totally new connotations and applications quite apart from the point of intellectuality. In his words:

> Creation is not a "making" of something, it is the struggle to regain equilibrium, as when atoms of cork are thrown to the bottom of a pail of water: they rush to the top singly and in clusters, and when all have reached the top and equilibrium has been regained, all motion or "life" ceases. So with creation; if equilibrium were reached, all change would cease and life, so-called, would end. Life must be accompanied with evil, for when the balance is regained, the world must end, as sameness and destruction are one. There is no possibility of ever having pleasure without pain, or good without evil, for living itself is just the lost equilibrium. What we want is freedom, not life, nor pleasure, nor good. Creation is eternal, without beginning, without end, the ever moving ripple in an infinite lake. There are yet unreached depths and others where stillness has been regained, but the ripple is ever progressing, the struggle to regain the balance is eternal. Life and death are but different names for the same fact, they are the two sides of one coin. Both are Maya, the inexplicable state of striving at one point to live and a moment later to die. Beyond all this is the true nature, the

> Atman. We enter into creation, and then, for us, it becomes living. Things are dead in themselves, only we give them life, and then, like fools, we turn round and are afraid of them or enjoy them! The world is neither true nor untrue, it is the shadow of truth.
>
> "Imagination is the gilded shadow of truth", says the poet. The internal universe, the Real, is infinitely greater than the external one, which is but the shadowy projection of the true one. When we see the "rope", we do not see the "serpent", and when the "serpent" is, the "rope" is not. Both cannot exist at the same time; so while we see the world we do not realise the Self, it is only an intellectual concept.[8]

For an extended view of imagination in terms of freedom and values, Vivekananda draws our attention to the concept of the Self, the Personal God:

> The Self is the eternal subject, and we are struggling all the time to objectify the Self. And out of that struggle has come this phenomenal universe and what we call matter, and so on. But these are very weak attempts, and the highest objectification of the Self possible to us is the Personal God. This objectification is an attempt to reveal our own nature. According to the Sankhya, nature is showing all these experiences to the soul, and when it has got real experience it will know its own nature. According to the Advaita Vedantist, the soul is struggling to reveal itself. After long struggle, it finds that the subject must always remain the subject; and then begins non-attachment, and it becomes free.
>
> When a man has reached that perfect state, he is of the same nature as the Personal God. "I and my Father are one". He knows that he is one with Brahman, the Absolute, and projects himself as the Personal God does. He plays—as even the mightiest of kings may sometimes play with dolls.
>
> Some imaginations help to break the bondage of the rest. The whole universe is imagination, but one set of imaginations will

> cure another set. Those that tell us that there is sin and sorrow and death in the world are terrible. But the other set—thou art holy, there is God, there is no pain— these are good, and help to break the bondage of others. The highest imagination that can break all the links of the chain is that of the Personal God.[9]

Freedom to develop one's potentiality is the highest and most respectable nature of religion. That adds flying colours to creation and imagination as efflorescent pointers to the march of man and society. A society dwarfed by narrowness of caste and creed makes freedom utterly meaningless and dangerous. It suffers from numerous ailings because it does not know the blessings of freedom playing a very optimistic and positive role in the society where the mind-sets of men with different castes do not pay heed to anything that acts as constraints to the role of freedom to work together for the all round welfare of man and society.

Elucidating on this point of the values of freedom in man and society in terms of the presence of a heterogeneous caste system in the Hindu society, Vivekananda states in a letter written from Chicago on 2nd November, 1893 to Alasinga:

> The Hindu must not give up his religion, but must keep religion within its proper limits and give freedom to society to grow. All the reformers in India made the serious mistake of holding religion accountable for all the horrors of priestcraft and degeneration and went forthwith to pull down the indestructible structure, and what was the result? Failure! Beginning from Buddha down to Ram Mohan Roy, everyone made the mistake of holding caste to be a religious institution and tried to pull down religion and caste all together, and failed. But in spite of all the ravings of the priests, caste is simply a crystallised social institution, which after doing its service is now filling the atmosphere of India with its stench, and it can only be removed by giving back to the people their lost social individuality. Every man born here knows that he is a *man.* Every man born in

> India knows that he is a slave of society. Now, freedom is the only condition of growth; take that off, the result is degeneration. With the introduction of modern competition, see how caste is disappearing fast! No religion is now necessary to kill it. The Brahmana shopkeeper, shoemaker, and wine-distiller are common in Northern India. And why? Because of competition. No man is prohibited from doing anything he pleases for his livelihood under the present government, and the result is neck and neck competition, and thus thousands are seeking and finding the highest level they were born for, instead of vegetating at the bottom.
>
> ** ** **
>
> Be of good cheer and believe that we are selected by the Lord to do great things, and we will do them. Hold yourself in readiness, i.e. be pure and holy, and love for love's sake. Love the poor, the miserable, the downtrodden, and the Lord will bless you.[10]

The new spirit of man in quest of freedom and values in perfect harmony of thought and action is one of his greatest identities and missions. So long as man lives in this world, this spirit acts as a driving force for excellence and ascent. Despite the fact that one cannot avert the thought of death and despondency, one must realise the spirit within oneself. Death will then be a welcome guest. Admitting the fact that death and despondency overpower us, one must stick to one's work because it is freedom—the value of all values— that is deathless and shows the way of efflorescence.

In explaining the value of freedom from the above-mentioned standpoint to Shri Surendra Nath Das Gupta, Vivekananda poignantly observes:

> At first, the heart will break down, and despondency and gloomy thoughts will occupy your mind. But persist, let days pass like that—and then? Then you will see that new strength has come into the heart, that the constant threat of death is giving you a new life and is making you more and more thoughtful by bringing every moment before your mind's eye the truth of the

> saying, "Vanity of vanities, all is vanity!" Wait! Let days, months, and years pass, and you will feel that the spirit within is waking up with the strength of a lion, that the little power within has transformed itself into a mighty power! Think of death always, and you will realise the truth of every word I say. What more shall I say in words![11]

The philosophy of values in terms of freedom and vice versa can be best understood through man and fatalism. Many people pay undesirable importance to astrology and fate as unavoidable and inevitable components in life. This is most irrational and unscientific. This simply devaluates man and dwarfs freedom to nothingness. As Vivekananda characteristically points out:

> Money is the only God of many beings. Weak men, when they lose everything and feel themselves weak, try all sorts of uncanny methods of making money, and come to astrology and all these things. "It is the coward and the fool who says, 'This is fate'"—so says the Sanskrit proverb. But it is the strong man who stands up and says, "I will make my fate." It is people who are getting old who talk of fate. Young men generally do not come to astrology. You *may* be under planetary influence, bit it should not matter much to us. Buddha says, "Those that get a living by calculation of the stars by such art and other lying tricks are to be avoided"; and he ought to know, because he was the greatest Hindu ever born. Let stars come, what harm is there? If a star disturbs my life, it would not be worth a cent. You will find that astrology and all such mystical things are generally signs of a weak mind; therefore as soon as they are becoming prominent in our minds, we should see a physician, take good food and rest.[12]

From the conceptual points of view, we are most often in an ambiguous position in understanding the real nature of virtue and vice. Our values come under scanner because we fail to understand the role of virtue and vice in life. Our freedom to realise virtue and vice suffers from clarity of vision, and thus all concepts of values in man become abstract and meaningless. Vivekananda's concept of freedom and values in terms of virtue and vice becomes very distinct with these invaluable words:

> This body is made up of two sorts of Karma consisting of virtue and vice—injurious vice and non-injurious virtue. A thorn is pricking my body, and I take another thorn to take it out and then throw both away. A man desiring to be perfect takes a thorn of virtue and with it takes off the thorn of vice. He still lives, and virtue along being left, the momentum of action left to him must be of virtue. A bit of holiness is left to the Jivanmukta, and he lives, but everything he does must be holy.
>
> Virtue is that which tends to our improvement, and vice to our degeneration. Man is made up of three qualities—brutal, human, and godly. That which tends to increase your divinity in you is virtue, and that which tends to increase brutality in you is vice. You must kill the brutal nature and become human, that is, loving and charitable. You must transcend that too and become pure bliss. Sachchidananda, fire without burning, wonderfully loving, but without the weakness of human love, without the feeling of misery.[13]

To become a real exponent of Sachchidananda without the least attraction of virtue and vice, and look upon the world as the loving and living citadel of inhabitants of the All Good is the best exercise of freedom transparent and transcendent in the real inherent spirit of man who adores the values of excellence and ascent. Naturally, a newer vista of freedom and values opens. Man becomes men and vice versa as the worthiest torch-bearer of God and truth. He never falters. Nor does he feel humiliated in failures and disappointments because these, under the untiring and dauntless spirit of truth, turn out to be the pathways of success. He becomes a new spokesperson of freedom and virtue, whose religion becomes the altruistic one of all religions blessed with the highest value of truth.

In one of his lectures, Vivekananda serenely observes and suggests:

> We cannot imagine anything which is not good. He is all that we can imagine with our five senses, and more. He is like chameleon; each man, each nation, sees one face of Him and at different times, in different forms. Let each man see and take of God whatever is suitable to him. Compare each animal absorbing from nature whatever food is suitable to eat.
>
> The fault with all religions like Christianity is that they have one set of rules for all. But Hindu religion is suited to all grades of religious aspiration and progress. It contains all the ideals in their perfect form, for example, the ideal of Shanta or blessedness is to be found in Vasishtha; that of love in Krishna; that of duty in Rama and Sita; and that of intellect in Shukdeva. Study the characters of these and of other ideal men. Adopt one which suits you best.
>
> Follow truth wherever it may lead you; carry ideas to their utmost logical conclusions. Do not be cowardly and hypocritical. You must have a great devotion to your ideal, devotion not of the moment, but calm, persevering, and steady devotion, like that of a Chataka (a kind of bird) which looks into the sky in the midst of thunder and lightning and would drink no water but from the clouds. Perish in the struggle to be holy; a thousand times welcome death. Be not disheartened.[14]

What, then, is the true value of religion? Wherein lies the essence of religion? How, as a human being, should everyone cultivate the values of religion? These and all other allied questions can be most appropriately answered in evaluating the role of man as Vivekananda suggests in terms of love and religion in course of his address on real worship:

> It is in love that religion exists and not in ceremony, in the pure and sincere love in the heart. Unless a man is pure in body and mind, his coming into a temple and worshipping Shiva is useless. The prayers of those that are pure in mind and body will be

> answered by Shiva, and those that are impure and yet try to teach religion to others will fail in the end. External worship is only a symbol of internal worship; but internal worship and purity are the real things. Without them, external worship would be of no avail. Therefore, you must all try to remember this.
>
> People have become so degraded in this Kali Yuga that they think they can do anything, and then they can go to a holy place, and their sins will be forgiven. If a man goes with an impure mind into a temple, he adds to the sins he had already, and goes home a worse man than when he left it. Tirtha (place of pilgrimage) is a place which is full of holy things and holy men. But if holy people live in a certain place, and if there is no temple there, even that is a Tirtha. If unholy people live in a place where there may be a hundred temples, the Tirtha has vanished from that place. And it is most difficult to live in a Tirtha; for if sin is committed in any ordinary place it can easily be removed, but sin committed in a Tirtha cannot be removed. This is the gist of all worship—to be pure and to be good to others. He who sees Shiva in the poor, in the weak, and in the diseased, really worships Shiva; and if he sees Shiva only in the image, his worship is but preliminary. He who has served and helped one poor man seeing Shiva in him, without thinking of his caste, or creed, or race, or anything, with him Shiva is more pleased than with the man who sees Him only in temples.[15]

Furthermore, in emphasising on the purity of mind and body sans selfishness for upholding the value of true religion, Vivekananda characteristically suggests:

> Let me tell you again that you must be pure and help anyone who comes to you, as much as lies in your power. And this is good Karma. By the power of this, the heart becomes pure (Chitta-shuddhi), and then Shiva who is residing in every one will become manifest. He is always in the heart of every one. If there is dirt and dust on a mirror, we cannot see our image. So ignorance and wickedness are the dirt and dust that are on the

> mirror of our hearts. Selfishness is the chief sin, thinking of ourselves first. He who thinks, "I will eat first, I will have more money than others, and I will possess everything", he who thinks, "I will get to heaven before others, I will get Mukti before others," is the selfish man. The unselfish man says, "I will be last, I do not care to go to heaven, I will even go to hell if by doing so I can help my brothers." This unselfishness is the test of religion. He who has more of this unselfishness is more spiritual and nearer to Shiva. Whether he is learned or ignorant, he is nearer to Shiva than anybody else, whether he knows it or not. And if a man is selfish, even though he has visited all the temples, seen all the places of pilgrimage, and painted himself like a leopard, he is still further off from Shiva.[16]

As a forerunner of values and freedom, Vivekananda advises to work unselfishly and nurse purity and wisdom, poignancy and perfection. Religion is never meant for a single individual but always for all. The religion thus valued in terms of all becomes a part and parcel of life. It responds to humanity most scientifically. In fact, the values of science and religion are not different but one, because true science and true religion are inseparable and tend towards the goodness of all.

Considering values in relation to good and evil through freedom exercised in purity, Vivekananda poignantly suggests:

> Those who are born in the wave and kept in it do not see the depression and what is there. Never think you can make the world better and happier. The bullock in the oil-mill never reaches the wisp of hay tied in front of him, he only grinds out the oil. So we chase the will-o'-the-wisp of happiness that always eludes us, and we only grind nature's mill, then die, merely to begin again. If we could get rid of evil, we should never catch a glimpse of anything higher; we would be satisfied and never struggle to get free. When man finds that all search for happiness in matter is nonsense, then religion begins. All human knowledge is but a part of religion.

> In the human body the balance between good and evil is so even that there is a chance for man to wish to free himself from both.
>
> The free never became bound; to ask how he did, is an illogical question. Where no bondage is, there is no cause and effect. "I became a fox in a dream and a dog chased me." Now how can I ask why the dog chased me ? The fox was a part of the dream, and the dog followed as a matter of course; but both belong to the dream and have no existence outside. Science and religion are both attempts to help us out of the bondage; only religion is the more ancient, and we have the superstition that it is the more holy. In a way it is, because it makes morality a vital point, and science does not.
>
> "Blessed are the pure in heart, for they shall see God." This sentence alone would save mankind if all books and prophets were lost. This purity of heart will bring the vision of God. It is the theme of the whole music of this universe. In purity is no bondage. Remove the veils of ignorance by purity, then we manifest ourselves as we really are and know that we were never in bondage. The seeing of many is the great sin of all the world. See all as Self and love all; let all idea of separateness go.[17]

To eliminate the self and visualise the Self in all stands for values that eliminate selfishness and welcome the All Beautiful. This also extends the horizon of values that cherish humane sensibilities. Goodness then becomes natural and spontaneous. Whatever evil is there in every walk of life is a pointer to address goodness anew and afresh. This acts as a splendid valuation of values. This also emerges as pure and supreme. The mind then acts like a bird free from all shackles and constraints. To tide over narrowness of the vision of apparent values shows the steadiness characteristic of every human being.

In his "Inspired Talks" on *Kathopanishad,* delivered on Saturday, July 1895, Vivekananda advises on how to learn and realise the value of the Self in terms of man free from ignorance of the self:

> Learn not the truth of the Self save from one who has realised it; in all others it is mere talk. Realisation is beyond virtue and vice, beyond future and past; beyond all the pairs of opposites. "The stainless one sees the Self, and an eternal calm comes in the Soul." Talking, arguing, and reading books, the highest flights of the intellect, the Vedas themselves, all these cannot give knowledge of the Self.
>
> In us are the two—The God-soul and the man-soul. The sages know that the latter is but the shadow, that the former is the only real Sun.
>
> Unless we join the mind with the senses, we get no report from eyes, nose, ears, etc. The external organs are used by the power of the mind. Do not let the senses go outside, and then you can get rid of body and the external world.
>
> This very "x" which we see here as an external world, the departed see as heaven or hell according to their own mental states. Here and hereafter are two dreams, the latter modelled on the former; get rid of both, all is omnipresent, all is now. Nature, body, and mind go to death, not we, we never go nor come. The man Swami Vivekananda is in nature, is born, and dies; but the Self which we see as Swami Vivekananda is never born and never dies. It is the eternal and unchangeable Reality.[18]

The quest for freedom and values in terms of 'unchangeable Reality' as suggested by Vivekananda makes inroads to inner awareness. To know that we are what we really are is the primary and essential point of freedom and values. Vivekananda's suggestions by means of highlighting the concept of the Infinite Man—Mukta Purusha— are invaluable from time to time with the bliss of freedom par excellence:

> The knower cannot be known, because if it were known, it will not be the knower. If you look at your eyes in a mirror, the reflection is no more your eyes, but something else, only a

> reflection. Then if this Soul, this Universal, Infinite Being, which you are, is only a witness, what good is it? It cannot live, and move about, and enjoy the world, as we do. People cannot understand how the witness can enjoy. "Oh," they say, "you Hindus have become quiescent, and good for nothing, through this doctrine that you are witnesses!" First of all, it is only the witness that can enjoy. If there is a wrestling match, who enjoys it, those who take part in it, or those who are looking on—the outsiders? The more and more you are the witness of anything in life, the more you enjoy it. And this is Ananda; and, therefore, infinite bliss can only be yours when you have become the witness of this universe; then alone you are a Mukta Purusha. It is the witness alone that can work without any desire, without any idea of going to heaven, without any idea of blame, without any idea of praise. The witness alone enjoys, none else.[19]

To achieve perfect freedom and endless joy as the value of all values is the vision of man. It is this vision that is idealised as the spirit of relentless devotion to an ideal selected or likely to be definitely selected. In elucidating this value from the standpoint of freedom, Vivekananda serenely suggests in Bhakti-Yoga:

> Very few indeed are those who are at once the possessors of an extensive sympathy and power of appreciation, as well as an intensity of love. We find, as a rule, that liberal and sympathetic sects lose the intensity of religious feeling, and in their hands, religion is apt to degenerate into a kind of politico-social club life. On the other hand, intensely narrow sectaries, whilst displaying a very commendable love of their own ideals, are seen to have acquired every particle of that love by hating every one who is not of exactly the same opinions as themselves. Would to God that this world was full of men who were as intense in their love as world-wide in their sympathies! But such are only few and far between. Yet we know that it is practicable to educate large numbers of human beings into the ideal of a wonderful blending of both the width and the intensity of love; and the way to do that is by this path of the

> Ishta-Nishtha or "steadfast devotion to the chosen ideal". Every sect of every religion presents only one ideal of its own to mankind, but the eternal Vedantic religion opens to mankind an infinite number of doors for ingress into the inner shrine of divinity, and places before humanity an almost inexhaustible array of ideals, there being in each of them a manifestation of the Eternal One. With the kindest solicitude, the Vedanta points out to aspiring men and women the numerous roads, hewn out of the solid rock of the realities of human life, by the glorious sons, or human manifestations, of God, in the past and in the present, and stands with outstretched arms to welcome all—to welcome even those that are yet to be—to that Home of Truth and that Ocean of Bliss, wherein the human soul, liberated from the net of Maya, may transport itself with perfect freedom and with eternal joy.[20]

The value of man is inherent in the spirit and exercise of freedom. It is freedom that is best represented in the spirit of self-realisation. What is the best way of self-realisation under any circumstances? How is freedom to be nurtured and strengthened so that the value of self-realisation stands supreme? How to overcome the physical limitations? To find an appropriate answer is very difficult. It is to prove that man and Atman are one and the same for the best valuation of man in terms of freedom. As Vivekananda reminds us:

> Man as Atman is really free; as man he is bound, changed by every physical condition. As man, he is a machine with an idea of freedom; but this human body is the best and the human mind the highest mind there is. When a man attains to the Atman state, he can take a body, making it to suit himself; he is above law. This is a statement and must be proved. Each one must prove it for himself; we may satisfy ourselves, but we cannot satisfy another.[21]

Chaste imagination and pure action are the positive values that stand for real freedom. The true religion of man lies in steadfast devotion to unalloyed freedom. As a matter of fact, religion does not mean dependence on some ideals but performance of activities independently so that the values inherent in these ideals become transparent and manifested as best as possible. In explaining the relationship between work and religion in terms of freedom and values, Vivekananda poignantly remarks:

> Doing work is not religion, but work done rightly leads to freedom. In reality, all pity is darkness, because whom to pity? Can you pity God? And is there anything else? Thank God for giving you this world as a moral gymnasium to help your development, but never imagine you can help the world. Be grateful to him who curses you, for he gives you a mirror to show what cursing is, also a chance to practise self-restraint; so bless him and be glad. Without exercise, power cannot come out; without the mirror, we cannot see ourselves.
>
> *Unchaste imagination is as bad as unchaste action.* Controlled desire leads to the highest result. Transform the sexual energy into spiritual energy, but do not emasculate, because that is throwing away the power. The stronger this force, the more can be done with it. Only a powerful current of water can do hydraulic mining.[22]

What, then, should be the guiding force of freedom and values? How should one direct oneself so that the best manifestation of freedom becomes an ever illuminating reality with the vibrant aura of values? What are the best avenues of exercise of freedom in harmony with the values which always stand the test of time and mind-sets? Assuredly, the answers to these and other allied questions are characteristically set forth in Vivekananda's incomparable poem entitled "Requiescat in Pace":

> Speed forth, O Soul! Upon thy star-strewn path;
> Speed, blissful one! Where thought is ever free,
> Where time and space no longer mist the view,
> Eternal peace and blessings be with thee!
>
> Thy service true, complete thy sacrifice,
> Thy home the heart of love transcendent find;

Remembrance sweet, that kills all space and time,
Like altar roses fill thy place behind!

Thy bonds are broke, thy quest in bliss is found,
And one with That which comes as Death and Life;
Thou helpful one! Unselfish e'er on earth,
Ahead! still help with love this world of strife![23]

When would we truly attune ourselves with the spirit of freedom and values as above?

References

1. Swami Vivekananda: *The Complete Works of Swami Vivekananda*, Advaita Ashrama, Kolkata, Mayavati Memorial Edition, 1989, Vol. I, pp. 10-11.
2. *Ibid.*, p. 115.
3. *Ibid.*, Vol. IV, pp. 322-323.
4. *Ibid.*, pp. 389-390.
5. *Ibid.*, Vol. II, pp. 7-8.
6. *Ibid.*, p. 150.
7. *Ibid.*, pp. 151-152.
8. *Ibid.*, Vol. VIII, pp. 29-30.
9. *Ibid.*, Vol. V, p. 266.
10. *Ibid.*, pp. 22-23.
11. *Ibid.*, pp. 329-330.
12. *Ibid.*, Vol. VIII, pp. 183-184.
13. *Ibid.*, Vol. VI, pp. 111-112.
14. *Ibid.*, pp. 120-121.
15. *Ibid.*, Vol. III, pp. 141-142.
16. *Ibid.*, pp. 142-143.
17. *Ibid.*, Vol. VII, pp. 102-103.
18. *Ibid.*, p. 70.
19. *Ibid.*, Vol. III, p. 419.
20. *Ibid.*, 62-63.
21. *Ibid.*, Vol. VII, p. 38.
22. *Ibid.*, p. 69.
23. *Ibid.*, Vol. IV, p. 389.

Index

Q

R

S